Motivation, Altruism, Personality, and
Social Psychology

Motivation, Altruism, Personality, and Social Psychology

The Coming Age of Altruism

Michael Babula
University of Greenwich, UK

First published 2013 by
PALGRAVE MACMILLAN

Palgrave Macmillan in the UK is an imprint of Macmillan Publishers Limited, registered in England, company number 785998, of Houndmills, Basingstoke, Hampshire RG21 6XS.

Palgrave Macmillan in the US is a division of St Martin's Press LLC, 175 Fifth Avenue, New York, NY 10010.

Palgrave Macmillan is the global academic imprint of the above companies and has companies and representatives throughout the world.

Palgrave® and Macmillan® are registered trademarks in the United States, the United Kingdom, Europe and other countries

ISBN: 978–1–137–03128–0

This book is printed on paper suitable for recycling and made from fully managed and sustained forest sources. Logging, pulping and manufacturing processes are expected to conform to the environmental regulations of the country of origin.

A catalogue record for this book is available from the British Library.

A catalog record for this book is available from the Library of Congress.

Dedicated to my parents, Raymond S. Babula and Ann M. Babula, whose guidance put me on the path to help others.

Contents

List of Figures and Tables

Figures

Tables

Preface

Congratulations, you just won a $300 million lottery! Use your imagination and contemplate this scenario for a moment.

Are you experiencing extreme joy knowing that all human needs are about to be satisfied? Will you be sitting on a warm Caribbean beach for months? Do your plans include endless tasty meals cooked by world-class chefs? Is that new car smell or the echo of entering your mansion for the first time starting to creep into your senses? These are all natural reactions. Sure, you might be thinking of giving some of the money away to help friends, relatives, or a charity, but research shows that people, especially those reared without wealth, are interested in spending on themselves.

Professor Michael Norton at the Harvard Business School published the results of an experiment which showed that people who spend money on others enjoyed greater happiness, while those who spent money on themselves did not (Dunn et al., 2008). It is also well established in the literature that larger lottery winnings do not make people happier than others, and, under certain circumstances, resulted in clinical depression, suicide, and divorce.

Two people had to be hospitalized for depression after large lottery wins. The researchers observed:

> Common to both patients was the fact that they were not hospitalized directly after winning the lottery, but only in connection with the plans engendered by the money and their realization. Thus, it should be considered whether it was not so much the prospect of the unexpected winnings, but the fear of failing at self-imposed projects. (Nisslé and Bschor, 2002, p. 185)

In June 1997, lottery winner Billie Bob Harrell Jr won $31 million in the Texas jackpot only to commit suicide 20 months later (Doll, 2012). It was also reported in that article that UK Lotto winner Michael Carroll spent his £9.7 million winnings on drugs, gambling, and "thousands of prostitutes." Similarly, Evelyn Adams spent $5.4 million on gambling. Juan Rodriguez won $149 million; a short while later his wife filed for divorce (FoxNews.com, 2012).

This research contributes to evidence that the drive to maximize self-potential and self-fulfilment can be illusionary and harmful to human psychological health. It has been found that large lottery winners are no happier than people who did not win the lottery and are less satisfied with regular daily life activities (Brickman et al., 1978). As an antecedent to the lottery example, David Myers argues, "We [Americans] are twice as rich and no happier. Meanwhile, the divorce rate doubled. Teen suicide tripled. Reported violent crime nearly quadrupled" (2000, p. 61). Myers also cited literature which suggests that "Depression rates have soared; especially among teens and young adults" (Klerman and Weissman, 1989; Seligman, 1989; Weissman et al., 1992, all cited in Myers, 2000). Are you starting to second guess your initial intentions of what to do with a large lottery win or the desire to strive for wealth alone?

It will be argued in this book that we are intrinsically motivated to do good, and, currently, there has emerged a sizeable minority of people who have progressed past self-interested needs pursuits, negated self-interest, and possess a purely altruistic mindset. Try to imagine what would happen if such a phenomenon starts to snowball over the next 10–30 years? Imagine a new governmental and economic order, established on self-control and cooperation, where resources are unlimited and the needs of humanity are not only met, but also exceeded. Rather than "wanting more," you are about to be challenged to "become more" as we discover uncharted human motivational development of the mind.

"The More" was discussed in early psychology by William James (1936 [1902]) as a calling or drive to learn and grow as one's identity develops. This work revises that concept to the extent that "becoming more" means that people achieve optimal psychological health by negating the self to live for others; in other words, we learn and grow to live for the other.

There are a few observations that can be delineated from the lottery example above. Psychologists have yet to locate the ego solely existing within the body. People can use the imagination to empathize and help people by negating the self, which, incidentally, produces greater happiness than operating from the first station of the self. The ability to step outside the self, to put oneself in the shoes of another person, makes us more than the by-product of human wants and desires. Humans are capable of achieving psychological development towards pure altruistic love and can thus fulfill the 'image' of divinity.

Recently, there has been a disturbing trend in social psychology to put people's mental state more on par with the image of Lucifer than God. In the *Lucifer Effect*, social psychologist Philip Zimbardo draws a comparison between Lucifer's descent as an angel and the ability of good people to easily turn evil when faced with bad situations. Zimbardo writes, "Lucifer, the 'light bearer,' was God's favourite angel until he challenged God's authority and was cast into Hell along with his band of fallen angels, 'Better to reign in Hell than serve in Heaven,' boasts Satan, the 'adversary of God' in Milton's *Paradise Lost*." (2007, p. 3). Zimbardo misses the point. Humans are not comparable with figurative images of angels and devils. People are born with intrinsic motivation for love, creativity, and cooperation, and are greater than the legendary images of angels.

Zimbardo completely overlooks that other angel in Milton's poem. The angel Michael defeats Lucifer in battle and casts him into hell. He is then given the task of leading Adam and Eve out of the Garden of Eden. Of course, Adam and Eve are understandably upset at having to leave the peace and security of Eden. After all, they are fully self-actualized in Eden with all human needs being satisfied by divine authority. They were living what we would envision as the "lotto dream." Michael advises as follows:

This having learnt, thou hast attained the sum
Of Wisdom; hope no higher, though all the Stars
Thou knew'st by name, and all th' ethereal Powers,
All secrets of the deep, all Nature's works,
Or works of God in Heav'n, Air, Earth, or Sea,
And all riches of this World enjoy'dst,
And all the rule, one Empire: only add
Deeds to thy knowledge answerable, add Faith,
Add Virtue, Patience, Temperance, add Love,
By name to come called Charity, the soul
Of all the rest: then wilt thou not be loth
To leave this Paradise, but shalt possess
A paradise within thee, happier farr. (Milton, 2012 [1677])

This is arguably the most powerful poetic statement made by Milton. Michael tells Adam that he has internally maximized all knowledge and self-interest. At last, Adam is instructed, among the seven virtues, to especially practise charity. Michael is informing Adam and Eve to negate the store of maximized self-interest acquired during their time in an illusionary paradise. The state of mind for a real and lasting paradise follows after Adam and Eve have been fully internally actualized.

The departure from the Garden of Eden pre-configures an outline for human psychological development more dependent on dispositional attributes than situational factors. Human development follows a false start to self-actualization, and, at this point, people can choose to negate self-interest in the pursuit of even higher psychological development. The stress, uncertainty, and rush of leaving the Garden of Eden are lesser secondary factors that prompt people to draw upon strong dispositional scaffolding to psychologically advance.

In contrast to humans, Lucifer got stuck in an illusionary paradise. Unlike Milton, I do not possess a sympathetic view towards Lucifer. Humanity left him behind as a bottom-feeder in the Garden of Eden. The view of Lucifer that arose during the Middle Ages is as a classic textbook psychopath who cannot see that by abusing others for personal gain, he is really harming himself.

A psychopath possesses no cognitive and emotional empathy, and advances only self-interest at the extreme detriment to others. Zimbardo (2007) correctly identified Lucifer's sin as *cupiditas*, "...the desire to turn into oneself or take into oneself everything that is 'other' than self. For instance, lust and rape are forms of *cupiditas*, because they entail using another person as a thing to gratify one's own desire; murder for profit is also *cupiditas*." The theological concept of *Cupiditas* fits nicely with the psychological definition of psychopathy and is the closest psychologists can get to observing true evil. The good news is that it is not a pandemic disorder among the general public—it likely occurs in less than 1% of the general population, and people do not easily transform into psychopaths based on situational whims.

The opposite of *cupiditas*, which Zimbardo briefly mentions in a footnote, is *caritas,* which is altruistic love and most identified with that famous saying "Do unto others as you would have them do unto you." How do we come to embody the golden rule? It's not like in the movies where a situational whim turns us into a glorified hero overnight.

My position on how we develop to live by the golden rule is influenced by Adam Smith, and extends beyond his philosophy. Smith was correct to argue that we use imagination when stepping outside the self and into a third impartial imagined station external to the self and the other to employ what he termed sympathy.[1] Station-switching is a progressive first step in using the imagination to place oneself in the shoes of another. Sympathy (herein described as empathy) results in an estimation of mental states outside the first station of the self.

We imagine another person's suffering externally to the self, and that mental image becomes our motive to end the other's suffering. In particular, we turn to negate a store of self-interest in order to meet the challenges presented to us by higher universal principles. These principles are universal because of their broad acceptability across cultures and aim to end suffering and promote happiness among all people.

As you continue reading, I am going to first unveil a new paradigm for human motivational development that will redefine optimal psychological health and provide a roadmap for how to achieve it. Evidence in the form of experimental research will be offered to support the notions of development advanced in this paradigm. Mass survey research will also be offered to show that this improved paradigm is better capable of predicting changes in political values over time and enabling governing systems to meet the needs of a given population. The findings of extensive survey research will suggest that the same old political institutions and power elites that rely on fear, quotas, and rewarding people based on extrinsic rewards (i.e. merit-based systems) need to be replaced in order to facilitate higher-order values development.

My plan is to end this ambitious undertaking by arguing that the West, which has based most institutions on self-interest and rugged individualism, got it wrong. The well-evidenced psychological paradigm offered here will give way to a series of recommendations for new governing, educational, and psychodynamic systems. The West continues to face calamity and turmoil, but it does not have to be this way. By recognizing our true intrinsic motivation to be good, and revolutionizing our systems around this concept, we could usher in the new order—an age of altruism.

Acknowledgments

Gratitude and thanks are extended to a series of colleagues that I have had the pleasure of working with over the years: Dr. Anastasios Gaitanidis, Dr. Herbert Blumberg, and Dr. Carl Levy.

Appreciation and thanks are also extended to Dr. Norman Markowitz and Dr. Hiroshi Obayashi at Rutgers University; Reverend Raymond Kemp at Georgetown University; Dr. Chuck Hill at Whitter College; Dr. Stephen Zavestoski, Dr. Renee Beard, Dr. Colin Silverthorne, and Dr. Stephen Zunes at University of San Francisco; Dr. Ellen Newman at St. Mary's College; and Dr. Del Dickson at University of San Diego. These scholars were instrumental in the administration of my political values survey.

Thanks are also extended to my former supervisor, Reverend F. Hank Hilton, SJ at Loyola University Maryland, and current supervisor Timothy Barry at the University of Greenwich for affording me to the opportunity to conduct important social science research.

Hundreds of university students have taken part in my research studies over the years and their voluntary participation has greatly contributed to the study of pro-social behaviour.

Part 1

Intrinsic Drive to Become Exocentric Altruists

1
An Unenlightened Developmental Psychology

The USA has a debt about to exceed $17 trillion. Part of that massive debt came from the US government's bailout of banks, the executives of which purposefully leveraged people 60–70 percent of their salaries, repackaged the mortgages when they noticed it was impossible to collect, and sold them off at a profit in the derivatives market. The lawyers working for major banks later admitted to falsifying thousands of foreclosure papers to illegally remove Americans from their homes.

We observe that the philosophies of modern Western systems mirror those of the Middle Ages. These self-interested beliefs are what are preventing human advancement to a new era of enlightenment. The Middle Ages witnessed the authoritarian rule of monarchies, the sale of indulgences by priests, and religious wars. This era was defined by substantial economic, cultural, and artistic decline.

The appropriate phrase 'Dark Ages' has been associated with an attitude expressed towards the values system of the Middle Ages. The historian Theodore Mommsen cited Lucia Varga, who had argued that "... the expression the 'Dark Ages' was never primarily a scientific term, but rather, a battle cry 'a denunciation of the mediaeval conception of the world, of the mediaeval attitude toward life, and the culture of the Middle Ages'" (Varga, 1932 cited in Mommsen, 1942).

We can generally expand upon the notion of darkness during the Middle Ages. A dark cloud fell over Europe when the ruling powers asserted that the universe revolved around man. People created extrinsic reward systems for governance, education, and salvation, which still exist in the modern era. The general belief of the Catholic Church, based on the Ptolemaic system, was that the sun and planets had revolved around the earth and that the earth was solely meant for man's survival (i.e. man was the master of his planet). Egocentrism ruled the day, and

3

vanity and pride had cast a figurative dark cloud over human development by promoting a materialist agenda.

The talents, capabilities, and genius of generations of people during the Middle Ages went towards strengthening domestic military apparatuses, wealth generation for aristocratic families, and encroachment on foreign lands because people thought it was their objective to maximize self-interest. Today, egocentrism within governing systems continues to blind large numbers of people from realizing their intrinsic motivation to negate self-interest and experience more optimal psychological health in doing so.

Ironically, it took the son of a wealthy merchant to challenge the central tenet of the Middle Ages. Nicolaus Copernicus challenged the Ptolemaic system that the earth was the center of the universe in *De Revolutionibus*. His work was suspended by the Catholic Church and, eventually, Copernicus' follower Galileo Galilei was placed under house arrest for heresy for supporting the position that the earth revolved around the sun. Despite a strong attempt by Church leaders to suppress Copernicus' theory, evidence of the truth soon emerged with technological advancements, and a period of enlightenment emerged not only in academia, but also in economics, literature, and the arts. The spark of enlightenment occurred when Europe started to upend egocentrism.

Today, the West has again developed a series of egocentric systems that promote extrinsic rewards over cooperation and thus stunt human psychological progression in a forward-moving direction. Such systems are keeping an era of enlightenment and personal growth at bay, while a minority of gamblers and artificial aristocratic families reap the rewards, and economic conditions become continually worse.

Despite the dark era in which we find ourselves, there is light at the end of the tunnel. An economic miracle following World War II permitted larger numbers of the population to progress from materialistic concerns, such as strong defense and economic security, to post-materialistic pursuits, such as healthcare, child care, and more say on the job (Inglehart, 1977). A higher level of egocentrism is developing, which aims to help people maximize their full potential. We are also simultaneously witnessing another unique phenomenon. Mass survey research in Chapter 10 indicates the rise of a third 'new values' type: those who have transcended egocentrism altogether and wish to build a society rooted in pure altruism. These exocentric altruistic value types favor redistribution of wealth and medications to the poor, and a declaration of Swiss-like military neutrality. These altruistic individuals are breaking the mold and challenging the dark era of self-interest, but so far their concerns remain unaddressed by ruling systems that have not kept pace with the populace's psychological development.

Disparities have arisen in the past between the psychological advancement of human populations relative to an inability of prevailing ruling systems to support such advancement. For example, soon after the Middle Ages, advancements in astronomy and the period of enlightenment were not to last long. Humanity started to face an inversion to the Copernican revolution with the philosophy of hedonism that was espoused by Thomas Hobbes. Hobbes was an adherent to the phrase 'war of all against all' (Kavka, 1983). His argument in *The Leviathan* is that people are self-interested and in a constant state of warfare, and Hobbes again resurrected the egocentrism of humanity. Under Hobbes' paradigm, we are called upon to give up our freedom in exchange for security from the state, and the state's responsibility towards us is to help maximize individual self-interest.

The American philosopher John Rawls places the father of capitalism, Adam Smith, in Hobbes' utilitarian camp and draws upon Smith's observations in *The Wealth of Nations* to argue that humans should be left alone to pursue self-interest. Arguably, a book more important than *The Wealth of Nations* was Smith's earlier work, *Moral Sentiments*. In that book, Smith identified how people could use their imagination to step outside the self and help others. For Smith, we are capable of stepping outside the self to sympathize with others through a would-be impartial spectator position (Smith, 1976 [1759]). It is in this position that we use conscientious decision-making to evaluate not only our own actions, but also the actions of others. Through this line of reasoning, Smith created the predecessor to developmental psychology although, over time, a lot of Smith's concepts about altruism were forgotten. Arguably, his economic philosophy never deviated from the utilitarian viewpoint and believed that leaving people to their own devices permits the 'greatest good.' However, a slight revision of Smith's viewpoint on altruism leads to a positive view of human development that is not aligned to utilitarianism—a point to which I will shortly return.

Arthur Schopenhauer refuted the utilitarian viewpoint in his work *On the Basis of Morality* (Schopenhauer, 1965). He argued that people use compassion to directly experience the suffering of others as the same as the self and all others. Thus, Schopenhauer did not believe that imagination plays a role.

My view agrees with Smith to the extent that we use imagination in a station outside the self to enter the shoes of the other. Rather than feeling the suffering of another as our own (which is the illogical conclusion of Schopenhauer's view), we empathize with the plight of the other, and that mental image becomes the motive to negate self-interest. It is important to note that my position is not utilitarian. My theory—that we psychologically develop to negate self-interest—demands new governing and economic systems that cultivate cooperation, rather than rugged individualism and extrinsic rewards.

Today, we are starting to witnesses increasing numbers of post-materialists taking interest in pure altruism as they come to experience the intrinsic motivation to help others. However, there also remains a sizeable minority within the population that, owing to inhibition or threats to human needs gratification, adheres to outmoded self-interest-based systems within the public and private sectors. We have yet to witness a replacement for these systems, which are subjecting humanity literally to a belief system reminiscent of Dark Age philosophies. The reason for this is because attempts at replacing such systems have lacked purpose and have failed to coalesce around our intrinsic motivation to cooperate. Modern day psychology that is rooted in egocentrism has gotten our psychological development wrong and contributed to slowing humanity's advance towards an inevitable altruistic age of enlightenment.

Sigmund and Anna Freud: The Counter-revolutionaries

A few hundred years after the Copernican revolution, the mysticism of the Church's faith healers had faded away, and—fast-forwarding to the twentieth century—humanity gets the birth of psychology as a replacement to the faith healers of the Church during the rise of industrialism in the West. Psychology emerges to guide individuals to better states of psychological health, but, as will soon be revealed, it has fallen into the same trap as the hedonists and utilitarian philosophers who inverted the Copernican revolution. We were subsequently left with a psychology directed and used for an outdated materialist agenda.

Let's start with the 'father' of modern psychoanalytic thought, Sigmund Freud. What did Freud have to say about the notion of *caritas* ("Do unto others as you would have them do to you")? He was highly averse to it:

> In consequence of this primary mutual hostility of human beings, civilized society is perpetually threatened with disintegration. The

interest of work in common would not hold it together; instinctual passions are stronger than reasonable interests. Civilization has to use its utmost efforts in order to set limits to man's aggressive instincts and to hold the manifestations of him in check by psychical reaction-formations. Hence, therefore, the use of methods intended to incite people into identifications and aim-inhibited relations of love, hence the restriction upon sexual life, and hence too the ideal's commandment to love one's neighbor as oneself—a commandment which is really justified by the fact that nothing else runs so strongly counter to the original nature of man. (Freud, 1961, p. 59).

We find Freud fully in agreement with Hobbes' view of humanity. Freud pointed to the violence of the Huns, the Crusades, and warfare to argue that humans were out to satisfy their own self-interest at the expense of others (Freud, 1961, p. 59). This negative view of human nature is completely flawed.

It was self-interest-based governing systems that thwarted people's intrinsic drive to be altruistic. Such systems establish a series of extrinsic rewards that run contrary to human psychological development and resulted in human violence against each other. Freud's incorrect interpretation of the nature of people provided us with a psychology that fed the industrializing era and unveiled a black curtain over Western civilization.

Freudian theory delineates human drives down to the basic-order instincts of sex and death. In his early publications, he defines humans as driven by sexual release and draws upon the myth of Oedipus to describe how male children unconsciously attempt to aggressively overthrow the father owing to sexual attraction for the mother. The sexual drive, or Eros, is described by Freud as the will to power over others.

Freud's later work revises his notion about the pleasure drive. He adopted the view of death as "... ultimately in the service of restoring or reinstating a previous state of undifferentiated internal being, a drive 'which sought to do away with life once more and to re-establish [an] inorganic state'" (Freud, 1933, p. 107 cited in Mills, 2006, p. 374). Freud believed that there existed a dialectical juxtaposition between Eros and death (Mills, 2006). This theory was not short on detractors. Abraham Maslow revised Freud's reductive theory that conflict is central for personality development, but accepts that people are initially driven by the pleasure they receive in satisfying human needs.

The Austrian-born psychoanalyst Heinz Kohut observed that "One of the most difficult emotional feats one has to make in understanding the pleasure principle is to be able to imagine, as Freud could, that the primitive unconscious contains nothing but wishes fulfilled. All there is in this primitive layer of the psyche is hallucinations" (Kohut and Seitz, 1963, p. 20). The instinctual drives for pleasure in the system unconscious are thus illusionary, even by Freudian standards—a point to which I will briefly return.

Anna Freud followed in her father's footsteps by describing all altruism as "altruistic surrender" (Freud, 1946). Her theory has caused many psychoanalysts to conclude that all altruism is pathological or, at the very least, should be viewed with extreme skepticism. She claims that we help others by projecting our desires onto the other. Anna Freud further posits that our unfulfilled wishes stem from the self's inadequacy. Her theory assumes that we gain pleasure by helping to satisfy our wishes in others rather than realize them ourselves. It is granted that some people do help to gain pleasure by vicariously living through others, and become overtaxed when their psychological resources fall short. In this regard, altruistic surrender defines only a very narrow form of egocentric (self-interested altruism) when a person's needs go unmet.

However, Anna Freud's pessimistic view of altruism cannot explain why healthy people have maximized the self-help others. I will discuss cases later in this book, such as multimillionaire Zell Kravinsky, who first maximized the self and then decided to help other people who were significantly different from himself.

Anna Freud failed to take into account human adaptations that constructively use imagination and reflection at higher states of psychological development. We regularly use higher universal principals that cross-cut cultures to reflect in a station outside the self and build a clearer view of the self and the other. Most healthy people who possess the capacity to use adaptive ability clearly recognize the distinctions between the desires of the self and the other, and become empathetically motivated to help the other beyond the aspirations of the self.

My position is that the illusionary drives for pleasure in the unconscious are serving a purpose. Such illusionary drives are building a store of maximized self-interest that a mentally healthy adult later uses to negate. Anna Freud failed to take into account that there may be different forms of altruism based on motivational development, and that a pure form of altruism contributes to improved mental health by counteracting pathology at higher states of human psychological development.

The Human Drive to Live for the Other

This first part of this book is a bold undertaking to formulate a purely altruistic human motivational paradigm. My observations will provide hope to humanity that not all is lost to the darkness of our present age, and, perhaps surprisingly, people who have maximized self-interest stand at the cusp of a profound cognitive shift. This work follows in the tradition of positive psychology to first identify the healthiest psychological state of existence and then to describe how best to bring people to that level of development.

Abraham Maslow originally developed a human motivation paradigm that was a breakthrough for its time, but he did not go far enough. He argued that man is a "wanting animal" who progresses through five stages along an ordered needs hierarchy. They include (i) physiological needs, such as hunger, sexual contact, and thirst; (ii) safety needs, such as protection from crime, authoritarian states, economic insecurity, and disease; (iii) belongingness and love needs, which take the form of friendship, companionship, and camaraderie; (iv) esteem needs, which represent competence, mastery of tasks, and recognition; and, finally, (v) self-actualization needs, which encompass self-fulfillment, knowledge, and maximization of self-interest.

However, Maslow's paradigm fell short at self-actualization. Despite revising Freud's notion that conflict was central to personality development, Maslow positions the peak of human motivation as arising initially around the pleasure principle. He neglected a pressing drive that extends beyond the pursuit of pleasure. Maslow argued that a dichotomy between selfishness and altruism "...is resolved in self-actualizing people" (Maslow, 1970, p. 157). Maslovian application of the needs hierarchy would classify people such as Oskar Schindler as a self-actualizer.

Schindler eventually acquired something very special and diametrically opposed to the maximization of self-interest, and yet he used self-actualization as a stepping stone to achieve a higher state of psychological development by living for the other. Schindler may be viewed as an untouchable icon of humanity—a larger-than-life personality—but, as we will soon discover, regular people who are unfettered in their needs development can progress beyond self-actualization.

Maslow erred in assuming that pure altruism stems from the first station of the self. His opponents were also wrong to suggest that pure altruism comes from a merging of the egos into a universal ego. Pure altruistic motivation occurs in a state outside of the self and the other's ego. It is a third imagined station where perspective-taking contributes to motivational development to negate self-interest. In order to make this discovery, we need to reverse-engineer human motivational pursuits to discover the dispositional scaffolds that support optimal psychological health.

The question becomes what is the ultimate good? The view adopted throughout this book is that ultimate good is living for the sake of others without expecting anything in return. The ultimate good that defines our psychological health requires a negation to the illusionary will for power. Empathizing with another's suffering becomes our motive to negate our own store of self-interest.

Altruism has been termed pathological, normal, necessary, and healthy by various academic discourses. Pathological altruism is defined as when the outcome has irrational and substantial negative consequences to the other or to the self (Oakley et al., 2012, p. 4). In contrast, the philosopher Auguste Comte argued that altruism was necessary and had "... maintained that the chief purpose of our existence was 'vivre pour auturi' (to live for the sake of others)" (Campbell, 1989, p. 31). Given all descriptions for altruism, what is it really? Does pure (selfless) altruistic motivation exist? Is there a separate transcendental state for pure altruism that exceeds the state of self-actualization through negation? Are purely altruistic motivations influenced more by situational (external environmental) factors or dispositional (inner) attributes?

Some social psychologists argue that we are easily led astray in harming others by environmental factors, as if we are puppets at the end of a puppet master's strings. These short-sighted claims offer little to understanding our true nature and potential to resist all forms of evil.

We need more multidisciplinary cooperation between psychology, neuroscience, and genetics to better understand the mind's ability to operate in complex states when defining optimal psychological health. There exist incredible and interwoven biological processes at work through evolution, and expanding far beyond evolution's original purpose and the higher meaning that humans have defined for themselves.

Cognitive Empathy Underpins Pure Altruistic Behaviour

In the last decade, we have witnessed a series of exciting discoveries in neuroscience which, when combined with our knowledge of humanistic psychology, confirms an underlying basis for the existence of pure altruism. Neuroscientists have discovered that there are three forms of empathy, which are distinct, and yet share some overlap with each other and underpin altruistic behavior. Human psychological health is heavily dependent on cognitive, emotional, and motor empathetic development. In particular, cognitive empathy is heavily employed as people psychologically develop to live for all others.

Motor empathy is the ability to mimic and synchronize facial expressions, vocalizations, postures, and movements in other people (Hatfield et al., 1994 cited in Blair, 2005). This form of empathy relies heavily on mirror neurons and is considered a lower form of empathy, which has a strong basis in evolution. It developed in primates as a mechanism to facilitate the parent–child relationship and promote survivability until the age of reproduction.

Emotional empathy can take two different forms. It can be a response to the emotional displays of others—such as facial expressions—and, in this form, heavily overlaps with motor empathy. Emotional empathy can also be a response to emotional stimuli (Blair, 2005). The various discourses in psychoanalytic theory or social neuroscience suggest that emotive empathy can arise in infancy (Benjamin, 1990).

To reiterate, cognitive empathy is perspective-taking or our ability to use imagination to estimate the mental states of others. One recent study found that by 2 years of age, toddlers begin to make appropriate judgment about others' emotional reactions, even without emotional cues (Vaish et al., 2009 cited in Decety and Svetlova, 2012). My theory, well supported by the literature, suggests that motor and emotive empathy are scaffolding the development of cognitive empathy. The ability to estimate the mental states of others becomes stronger over time as we progress through, and extend beyond, illusionary needs gratification.

The existence of cognitive empathy is supported by neuroscience. Neuroimaging studies have provided strong evidence that the medial prefrontal cortex (and especially the anterior paracingulate), the temporal–parietal, and the temporal poles within the brain play an internal role in representing the mental states of others (Brunet et al., 2000; Fletcher et al., 1995; Frith, 2001 Gallagher et al., 2000; Goel et al., 1995; Vogeley et al., 2001, all cited in Blair, 2005).

I cannot understate the importance of the role of cognitive empathy. This is especially true for high achievers. We must ask ourselves, 'Why do we have so much in our advanced industrialized societies, and yet so many people are so unhappy?' Witness the lives of Marilyn Monroe, Elvis Presley, Kurt Cobain, Heath Ledger, and Whitney Houston. There has been a lot of discussion in psychology about the dark side of Maslow's needs hierarchy. Never-ending pursuit of self-interested needs results in over self-gratification, boredom, apathy, and self-destruction

(Csikszentmihalyi, 1999). The mental resources spent on maximizing the self temporarily come at a cost for taking time to step outside the self and empathize with others.

It is for this reason that we desperately require a twenty-first century psychology to help self-actualizers develop their cognitive empathy the same way we physically strengthen world-class athletes. By assisting self-actualizers to recognize that their ultimate meaning and purpose for fulfillment is the same as others is a good first step on the way to overcoming guilt. Beyond this point, the ultimate goal is to encourage self-actualizers to become more than maximized potential.

As you read this book, try to discover how you have developed, and the types of internal energy that help you move forward in your daily life. Has it been expected that you will get married and start a family? Were you driven to start a business to obtain wealth? Were you told to become a poet, musician, or artist to maximize creativity and imagination? How have these drives to satisfy human needs influenced your decision-making when faced with choices of whether or not to help others? If you have attained self-actualization, are you now subject to decreasing marginal satisfaction and apathetic towards life?

We are capable of positive change by perceiving others' mental states and choosing to negate self-interest. Mohandas Gandhi was a successful attorney when he refused orders to get off a train. Karol Wojtyla was an up-and-coming actor when he disobeyed the Nazi occupiers and helped Jewish people escape. Businessman Zell Kravinsky made $45 million before he donated most of his estate to worthy causes. We see examples all around us of people who have developed strong cognitive empathy, which eventually leads to behavior and better states of psychological health beyond personal meaning.

You may be stuck in a rut of boredom after achieving self-actualization, or possess a faulty cognition that there is nothing further beyond satisfying the self's wants and needs. Do not despair! We are going on a journey that will give hope to all of us in a post-industrial era.

The field of psychology is stumped because it cannot figure out why firemen, knowing the South Tower had already collapsed, would sacrifice their lives by entering the North Tower on 9/11 to save people. Were these individuals adverse to Darwinian survival mechanisms? Or, more likely, did the firemen project outside of the self and make helping decisions to sacrifice their lives from a third imagined station by connecting to an altruistic drive?

Social scientists are also at a loss as to why certain soldiers will sacrifice themselves to save the lives of unrelated people. It seems inconceivable that other people will risk torture, ridicule, and prison to promote equality or blow the whistle on corruption. Together, we are about to view the human's true drive to help others. Let's see if we can perceive reality as it really is and win friends over to a psychological theory that helps people live for the other beyond self-actualization. You are about to be introduced to a positive view of human nature, which could, potentially, help revise our governing, educational, and healthcare systems to lift the dark cloud that has fallen over modern Western civilization.

2
Proposed Hyperbola Paradigm

Social psychologists have been trying to build the case that situational factors are more important than dispositional attributes in shaping human behavior. By trying to move beyond Maslow, psychologists may be throwing the baby out with the bathwater.

A more inclusive theory is that biology, learning, and cognition all influence human behavior to some degree (Franken, 1998). However, long before we face a particular situation, internal factors are scaffolding our decision-making ability. And altruistic motivation can be identified as the most important internal source to personality development, which has not only led to the advancement of our species on this planet, but also equips us with the ability to move past our own higher meaning.

Let's examine the case of Ayumu. He is a 7-year-old chimpanzee at Kyoto University who can perform better on certain memory tests when competing with people (Briggs, 2007). Let's assume that Ayumu's memory is better than ours. Why are we not ruled by a planet of the apes (no pun intended)? Direct observation provides us with the answer. Chimps are very poor at cooperation and certainly have not adapted higher cognitive skills, which redefine the purpose of life and the ability to negate that meaning in the service of others.

However, human life is not about ruling the planet, and our positive adaptations would have been wasted if that is the only outcome of developing skills to cooperate. The higher cognitive skills are nature's way of equipping us with the ability to not only redefine our own purpose beyond survivability, but also arrive at pure altruistic motivation to help all living creatures on our planet. Rather than ruling the planet, we follow an advanced developmental pattern to serve and enhance all life. Humans cause harm to themselves and the planet when they become frustrated in the pursuit of illusionary self-interest.

Advances in the social sciences have started to provide insight that the source of altruism is motivationally based. Genetic, trait, and general self-interested altruism fall under the rubric of endocentric altruism. The Polish psychologist Jerzy Karylowski defined endocentric altruism as motivated "...from considerations concerning one's own self-image" (Karylowski, 1984). Endocentric altruism is self-interested altruism. It compliments Maslow's needs hierarchy, builds our store of maximized self-interest, and equips us to succeed in life.

Exocentric altruism is wholly different from endocentric altruism and represents an anomaly to Maslow's self-interested needs hierarchy. Associate Professor of Economics at Monash University, Elias Khalil, states that "Smith discussed in detail how the impartial spectator... arises from station switching, i.e., how the ability to judge others impartially makes one an impartial judge of his own actions" (Khalil, 2004, p.119).

Karylowski builds upon Smith's logic by arguing that exocentric altruism arises "...when the source of gratification lies only in the improvement of the conditions of another person's need" (Karylowsi, 1984, p. 141). *Exo* means external and is a willing suspension of disbelief, by which we imagine what it would be like to be that kind of person (Wispé, 1991).

The social psychologist Daniel Batson took issue not so much with the notion that exocentric altruism exists, but rather that Karylowski as a researcher had never really differentiated in his participants whether they would help to relieve their own distress at watching another's unfortunate situation, or to improve the condition of the other person (Batson, 1991). In other words, Batson took issue with whether Karylowski's measurements of attitudes had reflected actual behavior. Batson does seem to favor more emotional empathy than cognitive empathy as underpinning altruistic action. This position appears unsupported by emerging neurologic evidence. While there is some neurologic overlap between all forms of empathy, it would appear that cognitive empathy very much improves as one ages and gratifies human needs. The newly emerging neurobiological research seems to confirm cognitive empathy as underlying exocentric altruistic behavior.

My recent publication on this subject described the three-station scenario as follows:

As seen in [Figure 2.1] the self, S, then examines the situation of the other, O, from the would-be impartial spectator position. We use imagination to step outside the self and enter a third station of what it would be like to be in the other's position. Residing in the third station creates an empathetic build up, which appears to be alleviated by helping others. (Babula, 2007, p. 319)

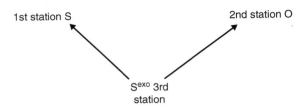

Figure 2.1 Three-station scenario. First published in Babula (2007) and adapted from Khalil (2001). Reprinted by permission

People are continually developing from endocentric altruism (i.e. helping to gain a benefit or relieve our own distress) to exocentric altruism (i.e. helping to benefit others' needs). However, this is not to say that the majority of us will advance to exocentric altruism overnight. Many people are empathy-impaired and will make poor decisions when faced with bad situations. Over-gratification or frustration of human needs blurs our ability to empathize with the suffering of others.

Only a small minority of people have thus far lived a life driven mostly by the true exocentric realm. But the importance of exocentric altruism, especially in an era when increasing numbers of people have become self-actualized, cannot be overlooked. It only takes a small number of exocentric altruists to reach the political realm or to become advocates for all others, and this can greatly affect the direction and psychological development of humanity.

Revised Motivation Paradigm

A decade before Maslow developed the needs hierarchy, the USA had just emerged from World War II, and psychologists overlooked a goldmine in defining optimal psychological health. There were numerous cases of self-sacrifice during that war which could not be explained by the maximization of self-interest. Let's review some of those cases here.

The case of US army sergeant Elmer J. Burr proves an anomaly to self-interested psychological paradigms. The official military record states that "During an attack near Buna, New Guinea, on 24 December 1942, 1st Sgt. Burr saw an enemy grenade strike near his company commander. Instantly and with heroic self-sacrifice he threw himself upon it, smothering the explosion with his body. 1st Sgt. Burr thus gave his life in saving that of his commander" (U.S. Army Center of Military History, 2011).

Another example from World War II is that of an injured solider named Richard Earl Bush. When the medical center he had been taken to came under attack, Bush sacrificed himself. According to the record, "Although prostrate under medical treatment when a Japanese hand grenade landed in the midst of the group, Cpl. Bush, alert and courageous in extremity as in battle, unhesitatingly pulled the deadly missile to himself and absorbed the shattering violence of the exploding charge in his body, thereby saving his fellow marines from severe injury or death despite the certain peril to his own life" (ibid).

William Robert Caddy also threw himself on a grenade to save others. The official record states that "a Japanese grenade fell beyond reach in the shell hole. Fearlessly disregarding all personal danger, Pfc. Caddy instantly dived on the deadly missile, absorbing the exploding charge in his own body and protecting the others from serious injury" (ibid).

Attacked by Japanese soldiers in the middle of the night, Anthony Damato also sacrificed himself to save others. The report tells the story: "When 1 of the enemy approached the foxhole undetected and threw in a hand grenade, Cpl. Damato desperately groped for it in the darkness. Realizing the imminent peril to all 3 and fully aware of the consequences of his act, he unhesitatingly flung himself on the grenade and, although instantly killed as his body absorbed the explosion, saved the lives of his 2 companions" (ibid).

John Fardy's actions also represent an anomaly to self-interested paradigms in psychology. It was reported that "Shortly thereafter, an enemy grenade fell among the marines in the ditch. Instantly throwing himself upon the deadly missile, Cpl. Fardy absorbed the exploding blast in his own body, thereby protecting his comrades from certain and perhaps fatal injuries" (ibid).

Thus far, I have reviewed only a handful of cases which indicate that humans will readily sacrifice themselves for people who are not genetically related to them. The official records are amazing in revealing the large numbers of people who have sacrificed their lives for non-relations during war.

Recently, extreme forms of self-sacrifice were also observed during the 11 September 2001 attacks. Father Mychal Judge went into the North Tower and administered last rites to the dying without concern for his safety or welfare; he was killed when the North Tower collapsed. These were common, everyday people like you and me who died so that others could live or be comforted. Were these individuals naïve or self-destructive? The emerging evidence suggests otherwise. These individuals were at the pinnacle of full human health.

The new paradigm proposed here adopts a hyperbola paradigm over the traditional textbook pyramid depiction of the needs hierarchy. Hyperbolas are observed in many facets of nature, such as comets in space, which have positive energy, or energy greater than zero. The faster a comet accelerates in speed, the more the particle approaches infinity and assumes a trajectory that is a hyperbola—a virtually never-ending movement in a forward-moving direction.

Gottfried Wilhelm Von Leibniz argued that "According to the hypothesis of the hyperbola, there would be no beginning, and the instants or states of the world would have been increasing in perfection from all eternity" (Beardsley, 1960, p. 301). The approach involved here is to adopt a hyperbola model to represent the complementary nature of certain pro-social behavior paralleling the needs hierarchy and extending beyond it.

Four forms of altruism, namely genetic/trait, egoistic, egocentric, and altercentric, parallel and compliment Maslow's original five needs and help people advance to full human potential. These types of altruism were described by Khalil, although, surprisingly, no one to date has observed their relationship with Maslow's needs hierarchy.

At the base of the hyperbola, people pursue basic survival needs, such as physiological and security concerns. It is here that our core consciousness is heavily at work to promote internal homeostasis. We may help protect immediate relatives from dangerous scenarios to secure the continuity of our gene pool. Or we might cooperate in armies or the police force to secure food, oil, or other land resources to further physical or security concerns. Mirror neurons and emotional empathy are at play in physical needs gratification, as the brain dedicates less energy to higher meaning and perspective-taking abilities.

We advance to love, and belongingness and self-esteem needs to achieve net gains. Evolution plays a large role in the development of our species to intermediate order needs. We inherited from our primate ancestors the ability to mimic emotional states in order to join collectives for survival purposes. From a game theory perspective, people at the level of social and self-esteem partake in egoistic altruism out of the belief that helping the group will eventually aid them. In other words, we may help others to gain a positive reputation, develop a larger social grouping, or attain advancement with the workplace.

For example, we might engage in charity so that our boss will read a positive review in the local newspaper and give us a promotion. It is here that humans' internal brain mechanisms are mimicking others' emotional states or responding to others' emotional stimuli in concert with motor empathy to bring about self-advancement. We are monitoring the other just enough to achieve our own security, social, and esteem goals.

The next stage on the hierarchy is self-actualization. At self-actualiza-tion, people desire to help others because it either gives them pleasure (egocentric altruism) or they believe it is their moral duty (altercentric altruism), or a combination of both. Maslow revealed that self-actualiz-ers are egocentric altruists, observing that "...the person doing his duty and being virtuous is simultaneously seeking his pleasure and being happy" (Maslow, 1970, p. 179). In this condition, an individual may help others to relieve his or her own distress at observing expressions or emotional stimuli of the other person. The inspiration for egocentric altruism is more related to motor and emotive empathetic reactions, or some combination thereof with less involvement of cognitive func-tion. For example, when we give money to a poor person on the street, it gives us a sense of euphoria and makes us feel better to alleviate the distress of another person.

Self-actualizers are also altercentric altruists. *Alter* implies 'other,' and Maslow states that:

> These individuals customarily have some mission in life...This is not necessarily a task that they would prefer or choose for themselves; it may be a task that they feel is their responsibility, duty, or obliga-tion...In general these tasks are nonpersonal or unselfish, concerned rather with the good of mankind in general, or of a nation in general, or of a few individuals in the subject's family.
>
> However far apart [the self-actualizer] is from [fellow humans] at times, he nevertheless feels a basic underlying kinship with these creatures whom he must regard with, if not condescension, at least the knowledge that he can do many things better than they can, that he can see things that they cannot see, that the truth that is so clear to him is for most people veiled and hidden. This is what Adler called the older brotherly attitude. (Maslow, 1970, p. 161, 166)

Self-actualizers help out of moral dictum or out of a sense of duty. The sense of duty becomes a moralistic drive when we believe that some superior knowledge would otherwise go to waste if unused. The alter-centric altruist draws upon the self to fulfill a self-projected duty on the other. In a sense, the altercentric altruist believes they are operating from the station of the other. However, motor empathy underlies alter-centric altruism, and this type of altruistic motivation is still derived from the first-person perspective.

For example, some Americans drew upon moral attitudes to donate food or rebuild shelter for the victims of hurricane Katrina. However, altercentric behavior is not pure altruism, and the helper's self-projection may cause him/her to overlook the recipient's requirements. Similar to egocentric altruism, people help out of altercentric altruism more to relieve their discontent with another's suffering.

In the case of hurricane Katrina, a lot of temporary Federal Emergency Management housing was unnecessary as the victims of the disaster voiced a need for greater investment in education, grants for small businesses, and free healthcare for poor communities. Unfortunately, while a lot of high-level government workers may have possessed good intentions, their moral dictum in an emergency to meet quotas caused them to overlook the intended recipients' actual needs.

How is it possible that self-interested needs of gratification and complimentary endocentric altruistic motivations contribute to the development of exocentric altruistic motivation? Neurobiology hints that the human capacity for higher cognitive empathy increases as we develop a cohesive sense of self. Some social neurobiologists claim that

> We stress the importance of maturation of the prefrontal cortex and its reciprocal connection with the limbic system and development of a sense of self to account for more complex forms of cognitive abilities such as mentalizing and language that interact with our older abilities (intersubjectivity and motivation to care for others). Compared to other species, humans indeed exhibit more advanced and flexible levels of empathy, tied to self-awareness and perspective-taking. These new levels of information processing provide both greater understanding of others' affective and mental states and flexibility in behavioral responses. (Decety and Svetlova, 2012, p. 3)

The field of social neurobiology is on the right track, but suggests that parental care and learning lead to the cohesive sense of self. The trend in academia is too often to forget or relegate the role of needs gratification in personality development as subsidiary to social factors, when the evidence suggests that needs gratification is still paramount.

It is also true that a person's mental state at self-actualization needs to be qualified because although there may be cognitive empathetic involvement playing a role among self-actualizers, it is certainly not as clear or pure as when a person moves to the state of exocentric altruistic motivation. Maslow was so close to defining optimal psychological health, but could just not see past the illusionary pleasure principle. And today, many neuroscientists and psychologists are still rigidly stuck in a first-person perspective of psychological health.

An advanced self-actualizer has gained functional autonomy and immunity to threats over time, and is less distracted by lower-order needs gratification (Maslow, 1970, p. 114). Maslow provided several examples arguing that depriving love is no great threat to a person loved their entire life. His argument is that lengthy needs gratification makes us immune to threats to lower-order needs gratification.

A self-actualizer's decision-making process is clearer than at any point along the needs hierarchy. The self-actualizer is better capable of discerning what it would be like to be in another person's shoes. And the self-actualizer has built up a maximized store of self-interest to be negated. What Maslow missed was that the human mind develops to step outside of the self through imagination, and thus to enter a third station. The third station is uncontaminated by the self or with the self's desire to merge its meaning with the other (i.e. altercentric altruism).

We develop the ability to represent the emotions of others from a state that is unaffected by relieving our own distress. Through clarity and a greater propensity to use imagination at self-actualization, cognitive empathy emerges as a more distinct factor that increases a person's motivation to help others.

This is not to say that people all along the needs hierarchy fail to satisfy some degree of exocentric altruistic motivation. Maslow was quick to point out that people are not a hundred percent satisfied in any one need at a time. He indicated that a person who has satisfied eighty percent of self-esteem needs and is beginning to pursue self-actualization needs would still test positive for self-esteem at the same time self-actualization starts to become a predominant motivator.

The concept that people advance along the needs hierarchy based on decreasing percentages of satisfaction holds true to the point of self-actualization. After reaching a heightened pursuit for self-actualization, the model opens up to a limitless motivational gratifier.

The hyperbola model in Figure 2.2 condones the concept of decreasing percentages up to a certain point, as shown with the inward bend toward self-actualization. At the point of self-actualization, the model opens up as we start to negate self-interests to live for the other. Despite being relatively less gratified toward the higher end of the hierarchy, we are capable of gratifying larger percentages of exocentric altruism than, say, self-esteem or self-actualization.

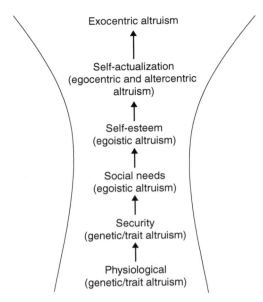

Figure 2.2 The pattern of motivational and altruistic development

Human Intrinsic Drive to Help Others

Maslow argued that "Man is a wanting animal and rarely reaches a state of complete satisfaction except for a short period of time" (Maslow, 1954, p. 69). The emerging evidence suggests this statement requires significant revision. Man is a giving animal with the capacity for pure altruism after acquiring a relative store of self-interest and choosing to negate it. We are at a very exciting point in human discovery of the mind. Human evolution has progressed far beyond the use of motor empathy for self-survival purposes, and people have moved beyond redefining our own sense of purpose. We are starting to step outside the confines of first-person consciousness through imagination to connect with an intrinsic drive to help others.

The ancient Greeks used to say *gnōthi seauton* ('know thyself'), or know one's place before the gods. That phrase has taken on a different meaning over time and people have been driven to discover the self alone. For the last sixty decades we have been told that the maximization of the self is our ultimate psychological goal. Now we come to realize with a more advanced scientific approach that living for the other surpasses the maximization of self-interest.

This knowledge of our ultimate purpose changes everything. It calls for major replacements of our self-interested-based governing, and educational and mental health systems with systems that are based on cooperation and tap our internal drive to be good.

3
Expanding the Scope of Biological Evolution

The psychiatrist Viktor Frankl, who authored *Man's Search for Ultimate Meaning*, had a difficult life. By the age of 39, he had lost his wife, mother, and brother during the holocaust. He emerged after the war, having languished in a concentration camp, to go on and contribute heavily to the development of existential theory. He claimed that better states of psychological health are obtained by locating meaning in life. A statement by Frankl has resonated with me for some time. He said that "No animal will ever raise the question whether or not its existence has a meaning, but man does..." (Anon, 2007a). An evolutionary theorist might take issue with this statement, but it does not conflict with evolution. Humans have adapted cognitive skills that enable them to define a purpose for themselves.

Frankl's shortcoming was not existentialist theory's incompatibility with evolution. His concept of higher meaning folds back into the framework for self-actualization. Under Frankl's paradigm, people find meaning in the suffering experienced by the self or others, and aim to reduce our own or another's suffering in order to advance our own purpose to live. We gain inertia or energy by helping others. Once the self is maximized, this can again result in boredom, over-gratification, or apathy unless new meaning is pursued. Because most people's talents tend to be specific, rather than eclectic, there are only so many different meanings one person is able to pursue before losing the inertia that comes with mastery.

My theory is that people develop personal meaning and build psychological resources to later negate it to live for all others. In this regard, Frankl's view was one step behind the theory offered here. People can advance to become resistant to potential existential crises that result from declining human abilities to sustain personal meaning, mastery,

24

and the maximization of the self. It is important to mention that my theory is also not incompatible with evolution.

The higher-order motivational pursuits in the hyperbola paradigm require an extensive expansion of biological evolutionary theory. A more constructive approach for evolutionary biologists is to recognize that the survival mechanisms provided to us by evolution served as the starting point to build the scaffolds for our higher cognitive development and the creation of our own purpose. Certain people have progressed past rewriting our own purpose by using positive adaptations to negate self-interest. The difficulty for the modern human is how to progress beyond their illusionary, albeit necessary, first steps toward locating personal meaning and development to the negation of self-interest at exocentric altruism.

Today, too many dogmatic evolutionary theorists are strengthening psychological illusions with the false assumption that our primary purpose is only aimed at inclusive fitness and survival. It is agreed that evolution created initial survival intention in humans, but we have developed and adapted to redefine our original purpose, and, eventually, some humans advanced to the negation of the individual will to power.[1] We became the creators of our own destiny only to later negate self-interest by choosing to live for others.

It is granted that evolutionary biology has come a long way since the days of Herbert Spencer and the concept of "survival of the fittest," but needs to progress much further if biologists are to better model human psychological development. Spencer's theory posited that the strong members of a given species survive, while the weak perish. Today, most evolutionary biologists concede that many mammals, and especially primates and humans, are highly social creatures and that success is dependent upon cooperation rather than competition.

However, a caveat is added by many evolutionary theorists that we are only altruistic when it suits our own 'purpose.' We must ask whether our purpose is solely developed by evolution's original design, or whether we evolved beyond these initial steps as conscious beings to create our own purpose and its negation. Once we have a say in the matter, this completely changes the entire picture of human evolution.

The position taken here is that humans have had the opportunity to define for themselves a higher purpose. They have also taken the liberty to negate self-interest stemming from their redefined meaning to helping others. Where is the evidence that we have adapted and redefined the purpose of our species? We can look to language and reflection with regard to our consciousness as the initial positive adaptations.

Today there exists apprehension in the biological sciences in recognizing that humans may have progressed beyond natural selection. The biologist Frans De Waal believes we are social animals for hedonistic reasons. De Waal argues that cognitive empathy has been "...made for [us] by natural selection. Weighing the consequences of behavior over evolutionary time, it has endowed primates with empathy, which ensures that they help others under the right circumstances" (de Waal, 2009, p. 115). He goes onto to say, "Yes, we derive pleasure from helping others, but since this pleasure reaches us via the other, and only via the other, it is genuinely other-oriented" (ibid, p. 116).

'Intentionality' relates heavily to De Waal's assumption. Evolution may have initially equipped us with the intention to help others for some personal gain. For example, let's say we really enjoy soccer. Under De Waal's paradigm, we might donate uniforms to a soccer team because watching the team play in it would provide us with pleasure.

But we possess language and adapted memory, and can reflect on our own consciousness to create our own vision of meaning. We can also step outside the self to use these same positive adaptations to negate self-interest. The beauty of evolution is that it has equipped us to progress past its own rules. And we have been redefining and breaking the rules in an effort to reconnect with the other.

Giacomo Rizzolatti's collaborative team effort in discovering mirror neurons in monkeys was a noteworthy accomplishment that helps to solidify evolution's original intention for humans to engage in social behavior for survival and reproductive purposes at lower stages of needs pursuits. Rizzolatti's team noticed that mirror neurons in the F5 region of the frontal cortex of a macaque's brain became activated when the monkey observed a human moving food around a testing box (Di Pellegrino et al., 1992).

Similarly, in 2011, researchers at the University of Chicago performed an experiment to see if a rat would release another rat from a cage without a reward (Bartal et al., 2011). Not only did the rat engage in such behavior, but when offered a reward the rat would also release its fellow vermin and share a chocolate treat.

De Waal is quick to point out that because motor empathy has been discovered in animals empathy and altruistic behavior are not uniquely human. As we will soon see, the use of motor empathy is derived in many species of mammals as a fulfillment of evolution's initial intention. It has enhanced parent–child relationships so that children can survive to a reproductive age and this purpose has served its ends. It has led to humans flourishing on the planet and has permitted us to develop higher cognitive facilities past other species, which make us unique.

Science requires a different approach to evolutionary theory. Cognitive neuroscientists argue that "Rather than replacing older structures with newer ones, evolution is a patchwork of additions. These additions are integrated into older elements, but do not replace them and do not necessarily control them" (Konner, 2010 cited in Decety and Svetlova, 2012). Recent neurological research is closing the chapter on the cognitive empathetic uniqueness of our species:

> ... children's mind reading abilities that interact with emotional circuits are implemented in a network of regions that include mPFC [medial prefrontal cortex], right pSTS/TPJ [posterior superior temporal sulcus/temporoparietal junction], and posterior cingulate cortex. That network supports rather complex cognitive processes that may be unique to humans, and these areas (especially the prefrontal cortex) follow an extremely protracted developmental course, with aggregate changes well into adolescence. (Casey et al., 2005, and Luna and Sweeney, 2004 cited in Decety and Svetlova, p. 14)

There is a host of factors that permit us to continually strengthen higher cognitive processes long past adolescence. In the case of parents who are struggling below the poverty line and incapable of putting food on the table or educating children, they are likely to be distracted by survival mechanisms. A person who is not accepted by others, unable to fulfill esteem needs owing unemployment, or incapable of achieving their dreams are similarly likely to encounter deficits and distractions. A person who becomes addicted to illusionary self-interested pursuits at self-actualization will stand a chance of negatively affecting their dopamine system in such a way as to self-destruct without realizing their higher exocentric altruistic potential.

The point that will be made in this chapter is that we are unique and that the initial intentions of evolution are at play when the illusionary drive for pleasure goes unmet. We will start by reviewing evolution's initial intentionality and how it continues to play a role in our development as we progress through the needs hierarchy. It will be concluded that people have rewritten the rules of evolution's initial purpose and our own defined higher meaning in an effort to live for the sake of others.

What Evolution Tells us About Empathetic Scaffolds

We have witnessed an explosion of research in cognitive neuroscience over the last decade. Researchers and students interested in the most recent review of the literature in this area are referred to Jean Decety and Margarita Svetlova's work on the matter (2012).

The emerging research indicates that some forms of empathy are shared with other mammals, while higher cognitive empathy is unique among humans. What Decety and Svetlova tend to leave out of the recent literature review is the importance of human needs gratification in the process.

My position is that evolution goes hand in hand with much of Maslow's needs hierarchy and self-interested altruistic compliments. The sequence of needs achievement helped us to meet evolution's initial purpose for our existence, and as early people started to gratify self-actualization we adapted personal reflection and imagination to create a higher meaning beyond the mechanistic intentions of evolution.[2] Today, some of those same adaptations are at play in deciding to negate the self-interest-produced higher personal meaning.

Let's take a moment to reflect upon our evolutionary development. Most research starts by citing Sober and Wilson's differentiation between evolutionary altruism from psychological altruism (Sober and Wilson, 1998 cited in Decety and Svetlova, 2012). Evolutionary altruism is when a species reduces its reproductive fitness relative to the reproductive fitness of one or more organisms (Decety and Svetlova, 2012). Psychological altruism is a motivational state with the goal of increasing another's welfare (ibid). It is in mammals that empathic-based altruism started to heavily arise with the intention that parental care would bring about reproductive success.

Decety and Svetlova state that "Basic affective circuits emerged much earlier in brain evolution than higher cognitive capacities" (2012, p. 4). The researchers cited studies as early as 1959 which showed that rats capable of pressing a level to obtain food would stop doing so if their action is paired with the delivery of electric shocks to another rat (Church, 1959, p. 132 cited in Decety and Svetlova, 2012). They also cited research studies where the skin temperatures of chimpanzees decreased as a result of watching emotionally-laden videos, or when other chimpanzees where injected with needles or viewed videos of needles themselves (Parr, 2001 cited in Decety and Svetlova, 2012). Chimpanzees react to emotional stimuli similarly to humans and render effective responses (Hatfield, 2009 cited in Decety and Svetlova,

2012). However, the chimps in the study experienced merely a basic form of simulated affective empathy, but in no way did these animals progress to higher-level adaptive skills, such as personal reflection or imagination.

The emerging evidence suggests that evolution's initial rules are no longer in play, as we have taken the liberty to rewrite them. Decety and Svetlova posit: "Moreover, empathy in humans is assisted by other abstract and domain-general high-level cognitive abilities such as executive function, language, and perspective taking which enhance and expand the range of behaviours that can be driven by empathy" (Decety and Svetlova, 2012, p. 4).

The actions of police officer Larry DePrimo, who used his income to purchase boots for a homeless man in New York City, or educator Victoria Soto, who shielded her students in the Newtown Connecticut shootings, hints at human behavior that has evolved far beyond inclusive fitness—our redefined search for meaning—and towards the utter negation of the self in the service of the other. We even have the ability as a species to empathize with those who are vastly different from us.

On 2 January 2007, Wesley Autrey, an African–American construction worker with two young daughters jumped onto the tracks at a New York Subway system to save the life of a white 20-year-old film student who had experienced a seizure. Autrey's young daughters watched the altruistic action of their father.

I also refer to the case of Maksymilian Maria Kolbe when referring to examples of people who help others outside our immediate familial circles. Kolbe was a Roman Catholic Priest in Poland during World War II. He was arrested by the Nazis for hiding 2,000 Jewish prisoners during the holocaust. He was eventually transferred to Auschwitz and received the prisoner number 16670.

On a visit to Auschwitz in 2001, Dean Richard Hunter from Seton Hall University's Business School took me on a tour of the cell where Kolbe had died and provided me the details of his death. Kolbe had volunteered to take the place of Franciszek Gajowniczek, a father and married prisoner who was sentenced to death by starvation because three unrelated prisoners had allegedly escaped. The guards had wanted to clear the bunker after 2 weeks and only Kolbe had survived the starvation. When the guards arrived to give him the injection, he lifted his arm in compliance.

Kolbe demonstrated the embodiment of true exocentric altruistic motivation. Of course, without evolution's originally stated intention, we would never have arrived at Kolbe's personality type in the first place. But we did arrive at him through the positive adaptation of cognitive ability, imagination, and reflection, which far transcends Darwinian survival mechanisms.

A true exocentric altruist has developed by silencing the will to power and all the pleasures associated with it—the ability to serve all others. This is not an easy task. It is difficult to deny the will and turn to the golden rule, practice patience with others, and turn the other cheek, but cognitive empathy becomes a very powerful motivator as a healthy person starts to place the self in the shoes of others.

Kolbe's actions represent the pinnacle for human mental development that our evolution, extending far beyond the animal kingdom, has been hurling towards at all along. We can confidently conclude that motor and affective empathies scaffold higher cognitive empathy and the use of imagination to step into the position of another person.

We must remember that higher-order needs gratification is not dependent on income alone and that any of us are capable of pure altruism, especially in emergency scenarios. Humans draw upon a source of maximized self-interest to negate the self and help others in an instant. But, as we will soon see, motor and affective empathies shared with the animal kingdom tend to invoke endocentric altruism, which helps us eliminate needs frustration and develop to the point of maximized self-interest. Once reaching self-actualization, we then have the ability to turn to its negation. The functionally autonomous exocentric altruist, who continually engages in pro-social behavior without consideration of the self, and rarely falters when faced with long-term deprivation such as Kolbe, tend to emerge in larger numbers from the well-developed self-actualized cohort.

Evolution and the Sequence of Needs Gratification

Currently, the field of evolution is far from a consensus on why humans are altruistic. Evolutionary theorists, such as Sober, Wilson, Dawkins, and many others, have offered various reasons for the existence of egoistic, egocentric, and altercentric types of altruism mentioned in Chapter 2. And, generally, disparate evolutionary theories fall short in capturing the big picture because they rehash evolution's initial purpose without considering the possibility that humans advanced far beyond its mechanistic rules.

What are we to make of all these theories? Rather than enhancing debate between evolutionary theorists, a more fruitful approach is to take a breath, step back, and explore the possibility of common denominators between evolutionary theories that help to explain how we developed to sacrifice for the other.

Let's start by exploring evolution at the very base of human existence. At a very basic level, humans gratify physical needs to ensure a state of homeostasis and regulation of bodily functions. A human who is starving or dehydrated will be primarily motivated for survival before concentrating on other needs.

David Brooks, a columnist for the *The New York Times*, wrote a most interesting piece on tribal customs that predate a lot of modern human society (Brooks, 2013). He recounted the story of Siriono Indians in Bolivia where a husband left his wife to die because she had become a burden on the tribe's ability to meet vital physical needs gratification. The husband did not even say goodbye to his wife as the tribe departed.

Does this mean that the tribe was somehow self-interested? The more likely scenario is that the tribe's form of pro-social behavior is defined mostly by evolution's original intention. These individuals view life and their role in the collective as a cyclical purpose for survival, rather than ascribing any form of individual or collective meaning and negation of meaning.

We can learn a lot about the precursors to our advanced mental development by studying tribal behavior. Humans in tribal societies very much practice motor and affective empathy as it aids their ability to gratify physical needs that are in short supply. Brooks mentions that tribal women nurse on demand and spend most of their time with skin-to-skin contact with their infants (ibid). Infants in tribal societies develop quicker neural–motor skills than people in modern societies, which serves their ability to hunt and gather to ensure survivability.

Today, many people's search for existential meaning and its negation is not completely detached from evolution's original purpose. When initially pursuing human motivational development from the illusionary vantage point, we are operating, to an extent, within the rules of evolution.

The literature mentions that attachment is "…defined as an innate biological system promoting proximity seeking between an infant and a specific attachment figure in order to increase the likelihood of survival to a reproductive age" (Sroufe, 2000 cited in Decety and Svetlova, 2012). Studies on the matter indicate that basic empathic responses underlie egoistic altruism, which has evolved to help us achieve security. In one study, "…the sense of security led participants to adopt a more empathetic attitude not only to close relationship partners, but also to non-intimate others" (Mikulincer et al., 2001 cited in Decety and Svetlova, 2012). A mother's smile that is reflected back by a child, joint giggling between a parent and child, and a child's ability to recognize a caregiver's voice or scent are all examples of motor and affective empathy serving as bonding mechanisms to enhance the offspring's sense of security. This use of basic empathy to gratify security needs progresses well into adolescence and beyond as we continually evaluate our fellow species' facial movements and emotions in order to obtain shelter, wealth, and protection for survival and reproduction.

When did our primordial need for security first arise? The human brainstem evolved from reptiles. Reptilians had evolved long necks and bodies to be able to see over competitors and obtain prey. This goes a long way towards explaining consumer behavior during the past decade of warfare. The thought among those desiring security is that we must obtain the next sports utility vehicle or Hummer to stay above our rivals. Of course, the initial intention of evolution becomes irrational to a human with higher reflection and imagination adaptations.

We continue through the rungs of evolution's original purpose as people advance to social and self-esteem needs gratification. A recent journal article caught my attention not because of its comical title ('Becoming a Vampire without Being Bitten'), but because it provided evidence that the human brain has evolved internal mechanisms to gain pleasure from using motor and affective empathy in the pursuit of social needs.

The narrative collective assimilation research tested whether reading caused college students to become part of the collective described by a written story. The results indicated that subjects who identified with the wizards in *Harry Potter* or vampires in *Twilight* did achieve higher levels of life satisfaction, and positive affect in doing so (Gabriel and Young, 2011). Humans have evolved as a social species in joining groups from a game theory perspective, and motor and emotional empathy are likely overlapping with cognitive empathy in producing this outcome.

Evolution's original purpose is also at work as people advance to the pursuit of self-esteem and self-actualization, although we see greater use of adaptive ability to define higher meaning and purpose at self-actualization. The drive for emotional recognition from peers helps to establish alpha males and females among our species for reproductive purposes. Have you ever witnessed that colleague who draws upon emotional intelligence to establish connections at work? Why do we act as good citizens in market transactions and stock trading? We measure up others and invest in them to receive benefits and pursue self-esteem in an effort to ensure survivability.

As we progress to satisfy higher percentages of self-actualization, people begin to engage adaptive abilities in defining higher meaning. Self-actualizers, in particular, are an inquisitive lot. Maslow's transpersonal psychology would suggest that the self-actualizer might metaphysically recognize that their meaning is shared by others, and engage in greater levels in altruism by doing so. There is evidence in support of this theorem. Self-actualization concerns heavily affect our dopamine system beyond social needs gratification. Self-actualizers spend a lot of energy maintaining heightened dopamine due to achievement, and one of the outlets to accomplish such a task is to help others out of pleasure. The self-actualizer's attempt to merge their meaning with the pursuit of collective satisfaction is also evident in that we have described self-actualizers as being moralistic and motivated by altercentric altruism.

However, all along the hyperbola paradigm, we witness one-off altruistic acts that cannot be explained by reciprocal motivation. Even when dealing with selfish and evil individuals, we see altruists such as Kolbe stepping up. He did not leave it to his neighbor to help. Kolbe's actions are evidence that free-rider issues are non-existent upon one's development of the motivation to negate the self.

Rather, what we are witnessing are the elements of pure altruism cropping up all along the hyperbola paradigm. The emergence of exocentric concerns is not explained by the mechanistic workings of evolution in relation to endocentric altruism. Some preliminary interest in exocentric altruism emerges, even as we advance through illusionary stages of self-interested needs pursuits and altruistic compliments, but it is not until we have mostly satisfied evolution's initial purpose that we become free to select a higher meaning and to use adaptive abilities to negate self-interest.

The human driven by self-interest alone will experience impermanence. Human satisfaction possesses a curvilinear relationship with Maslow's original needs hierarchy. As one hits the peak at self-actualization, the tendency for overindulgence and personal decline is present because individual meaning is deceptive and fleeting.

As intentional beings created by evolution, we adapted and rewrote the rules a second time to negate the will to power in the service of others, and, in doing so, achieved greater states of permanence. There is a huge difference between living to continually maximize self-interest and negating one's acquired store of self-interest. Exocentric altruists are continually growing, advancing, and increasingly resistant to over-gratification.

The exocentric altruist is essentially two steps ahead of the initial intentionality of evolution. We have come to create the healthiest of our own species by our own rules, and, more importantly, by breaking our own rules through negating self-interest.

4

'The unlikely Samaritans'[1]

When I was 16 years old, I went to see the movie *Schindler's List* for the first time and was perplexed by the story of Oskar Schindler, a Nazi party member and businessman who spent his entire fortune to save 1,100 Jewish people during the Holocaust. The movie and recollections of survivors never really pinpoint why Schindler suddenly gave away his fortune to save lives. The movie was an eye-opening experience and prompted me to address the question of the meaning of life.

We can infer a few things about Schindler. He was initially out to maximize full human potential as an entrepreneur. His initial meaning and purpose were defined by wealth acquisition. He also had a strained relationship with his wife, and turned to extramarital affairs. Maslow had observed that self-actualizers can sometimes seem cold by cutting off their spouse or friends. Schindler appeared to be a self-actualizer who violated evolution's intentionality under emergency conditions.

After 20 years, I find myself equally as interested in the historical character of Oskar Schindler as the movie's director and producer, Steven Spielberg. A biography of Spielberg indicated that he had rejected a salary for *Schindler's List* and believed the film would be a failure (McBride, 1997, pp. 424–7). It seemed irrational to me that a multi-millionaire, whose primary purpose for much of his life was to maximize financial gain, would spend a significant amount of time on a project without compensation. It was while pondering this thought that it hit me. Most psychology experiments surrounding pro-social behavior had concentrated on religious figures, seminarians, and others who were deemed to be of upstanding 'moral' character in the community. And often these experiments showed that situational variables affected more the helping behavior of participants than internal personality determinants. And, until now, we have been unable to demonstrate psychological advancement at the more advanced evolutionary process, which includes the negation of self-interest.

However, my observations of Spielberg's reasons for doing the Schindler project, and the actions of other businessmen, such as Zell Kravinsky (real estate tycoon), Thomas Monaghan (founder of Domino's Pizza), and Warren Buffet (founder of Berkshire Hathaway), in donating their time and fortunes to help others suggest that social scientists had studied the wrong cohort all along. These hurried businesspeople are heavily preoccupied with daily life and still appear to strive to negate self-interest in the service of others. They could easily say 'no' to helping other people. But they choose to help: not because they are pressured, but because strong internal attributes are scaffolding their drive to help the other.

My focus throughout this chapter is not to linger too long on the story of *Schindler's List* or its director/producer. Rather, there is a twofold objective in this chapter. First, my goal is rehabilitate the importance of dispositional attributes when studying human advancement along the hyperbola paradigm in relation to environmental factors. Second, I will investigate the relationship between helping behavior along an intrinsic versus extrinsic motivational paradigm to explore whether people are capable of over-riding evolution's initial intentionality and our own sense of meaning, and whether we regularly do so.

A discovery that intrinsic motivation is stronger than extrinsic motivation says a lot about how our society should be organized. Such a finding suggests that we replace extrinsic rewards and rugged individualism, which have come to define Western nations, with a culture of cooperation and recognition of intrinsic development.

Original Good Samaritan Study

Our point of departure starts by reflecting on one of the most famous social psychology experiments. In 1970, John Darley and Daniel Batson were two young researchers at Princeton University who wanted to explore situational versus dispositional variables in the helping behavior of Protestant seminarian students (Darley and Batson, 1994). The researchers turned to the Bible to find a "fresh perspective" on personality determinates for helping behavior. They cited the parable of the Good Samaritan as follows:

> 'And who is my neighbor?' Jesus replied, 'A man was going down from Jerusalem to Jericho, and he fell among robbers, who stopped him and beat him and departed, leaving him half dead. Now by

chance a priest was going down the road; and when he saw him he passed by on the other side. So likewise a Levite, when he came to the place and saw him, passed by on the other side. But a Samaritan, as he journeyed, came to where he was; and when he saw him, he had compassion, and went to him and bound his wounds, pouring on oil and wine; then he set him on own beast and brought him to an inn, and took care of him. And the next day he took out two denarii and gave them to the innkeeper, saying "Take care of him; and whatever more you spend, I will repay you when I come back." Which of these three, do you think, provided neighbor to him who fell among the robbers?' He said, 'The one who showed mercy on him.' And Jesus said to him, 'Go and do likewise.' (Luke 10: 29–37, RSV,[2] cited in Darley and Batson, 1994, p. 273)

The researchers inferred that there would be "situational and personality differences between the unhelpful priest and Levite versus the helpful Samaritan." They came to this conclusion after exploring the roles of these characters in the parable:

Both the priest and the Levite were religious functionaries who could be expected to have their minds occupied with religious matters. The priest's role in religious activities is obvious. The Levite's role, although less obvious, is equally important: The Levites were necessary participants in temple ceremonies. Much less can be said with any confidence about what the Samaritan might have been thinking, but, in contrast to the others, it was most likely not of a religious nature, for Samaritans were religious outcasts. (Darley and Batson, 1994, p. 273)

Darley and Batson hypothesized that the priest and Levite were in a rush to their destination, and were most likely using religion extrinsically as a means to an end. Extrinsic use of religion seeks to gain social status, approval of peers, and pleasure, and is thus most associated with endocentric altruism.

Darley and Batson correctly hypothesized that the Samaritan was using religion as an end in itself or as a quest, and this motivation was intrinsic. Intrinsic religiosity taps an exocentric altruistic dimension of personality. This is because "...it is motivation arising from goals set forth by religious tradition itself, and is thus assumed to have 'otherly,' nonmundane, even self-denying quality" (Burris, 1999, p. 144). Intrinsic religiosity involves rational perspective-taking by observing the other's position, not from the first station of the self, second station of the other, but from a third, imagined, station in order to alleviate the plight of another.

Over a series of frigid days from 14 to 16 December 1970, the researchers sent out forty unsuspecting seminarians to provide a talk on either the Parable of the Good Samaritan or about the application of seminary skills in the workplace. On their way to the talk, they passed a slumped victim planted in an alleyway.

The response variable was whether the subjects helped the person in need. The independent variables were how much of a hurry participants were in reaching their destination, the types of presentations they were supposed to provide, and Allport–Ross measures for religiosity.

Shockingly at the time, only forty percent of the seminarian students actually assisted the confederate, and their results did not show that intrinsic religiosity predicted helping behavior among that sample. They did find that the participants in the rush condition offered less help than the participants who were not in a rush. Darley and Batson stated that sixty-two percent of participants early for their talk helped compared with 10% who helped in the late condition.

Jost and Jost state:

> But 25 years later Batson (1998, p. 284) agreed that 'dispositional predictors have fared better than in earlier work,' citing Staub's (1974) research in which 'a prosocial orientation index (combining measures of feelings of personal responsibility, social responsibility, moral reasoning, prosocial values, and a low level of Machiavellianism) significantly predicted helping behavior across a variety of circumstances.' (2009, p. 253)

But even in Batson's original work we see some dispositional impact. Sixteen seminarians were identified as rigid; they refused to listen to the confederate and offered help of inappropriate character, which is consistent with using religion extrinsically and from an altercentric vantage point (i.e. they were out to satisfy some personal goal or objective, rather than offering otherly assistance).

My position is that Darley and Batson missed a major point in their research. A lot more can be inferred about the Samaritan than that he was taking a leisurely stroll and had more time on his hands compared with the priest or Levite. The Samaritan was likely a merchant, depicted as having money, and was also in a rush. Notice what he does at the end of the parable. He does not have time to spend with the person he just helped, but rather pays the inn-keeper to keep watch over the injured man until his return.

Overlooking the profession of the Samaritan has left us with a series of questions. What would have happened had Darley and Batson experimented on wealth-driven students? Would the results have been different? Would the findings have supported more the dispositional view of human behavior derived from human needs gratification than the situationalist perspective? Would wealth-driven college students be more influenced by intrinsic or extrinsic motivation? If intrinsic motivation showed up, would such students render affective responses beyond motor empathy or owing to a more advanced form of empathy?

In other words, are personality determinates shaping an 'otherly,' self-dying, and exocentric view of all others, or would wealth-driven students be using others for self-advancement as evolution would suggest? An opportunity to perform a similar experiment finally arose 38 years later at Loyola University in Baltimore, Maryland (USA).

Setting the Scene

Unbeknownst to Loyola University students preparing for economics exams on a mild spring day on 28 April 2008 they were about to be recruited for a research study that would challenge the prevailing position of an important social psychological paradigm. The majority of these students were not the youthful optimistic types out to change the world or aspiring future religious leaders.

Brief demographic items and questions pertaining to wealth acquisition and insider trading were administered to this cohort prior to the experiment. Seventy-two percent of the students reported wealth as a top priority in life. Fifty-six percent also self-reported that they would break the law by taking an insider trading tip. My objective to reach a sample that more resembled the mind of a merchant Samaritan had been achieved, and the question now was to explore how many of these students would help a confederate in need, and whether rushed conditions or personality determinants would more affect helping behavior. To a good extent, the students were already experiencing some anxiety about their upcoming exams, and were pressed for time generally.

Let's start by observing some of the situational factors that were affecting the country at the time of this experiment. By April 2008, mass home foreclosures had hit the USA hard, and gasoline prices were rapidly rising. Cracks were showing in the nation's fragile economy and many students at Loyola University had reported in their economics classes a strong sense of unease about the future of the country.

Adding to the pressures of a faltering economy were the wars in Iraq and Afghanistan, and discussions of increasing allied troop numbers in those countries. These students were also continuing to live under the daily threat of terrorism from al-Qaeda.

In hindsight, we can no doubt empathize that these young people were facing rapidly changing situational variables that have come to define one of the darkest eras in the USA's recent history. Applying the situationalist perspective, we might erroneously come to the conclusion that these students would shun altruism altogether and turn to the dark side of human nature. As we will soon observe, such an assumption is faulty.

Method

Prior to arriving on the day of the experiment, personality questionnaires concerning types of religiosity were submitted to the students. The experimental procedures were then started on the third floor of Sellinger Hall at Loyola University; the students were then asked to go to the opposite side of the building and proceed to a room located at the second floor of Sellinger Hall.

The experiment was slightly modified from the original Darley and Batson study. The students encountered a worried-looking victim planted in the hallway outside the room where each student was to speak. The confederate was played by a regular 'all-American' guy named Dan, who stood at 5 feet 11 inches tall and weighed about 170 pounds. He had dressed down on the day and looked a bit disheveled. Dan was not informed of the students' religiosity scale scores or the experimental conditions.

Departing from the original study, the victim would approach the student and state that a family member had been in an accident, that their cell phone had gone dead, and that they needed to use a cell phone or payphone. Given the time constraints, I needed a helping scenario that would take place within the building, would not draw too much attention from non-participants in the study, and permitted an easy escape option for participants. The easy escape variable was in itself a situational variable that needed to be explored in evaluating participants' behavior.

Participants

Questionnaires were given to fifty-four students at Loyola University taking an introductory course in micro- and macroeconomics. Of these, the data of four participants were not included in the analysis because they showed up late to the experiment.

The sample was fifty-six percent business majors (i.e. general business, accounting, finance, marketing, and public relations), twenty-six percent social sciences majors (i.e. economics, psychology, political science, history), twelve percent hard sciences (i.e. biology, chemistry, pre-medicine, engineering), and six percent undecided majors; fifty-four percent were of middle income, forty-four percent were of upper income, and two percent were of lower income; sixty-eight percent were Catholic, eighteen percent were Christian, four percent were Protestant, four percent were of no religion, four percent were of other religion, and two percent were Buddhist. Tuition costs at the time were approximately $36,240 per semester.

Judging from the income levels and ability of many of students' families to afford the tuition costs, we can surmise that many of these young people were raised by parents and older siblings who passed off their needs concerns to successive generations and effectively satisfied a larger percentage of needs. They had arguably inherited a strong sense of functional autonomy and immunity to threats, and possessed a store of self-interest to negate.

Personality Measures

Participants completed six measures: (1) the Allport–Ross extrinsic (AR-E) scale, measuring the use of religion as a means; (2) the Allport-Ross intrinsic scale (AR-I), measuring the use of religion as an ends; (3) the Batson, Schoenrade, and Ventis external scale of religious life (RELI-E), measuring the extent to which an individual's religion is influenced by others; (4) the Batson, Schoenrade, and Ventis internal scale of religious life (RELI-I), measuring the need for religious beliefs; (5) the Batson, Schoenrade, and Ventis doctrinal orthodoxy (D-O) scale, measuring endorsement of traditional Christian beliefs; and (e) the Batson and Schoenrade quest scale (Q) measuring motivation towards finding existential meaning in life (Allport, 1950; Allport and Ross, 1967; Batson and Schoenrade, 1991; Batson et al., 1993). A five-point Likert-type scale was used to rate items on the religiosity scales as follows: 1 = strongly disagree, 2 = disagree, 3 = somewhat agree, 4 = agree, and 5 = strongly agree.

Batson suspected that "... Allport's (1950) depiction of the 'mature' religious sentiment actually confounds two forms of religious orientation that are conceptually and empirically distinct" (Burris, 1967, p. 146). This is the reason the Batson and Schoenrade Q scale, and the RELI-E, RELI-I, and D-O scales were administered here. The objective was to tap "aspects of the extrinsic and intrinsic orientations that seemed implicit but unmeasured in [the Allport and Ross] constructs" (ibid).

Cronbach's alphas were used examine the reliability of the religiosity measures. AR-E and AR-I possessed moderate internal consistency in this study, with Cronbach's alpha equaling .64 and .82, respectively. Cronbach's alphas were .83 for RELI-E, .79 for RELI-I, .93 for D-O, and .84 for Q. These estimates of reliability indicate that the RELI, D-O, and Q measures possess high internal consistency.

Factor validity was assessed by factor analysis of AR, RELI, D-O, and Q scales using a principal-component analysis of Verimax rotation. As shown in Table 4.1, a three-factor solution is consistent with three distinct types of religiosity (i.e. religion as a means, religion as an end, and religion as a quest).

Religiosity as a means received a high loading from AR-E (.95) and continues to measure religiosity as a means to other ends. This component received a moderate loading from RELI-E (.52), which was consistent with Batson's prediction (1976). However, over time, it appears that RELI-E tends to positively correlate with the end dimension more than the extrinsic factor (Batson et al., 1993 cited in Burris, 1967). Because of a moderate factor-loading between AR-E and RELI-E here, an item-level analysis was conducted between RELI-E and other scale items, but for breadth purposes, the specific item-level correlations are not reported. It was observed that RELI-E items correlate strongly with each other without other scale items included in the factor analysis. RELI-E items possess weak-to-moderate correlations with several AR-E items, and possess stronger positive correlations generally with AR-I items. Because RELI-E items showed some positive correlation with several AR-E items, a decision was made to run two logistic regression models. The first model includes RELI-E in the dimension measuring religion as a means, whereas the second model excludes RELI-E from

Table 4.1   Construct validity (factor analysis) for religiosity scales[a]

	Religion as a means	Religion as an end	Quest
AR-E	.95		
AR-I		.92	
RELI-E	.52	.68	
RELI-I		.93	
D-O		.90	
Q			.99

[a]Correlations < .30 are omitted.

the extrinsic dimension and includes it with the dimension measuring religion as an end in itself. The following results will show that RELI-E generally had no affect in significantly predicting helping behavior among this sample.

Religion as an end in itself received high loadings from AR-I (.92), RELI-I (.93), RELI-E (.68), and D-O (.90). This component remained consistent with the Darley and Batson findings (1994), and with the predictions made by Batson et al. (1993).

The Q scale (.99) received a high loading on the third factor. It would appear that this scale taps the drive for existential meaning.

Scheduling of the Experimental Study

The entire experiment was staged indoors on 28 April 2008 between 10:00 AM and 7:00 PM. Although the schedule was tight, using the same building lessened the amount of time it took to complete the study compared with the Darley and Batson Samaritan study.

Procedure

The order of the questionnaires was as follows: AR, RELI, QS, D-O. It might be useful for researchers to consider varying the order of these measures to further explore reliability and validity estimates in future studies. Participants completed the questionnaires prior to their arrival for the experiment. The sample was one of convenience. The researcher asked each participant to read a statement that they were participating in a study about future career aspirations. The directions stated:

> You are participating in a study about career choices for college students with completed economics coursework. What we have called you in for today is to provide us with some additional material of the role of religion in choosing your career than does the questionnaire material we have gathered thus far. Questionnaires are helpful, but tend to be somewhat oversimplified. Therefore, we would like to have you provide a 3–5-minute talk based on the following passage...

A. Message Variable

In the task-relevant condition, the passage stated:

> With increasing frequency the question is being asked: What jobs or professions do students studying economics subsequently enjoy the most, and in what jobs are they most effective? The answer to this question used to be so obvious that the question was not even asked.

Economics students were being trained for investment banking, and since both society at large and the economic student had a relatively clear understanding of what made a 'good' economist, there was no need to even raise the question of what other jobs economics experience seems to be an asset. Today, however, neither society nor many economists have a very clearly defined conception of what a 'good' economist is or of what sorts of jobs and professions are the best context for economists. Many students, apparently genuinely concerned with making money seem to feel that it is impossible to perform any other function such as teaching, journalism, or non-profit employment. Other students, no less concerned, find investment banking the most viable profession for economists. But are there other jobs or professions for which economics experience is an asset? And, indeed, how much of an asset is it for investment banking? Or, even more broadly, can one make money using their economics experience in a different field or in starting a business?

In the helping condition, participants were given the version of the parable of the Good Samaritan used by Darley and Batson and told:

You can say whatever you wish based on the passage. Because we are interested in how you think on your feet, you will not be allowed to use notes in giving the talk. Please let the project director know whether you understand what to do. If not, the project director will be happy to explain.

After a few minutes, the researcher returned, asked if there were any questions, and explained that space was limited on the third floor to record participants' discussions. The researcher instructed the participants, one at a time, to use the stairwell to go to a room on the second floor, where a volunteer was waiting in the room to record the participants' comments. Runners were employed to guide the students in the correct direction and to help space the time between each participants' arrival at the helping scene. A participant was not permitted to depart for the task until a runner returned from the previous participant's recording. The students did not run into each other while encountering the confederate and giving their recording.

B. Hurry Variable

The hurry condition resembled the one used by Darley and Batson. The researcher looked at his watch and said "You are running late. We are really backed up. The assistant is waiting for you, so you'd better hurry." In the low-hurry condition, the researcher stated, "It will be a little while before they're ready for you, but you can head over now."

C. The Incident

When the participants came close to the room where they were to give the talk, an anxious and worried-looking confederate would approach them. The confederate would approach the student and say, "My cell phone just died. My family member was in an accident. I really need to make a call and have no change on me for the payphone." If the participant gave them a cell phone to use, the confederate thanked the participant, called another volunteer, and received confirmation that the accident was minor and that his relative was OK. The confederate then thanked the participant. If the student gave money for a payphone, the confederate would again thank the participant. The students then continued on to the prearranged talk.

D. Helping Ratings

The confederate rated each participant on a scale of helping behavior as follows: 0 = failed to notice the victim as possibly in need at all; 1 = perceived the victim as possibly in need, but did not offer aid; 2 = did not stop but helped indirectly (e.g. by telling the assistant about the victim; 3 = stopped, listened to the direct request, but refused to pass the victim off to a bystander; 4 = after stopping, insisted on taking the victim to a pay phone, but then left the victim and/or provided him/her with money for a pay phone and left him/her; 5 = after stopping, refused to leave the victim and/or provided the victim with a cell phone.

E. The Speech

Participants then proceeded to their talk. A separate volunteer greeted students arriving at the room. This volunteer set up the tape recorder for the students to give their talk.

F. Helping Behavior Questionnaire

In the Darley and Batson study, participants were given another brief questionnaire after their recorded talk, which asked " '(a) When was the last time you saw a person in need and helped? (b) When was the last time you stopped to help someone in need? (c) Have you had experience helping persons in need?' " (1994, p. 104). An additional four questions were added in my study for exploratory purposes. These included: (d) "If you could get away with a victimless crime (i.e. such as insider trading) and collect a $2 million pay-off, would you take the tip? Yes/ No"; (e) "Is one of your top goals in life to achieve material wealth? Yes/ No"; (f) "What is your religious preference?"; (g) "How would you categorize your family's income?"

G. Debriefing

The participants were later debriefed by the researcher in their classes. They were told the planned deception and the reasons for it. The participants did not report any stress as a result of the study, and were quite interested in the concepts behind it.

Results

The frequencies here showed that among the participants, thirty-nine (78%) offered some form of direct or indirect aid to the victim (coding categories 2–5), and eleven (22%) did not (coding categories 0–1). The data also showed that thirty-three (66%) participants refused to leave the confederate and/or provided the confederate with a cell phone (coding category 5). These results contrasted heavily with the findings of Darley and Batson.

Darley and Batson reported that of forty seminarian participants, sixteen (40%) offered some form of direct or indirect aid to the victim and twenty-four (60%) did not. The data from my study showed that of fifty participants, twenty-eight (56%) would engage in a crime and take a $2 million insider trading tip compared with twenty-two (44%) who responded 'no.' Although the descriptive statistics are subjective, the preliminary data suggest that the majority of participants were somewhat ethically challenged. The data also showed that thirty-six participants (72%) reported that obtaining wealth was a top priority in life, thirteen (26%) reported that it was not a priority, and one failed to respond. The situational variable showed that eighty-four percent helped in the low-hurry group, seventy-two percent helped in the high-hurry group, eighty-two percent helped in the relevant-message group, and seventy-four percent helped in the task-relevant group. To reiterate, whereas the message-relevant group gave a talk directly about the parable of the Good Samaritan, the task-relevant group discussed potential careers for economics students.

t-tests were conducted on the situational factors. The hurry and message variables served as predictors, and the helping variable as the response variable. The Levene statistic showed that the data were normally distributed, but the *t*-tests did not show any significant difference between the hurry groups and message groups and the amount of help offered to the confederate. In separate *t*-tests, variables such as taking an insider trading tip and the drive for wealth were entered as predictors, and the helping ratings served as a response variable. In these tests, the data were not normally distributed, and follow-up Mann–Whitney tests failed to show a significant association between the variables. A one-way analysis of variance was used to check for significant differences between majors, income groups, and religious preferences and helping ratings. The Levene statistic demonstrated that the data for majors and income groups were normally distributed, but there existed no significant differences between these groups and helping behavior. The data were not normally distributed for religious preferences. Follow-up Kruskal–Wallis tests demonstrated no significant difference between religious preference and helping ratings.

Darley and Batson originally utilized two multiple regression models to explore the association between predictor variables and helping behavior. However, multiple regression models are not the most appropriate analysis given the types of variables involved here. The graded helping is an ordinal response variable, and the differences between the levels of an ordinal variable are uneven. The responses to the religiosity measures were also ordinal. A more appropriate form of analysis for these types of variables is logistic regression. The objective is to explore whether participants belong to a helping versus non-helping category given the responses to situational and dispositional variables. Two five-block, forced-entry logistic regression models were run to examine the influence of predictors on the helping response variable. For the first model, the level of hurry was entered in the first block; the situational task category (i.e. task-relevant vs helping-relevant) was added to the second block; Q scores were added to the third block; AR-E scores and RELI-E were added to the fourth block; and AR-I, RELI-I, and DO scores were added to the fifth block. For the second model, the variables were entered in the same sequential order with the exception that RELI-E was excluded from the fourth block and moved to the fifth block.

The overall method of entry was chosen to generally test the theory concerning the affect of situational and dispositional variables on a dichotomous helping response variable based on past research. Darley and Batson's stepwise regression models were used to determine the order of entry for items in each of the blocks in the logistic regression models. In stepwise regression, the order of predictors follows mathematical criterion. Darley and Batson used the size of the *F* values for each construct to sort five predictors in the following order for two step-wise regression models: hurry, message, quest, religion as means, and religion as an end. Whereas single items measure the hurry, message, and quest variables, there are several potential variables that measure religion as a means to an end (i.e. AR-E and, possibly, RELI-E scores) and religion as an end in itself (i.e. AR-I, RELI-I, RELI-E, and DO scores).

The factor analysis in this research helped determine the placement of items in blocks four and five for both logistic regression models. RELI-E scores were added to the fourth block in the first model because the factor validity suggested that this item might be somewhat measuring religion as a means to an end. The second logistic regression model excluded RELI-E from the fourth block and added it to the fifth block for general comparison purposes. AR-I, RELI-I, and DO scales loaded well on the religion as an end construct and, hence, were included in block five for both models to explore the end dimension as a predictor of helping behavior.

Tables 4.2 and 4.3 report the results of logistic regression analysis using a dichotomous helping variable and dichotomous dummy religiosity variables. Some data transformation took place to facilitate logistic regression analysis. A dichotomous helping variable was determined as follows. Ratings representing no form of assistance were coded 0, and ratings for indirect or direct assistance were coded 1. Mean scores were calculated for the five-point Likert scale responses on the religiosity measures. Dummy variables were created from the mean scores as follows: disagreement with an item on a religiosity measure was coded 0, and agreement or strong agreement with an item on a religiosity measure was coded 1.

Whether participants were in a rush did not significantly predict helping behavior [$\chi^2 = 1.23$, degrees of freedom (df) = 1, $p > .05$] in both logistic regression models. It is important to note that this finding may be attributed to a statistical lack of power owing to a small sample size because the descriptive statistics showed that ten percent more participants helped in the low-hurry group than the high-hurry group. The task-relevant item also failed to predict helping behavior ($\chi^2 = 1.75$, df = 2, $p > .05$) in both models. The quest item did not significantly predict helping behavior ($\chi^2 = 1.90$, df = 3, $p > .05$) in either model. The use of religion as a means to an end also failed to predict helping behavior ($\chi^2 = 7.60$, df = 5, $p > .05$) for model one (i.e. RELI-E included) or for model two (i.e. RELI-E excluded) ($\chi^2 = 2.80$, df = 4, $p > .05$). Surprisingly, using religion as a means to an end positively predicted helping behavior ($\chi^2 = 16.54$, df = 8, $p < .05$, Nagelkerke $R^2 = .44$)

for both models. The results indicated that intrinsic religiosity ratings had an additive effect on the fifth block (χ^2 = 8.94, df = 3, $p < .05$). This means that the odds of a participant who is intrinsically motivated also helping the confederate are thirteen times higher than those of a participant who is not intrinsically motivated (see note 'c' in Tables 4.2 and 4.3 for identifying the proportionate change in odds).

Table 4.2 Hierarchical logistic regression analysis of situational and dispositional variables with RELI-E included in block four

Step	NGS[a]	R[b]	Scale	B	SE	Sig.	Exp. b[c]
1. Hurry	.038	.024	HURRY	.771	.707	.275	2.162
			Constant	.116	1.051	.912	1.123
2. Group	.053	.033	HURRY	.770	.710	.278	2.160
			GROUP	−.499	.698	.474	.607
			Constant	.858	1.485	.563	2.359
3. Religion as quest	.058	.036	QUEST	.381	.946	.687	1.464
			HURRY	.786	.713	.270	2.195
			GROUP	−.469	.703	.504	.625
			Constant	.468	1.779	.792	1.597
4. Religion as means	.219	.146	AR-E	−.177	.977	.856	.838
			RELI-E	−20.453	12919.315	.999	.000
			QUEST	1.139	1.105	.303	3.122
			HURRY	.697	.750	.352	2.008
			GROUP	−.510	.787	.517	.601
			Constant	20.307	12919.316	.999	6.593×10^{-8}
5. Religion as end	.437	.317	AR-I	2.589	1.171	.027	13.318*
			RELI-I	21.393	12303.137	.999	1.953×10^{-9}
			D-O	−5.639	25727.476	1.000	.004
			AR-E	.414	1.055	.695	1.513
			RELI-E	−39.398	17399.262	.998	.000
			QUEST	1.424	1.316	.279	4.154
			HURRY	1.314	.944	.164	3.720
			GROUP	−.123	.909	.892	.884
			Constant	19.393	22595.039	.999	2.644×10^{-8}

Sig., significance; SE, standard error; Exp. B, exponentiation of the B coefficient (odds ratio).
[a]Nagelkerke R^2 (NGS) is reported for effect size.
[b]R_L^2 = −2LL(model)/−2LL(original), as described in Hosmer and Lemeshow (1989).
[c]The predicted change in odds for a unit increase helping ratings. *$p < .05$.

Table 4.3 Hierarchical logistic regression analysis of situational and dispositional variables with RELI-E excluded in block four

Step	NGS[a]	R[b]	Scale	B	SE	Sig	Exp. b[c]
1. Hurry	.038	.024	HURRY	.771	.707	.275	2.162
			Constant	.116	1.051	.912	1.123
2. Group	.053	.033	HURRY	.770	.710	.278	2.160
			GROUP	−.499	.698	.474	.607
			Constant	.858	1.485	.563	2.359
3. Religion as quest	.058	.036	QUEST	.381	.946	.687	1.464
			HURRY	.786	.713	.270	2.195
			GROUP	−.469	.703	.504	.625
			Constant	.468	1.779	.792	1.597
4. Religion as means	.085	.053	AR-E	−.829	.914	.365	.436
			QUEST	.641	1.006	.524	1.898
			HURRY	.812	.719	.258	2.253
			GROUP	−.348	.718	.628	.706
			Constant	.655	1.791	.714	1.926
5. Religion as end	.437	.317	AR-I	2.589	1.171	.027	13.318*
			RELI-I	21.393	12303.137	.999	1.953×10^{-9}
			RELI-E	−39.398	17399.262	.998	.000
			D-O	−5.639	25727.476	1.000	.004
			AR-E	.414	1.055	.695	1.513
			QUEST	1.424	1.316	.279	4.154
			HURRY	1.314	.944	.164	3.720
			GROUP	−.123	.909	.892	.884
			Constant	19.393	22595.039	.999	2.644×10^{-8}

Sig., significance; SE, standard error; Exp. B, exponentiation of the B coefficient (odds ratio).
[a]Nagelkerke R^2 (NGS) is reported for effect size.
[b]$R_L^2 = -2LL(model)/ -2LL(original)$, as described in Hosmer and Lemeshow (1989).
[c]The predicted change in odds for a unit increase helping ratings. *$p < .05$.

Because some large standard errors are present in the fourth and
fifth logistic regression models, follow-up collinearity diagnostics
were performed. It has been suggested that tolerance values < .1 may
indicate a collinearity problem (Maynard, 1995). The tolerance values
for these data ranged from .3 to 1. It has also been suggested that
variance inflation factor (VIF) values > 10 may indicate a collinearity
problem (Myers, 1990). The VIF values for this data ranged from 1 to

4. The variables did not present high variance proportions with regard to eigenvalues. Thus, collinearity problems did not appear to be overly present.

It is worth mentioning that the use of religion as a means to an end (i.e. extrinsically as measured by AR-E) was supposed to represent the priest or Levite mindset. These personality types are likely using religion for social status, approval of peers, and pleasure. The results suggest no significant finding with regard to a sample of wealth-driven college students at Loyola University using religion extrinsically to help or not help a confederate in need. The use of religion intrinsically (i.e. as measured by AR-I) likely resembles the Samaritan mindset more because the participant is using religion as an end in itself. The source of intrinsic motivation arises from following religious tradition which calls for altruism and self-sacrifice. This significant finding offers an upbeat note that wealth-driven individuals in this sample may possess the Samaritan-like mindset. The effect of this research could be far reaching for the development of social responsibility courses within a business curriculum, or within the context of better understanding the pro-social motivation generally among the wealth-driven laity. Perhaps, more training could be offered to foster positive intrinsic motivation.

The internal scale that measures the need to believe in religion, the external scale that measures social influences, the quest scale that measures existential questions, and the doctrinal orthodoxy scale that measures support for traditional Christian beliefs theoretically tap religion as an end in itself dimension. However, the results suggest that these scales failed to show a significant relationship with helping behavior. This may be a further promising finding because Darley and Batson found that seminarians who scored high on doctrinal orthodoxy, in particular, offered a different type of help. In that study, seminarians scoring high on doctrinal orthodoxy were identified as super-helpers, possessed an inappropriate character, and were rigid in regard to listening to the confederate's needs.

The significant relationship between intrinsic motivation and helping behavior in this research appears to demonstrate a more appropriate character in line with traditional religious teachings about self-sacrifice. You may ask where should we turn when environmental factors fail to explain helping behavior? We must turn to personality determinates. Immediately after the experiment, I had the opportunity to ask Dan, the confederate, "How would you describe the subjects who helped you?"

Dan responded, "The guys who helped really looked concerned."
Interrupting Dan, I asked, "Did they try to impose help on you?"
Dan looked a bit perplexed and asked, "Impose? Do you mean tell
me what to do?"
"Yes," I responded.
Dan continued, "No, not at all. Some of them were rushed. But those
that helped were listening to me."

Discussion

What can be said of the non-helpers? Not much in this instance. The
numbers of non-helpers were especially small, and inferential analysis
did not pick up any significant differences between non-helpers and
religiosity scores or situational variables. Hypothesis testing showed
that there were no significant differences as to whether helpers versus
non-helpers were more wealth-driven or likely to take an insider trading tip. The majority in both groups were wealth-driven and ethically-
challenged with regard to the insider trading tip.

These findings were perplexing at first. Evolutionary theory tells us
that people use motor empathy to help others for survival purposes.
Had that been the case here, extrinsic scores would have had an effect
on the unlikely Samaritans' behavior. Or, the participants would have
demonstrated rigid doctrinal helping behavior, which was totally absent
in this study.

Was traditional evolutionary theory falling short? To reiterate, sixteen
helpers in the original Darley and Batson study had helped for seemingly rigid extrinsic reasons. The seminarians in that study are like many
other people today who continue to be needs frustrated, engaged in limited motor empathy, and operating from the first station of the self.

With the unlikely Samaritans, we witnessed a truly unique human
phenomenon. Evolution is playing a role, but we have adapted skills to
define meaning and its negation. Motor empathy and the gratification
of human needs, namely social, esteem, and actualization are scaffolding development to exocentric altruism and the eventual negation of
the self.

The height of our evolution does not peak in simply moving beyond
other primates by joining collectives and dominating the planet. Nature
has equipped us with adaptations that are playing a much more interesting role in our development. We can infer that intermediate-order needs
were no longer motivating some of the unlikely Samaritans during an
emergency situation because once a need is gratified it is no longer a

pressing concern for the individual. Maslow originally described the metaphysical nature of needs gratification where lower-order needs become less pressing as they are gratified (Maslow, 1970, p. 30).

Evolution has taken us on a wonderful path to achieve free will by entering a station for decision-making outside the body. We are subsuming our endocentric existence, which helped us move past primates and advance towards something completely new and not yet observed in the animal realm. The reason why this phenomenon has not been more widely observed is that social scientists have been searching for exocentric altruism in the wrong places. The pious religious leader, upstanding politician, or petit bourgeoisie academic are frustrated by intermediate-order needs for personal gain, and are thus extrinsically motivated and less resistant to negative situational factors. Many of these individuals can barely help themselves, so how could we possibly expect them to engage in exocentric altruism?

It may seem very conflicting that wealth-driven young people are capable of exocentric altruism. But this satisfies the old axiom that we learn to help the self before helping others. It is certainly possible that among the sample, guilt may be playing a role. However, the correlation between intrinsic motivation and helping behavior suggest a noticeable subgroup at higher-order motivational development have arguably empathized with the other's suffering as their motive to help.

Limitations

The small, non-random sample precludes generalizing this study to the general population of undergraduate students in the USA or internationally. Nevertheless, economics is a popular course at Loyola University, so the overall pool of participants was a relatively random sample of undergraduates at that university.

Where do we go from Here?

The experimental research conducted here is exploratory and raises a series of new areas to consider. The first area for exploration might be to examine the motivations of people who choose not to help.

The results here did not show significant findings with regard to the helping motivations of the non-helpers, especially with regard to the fourth block of the logistic regression models, which explored the effect of extrinsic motivation. This might have been owing to the small numbers of non-helpers among the sample size, and a larger sample might show that extrinsic motivation negatively correlates with helping behavior.

The use of deductive reasoning, though not necessarily accurate, might suggest that upon graduation from university, the small minority of non-helpers would eliminate their competition quickly, resulting in a business world hierarchy that is self-interested. This type of belief supports rewarding people extrinsically. However, the emerging literature does not support this theory.

Kanungo and Conger summarized the general stereotype by stating that "The path to profits, it is widely believed, is not paved with caring concern but with Darwinian cleverness" (1993, p. 37). These researchers challenge the stereotype by arguing that "The greater complexity of today's global marketplace will demand within organizations a higher degree of interdependence than independence, more attention based on cooperation than competition, and greater loyalty to the organization than to the individual" (ibid).

The famous statistician W. Edwards Deming argued that US corporations had lost a competitive edge due to fostering individualism and competition over cooperation. The Total Quality Management philosophy has spread over time, and today includes the concepts of transformational and servant leadership styles. These styles are seen as giving a corporate leader a competitive edge over those who follow the traditional individualistic models of corporate leadership. Transformational leadership is concentrated on "... creating a shared vision and motivating followers to sacrifice themselves for the greater good of the organization" (Early and Davenport, 2010, p. 60). Servant Leadership "... operates from the position that a person is drawn to serve and through this attitude of service naturally assumes leadership roles" (Greenleaf, 1977 cited in Early and Davenport, 2010, p. 61). In contrast, transactional leadership is identified as hierarchical leadership that "rewards or disciplines a follower depending on the adequacy of the follower's performance" (Early and Davenport, 2010, p. 60).

A study was conducted to discover which leadership abilities were thought most important for leaders in Certified Public Accounting (CPA) firms to exhibit (Early and Davenport, 2010, p. 61). The results in this study were rather surprising. Out of 266 responses, sixty-six percent of respondents self-identified as transformational or servant type leaders. Sixty-two percent of respondents stated that their supervisor was more transactional.

However, responses to the individual characteristics of servant leadership suggested that ninety percent of CPA respondents ranked empathy as the top attribute for leaders. The listing of empathy as a top attribute by CPAs is important because it highlights the importance of tapping our intrinsically-based altruistic motivation for any type of corporate, government, educational, or therapeutic system to succeed.

The results of Early and Davenport generally call for further experimental research to see if Samaritan-like business leaders might be more successful than self-interested colleagues based on an ability to better motivate staff. Sixty-four percent of respondents thought they would be more responsive if supervisors were more transformational. Ninety-eight percent of CPA respondents thought that leaders should possess an attitude of service toward other people.

The next part of this book will shed some light on people who do not help others, or whose endocentric (self-interested) altruism becomes a source of illness. We must now turn to the flip side of the human condition to probe the factors that cause us to turn against our nature to become altruistically good. We are about to encounter a sobering reminder that many people remain susceptible to evil actions because psychologists have not yet made a series of important connections between pathology and threats to illusionary self-interested desires. A paradigm shift in the way we view pathology will be recommended. I will explore how weak dispositional scaffolds can be obliterated by a minority of psychopathic predators who are very much born as 'bad apples,' and lurk and wait to inflict harm on individual psychological advancement and, by extension, the larger society.

Part 2
A Fresh Look at Pathology

5
Pathological Self-interest

A newly edited book entitled *Pathological Altruism* pulled out the 'big guns' in psychology and evolution to argue that "Altruism can be the back door to hell" (Oakley et al., 2012, p. 4). The phrase 'pathological altruism' is intended to mean that, despite good intentions, a pro-social act can harm the self or others.

The authors of *Pathological Altruism* argue that altruism arises only from the original intentionality of evolution and that every altruistic act is reward-based (Homant and Kennedy, 2012). The value in this work resides in describing pathologies that arise as a result of faulty endocentric altruism and its association with needs frustration.

However, *Pathological Altruism* should be read with caution because the authors over-reach in many areas, and draw assumptions that are simply unsupported. It is a mostly one-sided exploration of self-interested pro-social behavior that fails to take into account the existence of exocentric motivation. Without exocentric altruism, there cannot be a definition or understanding of pure altruism.

In light of the sequence of development predicted along the hyperbola paradigm, this chapter argues that the notion of 'pathological altruism' and the causes of pathology generally need to be revised. It should more aptly be referred to as 'pathological self-interest.' Endocentric altruism can become pathological and harm the recipient or helper in under-developed people whose individual needs pursuits and self-interested altruistic compliments are threatened or inhibited, whereas exocentric altruism counteracts pathology altogether and is the pinnacle of human health. It is important to remember that self-interested needs pursuits are illusionary, and, typically, these pursuits can become unachievable when people try to attain standards set for them by self-interest-based governing, educational, or healthcare systems.

In this chapter, I will briefly explore how stress is often viewed as a challenge or growth opportunity for self-actualizers and can operate as a catalyst to exocentric altruistic development. I am also going to explore how exocentric altruism renders a person resistant to pathology by delving into a recent study of Tibetan monks. The Tibetan monks demonstrate the counteraction between exocentric altruism and pathology. I will also explore cases of exocentric personalities and their apparent lack of pathological symptoms to conclude that exocentric altruism counteracts pathology, while frustrated self-interest in the form of endocentric altruism can produce pathology under certain conditions.

Stress as a Catalyst to Development

Exocentric altruism is the result of positive adaptations through advanced decision-making once threats to illusionary needs gratification are overcome. One of these adaptations is the ability to positively reappraise and cope with stressful situations.

Exocentric altruistic adaptations are not easily over-ridden when a person faces a harsh environment. Biologist David Sloan Wilson makes the argument that survival mechanisms override conscious decision-making at a cost to others (2012). The position here is that Wilson's view is overly pessimistic and that higher evolved humans, living for the other, are resistant to the stress produced by harsh environments. They will not flip off decision-making ability when deciding whether to do the right thing in any given stressful circumstance. Witness the countless numbers of soldiers who threw themselves on grenades that were a safe distance away to save non-relations. A pure altruist has gained functional autonomy to continue to negate self-interest, even in the face of violence and threats.

This is not to say that exocentric altruists are perfect humans, rather that pathology is counteracted in exocentric altruists. For example, exocentric altruists may occasionally break the law, but this action does not necessarily equate to pathology or illness. One study explored whether empathetic participants would move a financially-impaired child up a waiting list for an organ donation. The findings allege that empathy can become a source of immoral judgment (Batson et al., 1995).

However, Socrates, Mohandas Gandhi, and Martin Luther King all broke unjust laws and were considered 'immoral' by some of their contemporaries, but their pro-social actions could not in any way be classified as pathological. On the contrary, they seized upon stressful situations and their coping strategies greatly benefited wider society.

The contrast between pathological, frustrated, endocentric altruists and healthy, exocentric altruists comes into perspective we look at how humans tend to cope with stressful events. The authors of *Pathological Altruism* adopt a one-sided view of stress and argue that caregivers can become overtaxed, experience distress, and become ill themselves (Li and Rodin, 2012). It is argued that "...inattention to one's needs and emotions may contribute to physical illness via biological pathways" (Mate, 2003 cited in Li and Rodin, 2012, p. 151).

It is readily agreed that society should do a better job of helping to meet the physical and emotional needs of under-developed people who face helping scenarios, and social work and counseling is a good way to go about that. However, at the same time, we must be cognizant of people's different reactions to stress according to human motivational development, and tailor assistance accordingly.

Once upon a time, it was suggested that all forms of stress were crippling and destructive for human performance. However, Richard Lazarus pioneered a series of research studies that overturned much of that one-sided approach to stress. He found that some individuals' performance thrived under stressful conditions, while the performances of others were reduced. Lazarus, working together with colleagues, developed a transactional paradigm to explain human reactions to stress (Lazarus and Launier, 1978; Lazarus and Folkman, 1984).

The transactional model involves cognitive appraisal [a prevailing view is that there is a (variable) "optimal level" of stress associated with maximum performance, but personality, as well as some situational variables, presumably underlie the positioning of the optimal point (in any given instance) of stress as a two-part process that involves primary appraisal and secondary appraisal]. In primary appraisal, an individual makes an evaluation to determine whether an event is stressful.

The stressor can be viewed as beneficial, detrimental, or immaterial. A stressful event is then further evaluated and categorized as harmful, threatening, or challenging. A harmful category is when damage (possibly psychological) has already taken place. Threats are events that could produce harm; challenges refer to the opportunity to realize growth, mastery, or benefit from a stressful event.

A well-formed altruistic personality is more likely to categorize a stressful event as a challenging growth opportunity. Let's apply the transactional model through the lens of human needs gratification to explore this point. The frustration of lower-order needs renders people at physical, security, and social levels unable to renegotiate stressful situations into positive outcomes. Maslow wrote:

> Apparently the organism is most unified in its integration when it is successfully facing either a great joy or creative moment or else a major problem or threat or emergency. But when the threat is overwhelming or when the organism is too weak or helpless to manage it, it tends to disintegrate. On the whole when life is easy and successful, the organism can simultaneously do many things and turn in many directions (Maslow, 1970, p. 29–30).

Self-actualizers are largely impervious to stress and better capable of viewing it as a challenge. In theory, stress can take on a role as a catalyst for exocentric altruism because self-actualizers may reappraise stressful situations into positive outcomes by drawing upon the imagination to cope with negative life events.

Recently, a most interesting study published by O'Connor et al. (2012) strongly suggests that pure altruists are models for human psychological health. The researchers in that study compared anxiety and depression scores for ninety-eight Tibetan meditation practitioners. The results indicated that practitioners who were other-focused in their meditation scored significantly higher in cognitive empathy (perspective-taking) and significantly lower in anxiety, depression, and empathetic distress than individuals whose meditation was self-focused (ibid). This is critical because it suggests that the ability to step outside the self through imagination to empathize with another's suffering represents better states of psychological health.

Were the Tibetan Monks born possessing higher cognitive empathy? It is safe to assume that they advanced, like other people, through self-interested needs concerns, but, owing to psychologically-based theological teachings, may have arrived at using positive adaptations, such as personal reflection through meditation, somewhat earlier than those of us born in the West. In light of more advanced stress paradigms and emerging evidence that cognitively motivated exocentric altruism is a very real phenomenon that counteracts pathology, psychologists are strongly advised against labeling pure altruism as pathological.

Even self-interested forms of altruism that compliment self-interested needs should not be treated as pathological unless they are frustrated. Imperfect altruism can lead to a lot of physical and mental health benefits as one satisfies human needs and advances on the way to the negation of self-interest. Humans can enjoy a series of mental and physical

health benefits through pro-social behavior generally. Extensive lon-
gitudinal studies have been largely conclusive that altruism generally
increases our happiness, well-being, and longevity (S. G. Post, 2005).
Altruism also mitigates stress.

Helping others acts as an inhibitory factor to stress, which is widely
recognized as a leading cause of cellular aging. These findings are
backed up by studies such as those by Moen et al. (1992), Musick et al.
(1999), and Oman et al. (1999) (all cited in S. G. Post, 2005), which all
found a link between volunteerism and longevity. It also appears that
older volunteers (aged 65 years and older) experience lower levels of
depression, anxiety, and somatization (Hunter and Linn, 1980 cited in
S. G. Post, 2005). It appears that when individuals establish achievable
targets through endocentric altruism to find meaning, this too leads to
better health outcomes.

I will now turn to two brief cases that demonstrate development from
endocentric to exocentric motivation, and observe how healthy psychological development is inhibiting to pathology. My position is that
we find no pathology whatsoever in exocentric altruists who follow a
pattern of building a given store of self-interest only to later negate the
self.

Is Dr. Zell Kravinsky Psychologically Healthy?

Dr. Zell Kravinsky, at the age of 49 years, became a very public altruist.
He was cited as an example in President William Jefferson Clinton's
book, *Giving*, and also featured in various news articles throughout the
USA. As you read on, try to evaluate whether you believe Kravinsky's
altruism is pathogenic or healthy. The evaluation of Kravinsky's pro-
social behavior is supported by material published in the *Los Angeles
Times* (Schwartz, 2003).

Kravinsky's early childhood activities provide a few insights into his
early needs gratification. He purchased his first shares of stock by the
age of 12, and was well satisfied in material physical and security needs
(ibid). His father was a successful printer and his mother was a teacher.
Kravinsky appeared well satisfied in physical, security, and social
needs gratification, and was likely developing strong interests in self-
esteem and self-actualization concerns at a young age. Interestingly, at
around this same age, as his needs pursuits were being met, Kravinsky
demonstrated strong cognitive empathetic ability when he picketed
Philadelphia's City Hall, demanding that low-income housing be built
in the city where he lived (ibid).

We next see Kravinsky focusing heavily on self-actualization concerns and developing a higher sense of meaning as a young adult. He would go onto to obtain two doctorates in rhetoric and Renaissance literature (ibid). Upon graduation, he decided to teach emotionally disturbed kids in the slums of north Philadelphia before lecturing at Penn State University (ibid).

A pattern appears to emerge as Kravinsky gets married and starts a family. He made his first significant investment in an apartment building for African–Americans and minorities. His friend observed that Kravinsky always "lived in the worst apartment of his own building" (ibid).

Eventually, Kravinsky's real estate empire blossomed. He earned $45 million and continued to drive around in a beat-up 1986 Toyota (ibid). Upon his sister's death, he donated $6.2 million to the Adria Kravinsky Endowment for Public Health, but there was one problem (ibid): Kravinsky did not have a suit to wear at the announcement and rushed out to purchase a $20 suit at nearby thrift shop (ibid). He eventually donated most of his fortune to healthcare charities.

You are probably already shocked by Kravinsky's generosity, but there is a lot more to the story. He read an article from the *Wall Street Journal* about kidney donations and noticed that 3,491 individuals died in 2002 while waiting for a donation (ibid). African–Americans comprised about a third of the deaths due to kidney disease (ibid). Despite the best efforts of his wife, who wanted Kravinsky to retain both kidneys in case one of his three children needed a transplant in the future, he thought that it was more important to make the donation. Kravinsky reasoned that the children would probably get a better organ from each other rather than him at some point in the future. He also asked why his own children were any more important than other members of the society. Here we start to witness the negation of self-interest entirely as Kravinsky empathizes with others' suffering.

The Albert Einstein Medical Center tried to talk him out of it. Kravinsky was interviewed by a battery of doctors, including a psychiatrist to ensure his sanity (ibid). In the end, Kravinsky made the kidney donation to a lower-income African–American woman named Donnell Reid (ibid). Ms. Reid was orphaned at the age of 8, suffered through an abusive relationship, and underwent 8 years of kidney dialysis (ibid).

What can we gather from the Kravinsky donation? A psychiatrist apparently did not report any pathological motives for Kravinsky's donation. He has subsequently become the target of press pundits, such as Kate Fratti, who labeled Kravinsky's behavior "selfish" (ibid).

Kravinsky's response was that "I'm not generous, and I'm not insane. Maybe the sanest thing I do is to give things away" (ibid).

Kravinsky is a bit different from most of us in that "he takes the equal value of all human life as a guide to life, not just a nice piece of rhetoric" (Singer, 2006). Kravinsky may have been influenced by the endocentric motivation of his parents and inherited, at an early stage, their advanced human psychological development, but he did not become settled in the pursuit of illusionary drives. A strong sense of meaning and self-actualization led Kravinsky on a path to eventually negate the self, and we cannot find any reports of anxiety, depression, or stress as a result of his mental development.

On the contrary, the psychiatrist who evaluated Kravinsky for the kidney donation viewed him as mentally healthy and competent. We very much have an example of an individual who has mitigated and reduced negative emotional factors perhaps better than the rest of us.

Was Liviu Librescu Psychologically Healthy?

Let us briefly review the case of a deceased individual who also, arguably, reached the level of exocentric altruistic personality development. Details about Professor Liviu Librescu's life have been obtained from press reports with his family. An exploration of Librescu's life is based on published news and video materials, rather than any personal knowledge of Librescu or his research.

Librescu, 1930–2007, was an aeronautics expert at Virginia Tech University (Anon, 2007b) Librescu's motivational development followed a path differently from Kravinsky. Librescu was a holocaust survivor who eventually fell out of favor with Dictator Nicolai Chauchesku's Romanian regime (ibid).

Described by family and colleagues as a scientific genius, Librescu was a self-actualizer who heavily accommodated visiting academics from around the world. He clearly had a love of knowledge and interacting with other high-level achievers. In 1985, he relocated while on sabbatical to the USA and took up a professorship at Virginia Tech University (ibid).

On 17 April 2007, Librescu's wife dropped him off at work. A short while later, a mentally ill student named Sueng-Hui Cho made his way into Norris Hall with a 9-mm Glock, P22 automatic handgun and barricaded the door (Anon, 2008). On that fateful day, Cho started shooting at everyone he encountered.

Librescu peeked through his classroom door and requested that students call the police. When Cho attempted to enter the classroom,

Librescu stayed to hold the door shut and ordered his students out of the classroom. A student named Yam King states: "I definitely thank him for my life, even though I ran. He could have easily run with me and he stayed and he tried to help the other students who were in there. He felt that all the students in there had a future. To do that human sacrifice, like to give himself up...you can't really measure that" (ibid). Librescu was shot through the door four times and is credited with saving the lives of twenty-two students that day (ibid).

A traditional approach by some social scientists would allege that Librescu made a poor choice, or that he was pathological to give up his own life. However, Librescu was a well-fortified self-actualizer who turned to the negation of the self. In particular, through the negation of the self, Librescu achieved what so many of us aim for—an honorable death that saves the universal other by becoming a symbol of sacrifice.

Frustrated Self-interest as the Root of Pathology

It is not Kravinsky or Librescu who are pathological. These individuals have overcome the illusionary pleasure drive and advanced to its negation. They are the epitome of psychological health. It is interesting that members of the media, who operate based on a corporate system rooted in self-interest, have attacked Kravinsky as selfish.

While we can locate pathology in the individual, it is society's governing, educational, and healthcare systems that cause pathology owing to the philosophy of valuing self-interest. A society that promotes individual self-interest sets unachievable goals through a consumer culture and is blocking people from empathizing with others.

This evidence suggests that America's antiquated federal government, so focused on self-interest and producing fear and competition among its populace, is crippling the psychological development of its populace by denying the human intrinsic drive to cooperate. When people peacefully protest and request that the governing system addresses social inequality caused by artificial aristocracy, modern Western governments allegedly collaborate with the private sector to wage direct violence at innocent civilians and further frustrate the populace. If the self-interested basis of the public and private sectors is not contributing to pathology among underdeveloped individuals, then what is?

For example, the governing system permitted peaceful university students at the University of California, Davis, to be mass pepper-sprayed for protesting economic inequality (Stelter, 2011). Modern society's sickness was also evident when an 84-year-old woman named Dorli

Rainey was pepper-sprayed by police in Seattle (Kehoe, 2012). Rather than cooperate and attempt to address the very serious and legitimate concerns of the protestors, the self-interested status quo is concerned with protecting its self-image.

One might claim that these were random incidents, but recently-obtained Federal Bureau of Investigation (FBI) documents allege otherwise. The most disturbing documents come from the Domestic Security Alliance Council. This document was recently posted online and described the US federal government's activities as "a strategic partnership between the FBI, the Department of Homeland Security and the private sector," discussing the Occupy Wall Street (OWS) protests at the West Coast ports to "raise awareness concerning this type of criminal activity" (Anon, 2012).

Look at the case of an adult trying to care for an elderly, bedridden parent in the USA. Now, let us hypothetically examine the pressures exerted upon this individual. This individual is likely facing an employment crisis and simultaneously encountering a host of medical bills, and cannot pay their mortgage, student loans, or save for their own children's education. Society is telling them that they must meet its established indicators or standards (i.e. possess a certain amount of savings, a retirement account, and own a home). Of course, such a person's development to higher purpose and its negation is going to be compromised because the extrinsic quotas are unachievable owing to intrinsic motivation being inhibited.

Thwarted self-interest can easily produce negative adaptations to harsh environments under certain circumstances. For example, a person who is experiencing physical- and security-order needs frustration and helping others from an egoistic perspective may become overtaxed by caregiving if they hit financial hardship or lose a job. A person who is encountering loneliness or boredom from a lack of social relations may unconsciously take on the role of a victim in dangerous helping scenarios to gain attention. Social needs frustration overlapping with the impairment of the pursuit of self-esteem and recognition also enhances susceptibly to cult leaders who prey upon the insecure. Even moral ascription at self-actualization has the potential to cause people to doctrinally help others and overlook the recipient's needs. But we must qualify negative adaptations as belonging directly to threats and inhibition to illusionary needs that have not yet been overcome.

Obtaining better states of mental health is dependent upon erecting solid dispositional scaffolds, and when society prevents or inhibits development of our internal scaffolds, pathology emerges. We do not need to treat the altruist, but reverse the doctrine that we are solely driven by self-interest and create governing, educational, and therapeutic systems based on cooperation and altruism.

Duality of Maladaption Versus Healthy Adaptation

As the literature review suggests, there exists a disturbing tendency among academics to place too much emphasis on an association between pathology and altruism. Wilson asserts that the only way for altruists to "survive in a Darwinian world is by interacting with other altruists and avoiding interacting with selfish individuals" (Wilson, 2012, p. 407).

Wilson goes onto to argue for the need to create a social environment that would foster altruism, and he mentions the tragedy of the commons. Essentially, he wants to see mechanisms, such as quotas, to reward altruists and sanctions to punish self-interested transgressors. Such an artificial environment would produce fear and unachievable goals because it views altruism as extrinsically motivationally based on self-interest. Evidence of our intrinsic drive to cooperate challenges Wilson's flawed assumption that human behavior is about winning and losing from a mechanistic survival perspective.

Humans have formed the cognitive ability beyond mechanistic intentionality to redefine the notions of winning versus losing, and they can set themselves as examples for the rest of us to emulate. Kolbe lost his life at the hands of the Nazi occupiers, but became an inspiration of hope for remaining prisoners. He became a symbol of defiance against oppression and may serve as a source of inspiration for future individuals to defy unjust authority. Did Kolbe lose in sacrificing the self for others?

Evolution's initial intentionality does not over-ride advanced conscious decision-making skills in well-gratified and psychologically strong individuals when the going gets tough. We have too many instances of people who become immune to environmental threats. The evidence has started to demonstrate that positive adaptations are more influential at higher motivational development than negative adaptations, and render humans resistant to evil.

Rather than create an extrinsic systems of self-interested rewards for altruists, let us form intentional systems that foster our intrinsic motivation to cooperate. This should be accomplished by developing clear and concise pro-social purposes for such systems that use the scientific method to ensure that the systems are fulfilling their purpose.

We are all going to encounter bad situations, but this does not mean we will be defined by them. We may lose a job, fail at a course, or get divorced. We may face famine, war, or natural disasters. Our reaction to various challenges, and our ability to thrive in adverse conditions and become psychologically immune to threats rests primarily on dispositional altruistic development. Psychologists are wasting too much valuable time by improperly defining all altruism as self-interested and attaching labels to it, such as 'pathological.' Pathology does not stem from pure altruism, but threats to self-interested needs. Thus, the phrase for 'pathological altruism' should be revised to 'pathological self-interest.' My preference is to study and understand the dispositional features that make us triumph in the face of evil. This means strengthening internal scaffolds so that people arrive at health exocentric altruistic motivation.

6
Needs Frustration and the Mindset of the 9/11 Jihadists

Throughout this book, the case is being made that it is against our will to act to the detriment of others. You may be wondering if it is against our will, why do people so often harm others? After all, the human track record in Nazi Germany, Stalinist Russia, Rwanda, Guantanamo Bay, Abu Ghraib, and rendition camps worldwide has been quite horrific.

In addition to the horrors of mass direct violence, we also need to consider child abuse, spousal abuse, and individual discrimination and racism. We know that aggression does not occur in a vacuum, and we certainly see incidents of child and spousal abuse increase during hard economic times. Several important questions emerge here. Do strong dispositional scaffolds make us resistant to negative situations? Can we trace our behavior back to a unifying factor that weakens or strengthens our dispositional altruistic scaffolds? How psychologically resistant and strong can we make an individual who may face a negative life event? Society plays a role in that its sickness can damage the individual's dispositional scaffolds. My position is that if we find the commonality at the root cause of various pathologies, it becomes possible to generate a solution that rectifies multiple problems at once.

The popular social psychologist Philip Zimbardo compares the dispositional approach to a medical model of health and the situational approach as a public health model (Zimbardo, 2007). But his position in over-emphasizing the situational may be overly simplistic. Granted, the medical model looks for pathologies and cures within the person. This much we know. For example, take the case of viruses. The medical model, through vaccines, provides us with eradication of certain viruses much better than keeping the environment clean.

Rather than take the position of a public health model over the medical model, perhaps we require a different way of viewing illness. Maslow states that "Perhaps what we now speak of as separate disease entities on the medical model are actually superficial and idiosyncratic reactions to a deeper general illness, as Horney (1937) claimed" (Maslow, 1970, p. 80). We see the medical model breaking down and find commonalities between pathologies; today, virologists are developing vaccines that contain multiple strains of various dead viruses. As technology improves, we may one day have an all-inclusive antiviral vaccine. In comparison to psychology, we may have already identified the common theme for pathology, but we have been too lax over the last six decades to do anything about it. Maslow indicated that commonality is threats and inhibition to the gratification of basic order needs and meta-needs.

The position taken here mostly agrees with Maslow's approach, with the exception that overcoming threats to the development to self-actualization is not sufficient. Psychologists need to help people to overcome threats, or inhibition to exocentric altruistic personality development and motivation. We need to (a) ascertain whether such threats to individuals form a general pattern, and (b) rectify any remaining issues within the governing system to eradicate threats to needs gratification and, especially, the negation of the self.

It is rare that a psychologically strong individual with solid dispositional scaffolds will succumb to environmental pathogens. To reiterate, I argue in this chapter that most human psychological pathology occurs within the individual when a faulty self-interest system of governance indirectly and directly produces threats, and inhibits basic- and higher-order needs.

As psychologists, we can help individuals achieve needs gratification, and—more importantly, upon achievement—negation of the will. And for the last few decades, an often overlooked discipline within psychology has been leading the way on this important goal. Peace psychology has been developing methods to reduce conflict and threats to needs gratification, but without a definition of optimal health, peace psychologists arguably lack a cohesive mission. They have come up with all sorts of methods to help end needs frustration and direct violence, but have had very little effect in reducing actual violence—some of the worst human genocides and the march towards nuclear annihilation have occurred since the advent of peace psychology.

Today, peace psychologists are well advised to continue to identify threats and solutions to indirect violence, which inhibit development to self-actualization. But, more importantly, they require the hyperbola paradigm to coalesce around a testable centralized theme. All the other pieces of the puzzle or solutions could be matched and tested for success based on how far they align people with the intrinsic desire to become altruistic.

Because of the addition of exocentric altruism as a higher-order motivation to self-actualization, it is no longer sufficient for social scientists to argue for overcoming threats and inhibition along the original needs hierarchy. We must know that individual experiences of threat produce an inability to develop to exocentric altruistic motivation. Certainly, people are encouraged to engage in peaceful civil disobedience to challenge the philosophies of self-interest-based systems of governance, but they must be aware not to overthrow the systems they fight with unworkable replacements that lack purpose.

Applying Maslow's Take on Pathology to the 9/11 Hijackers

We now have more than six decades of data since Maslow's view of pathology to explore the accuracy of his theory, and the data suggest that his preliminary understanding of the causes of pathology were highly accurate.

A good starting point in exploring this phenomenon is in the backgrounds of the nineteen hijackers on 11 September 2001. The actions of killing thousands of people at the World Trade Centers, Pentagon, and on United Flight 53 represented a pure act of evil. What made them do it? Were these individuals easily swayed by bin Laden's uniform or his desert outpost to follow orders? I am being a bit facetious here, but there are much stronger dispositional factors to take into consideration than the situation when exploring why people commit evil acts.

A review of the 9/11 Commission Report is highly insightful in helping us to understand the motivations of the hijackers. Twelve of the thirteen "muscle hijackers," or stooges, came from poor areas in Saudi Arabia (Anon, 2004, p. 231). The royal dictatorship in that nation had cut off welfare payments to its population. In addition to food shortages and extreme poverty, there were rolling blackouts outside the capital city of Riyadh throughout the 1990s. Owing to religious and societal beliefs, these young men were under extreme pressure to satisfy extrinsic motivation to marry and obtain a job. The report goes on to state:

> Saudi authorities interviewed the relatives of these men and have briefed us on what they found. The muscle hijackers came from a variety of educational and social backgrounds. All were between 20

to 28 years old; most were unemployed, with no more than a high school education and were unmarried.

Four of them—Ahmed al Ghamdi, Saeed al Ghamdi, Hamza al Ghamdi, and Ahmed al Haznawi—came from a cluster of three towns in the al Bahah region, an isolated and underdeveloped area of Saudi Arabia...None had a university degree.

Five more—Wail al Shehri, Waleed al Shehri, Abdul Aziz al Omari, Mohand al Shehri, and Ahmed al Nami—came from Asir Province, a poor region in southwestern Saudi Arabia that borders Yemen; this weakly policed area is called the 'the wild Frontier.' All five in this group began university studies [only Omari managed to succeed in obtaining a degree. The others dropped out, demonstrating low emotional intelligence and needs insecurity to complete higher education].

The three remaining muscle hijackers from Saudi Arabia were Satam al Suqami, Majed Moqed, and Salem al Hamzi...Suqami had very little education, and Moqed had dropped out of university. (Anon, 2004, pp. 231–2)

In addition to the 9/11 report, it has emerged that Waleed al Shehri and Wail al Shehri had no television or contact with women (Anon, 2004, p. 162; Sennott, 2002a). The 9/11 Commission Report presents few details about Fayez Banihammad, who was from the United Arab Emirates, but it is assumed that he was also likely unemployed. Hani Hanjour was rejected for multiple jobs in the airline industry (Sennott, 2002b). His brother described him as becoming progressively depressed by employment failures (ibid). Nawaf Hamzi experienced significant threats to social needs frustration. It was reported at the time that Hamzi "...was stuck in what was seen by Saudis as a humiliating job working as a stock boy in a housewares shop" (ibid).

Ziad Jarrah's father only earned about $21,000 per year, and was the breadwinner for the household (Walker and Dorsey, 2001). It was initially alleged by the media that Jarrah came from an upper-class family, but this was obviously not the case. Jarrah had, reportedly, wanted to become an airline pilot from a young age and was heartbroken when his father forbade his desired career; arguably, this inhibited Jarrah's social and esteem needs pursuits (ibid).

Only one of the hijackers, Khalid al-Mihdhar, came from a mostly affluent family. He had fought in Bosnia, where he may have become hardened towards direct violence (Anon, 2004, p. 155). It is interesting that the 9/11 Commission Report indicates that only Mihdhar went

AWOL for a brief period, and that al Qaeda leaders wanted to oust him from the mission (Anon, 2004, p. 237). He did not fit the category of a suicide attacker, and we can only surmise that a catalyst had set him off. Typically, such catalysts can be witnessing family members or friends die at the hands of perceived enemies. Perhaps, witnessing the deaths of friends in Bosnia had operated as a trigger.

Two of the 11 September ring-leaders were Mohamed Atta and Marwan al Shehhi. Mohamed Atta's social needs were frustrated at a young age. Investigative reporter Liz Jackson wrote an in-depth piece on Atta. After noting that his hometown was in significant decline, Jackson stated, "Our translator Hanadi and I met up with one of Atta's schoolmates in a cafe nearby. He recalls him as a studious teenager with no really close friends and not interested in girls" (Jackson, 2001). Shehhi obtained a military scholarship after his father's death, but was unable to sustain decent grades at university in Germany (Anon, 2004, p. 162). During studies abroad, Shehhi's finances dwindled and he began to wear inexpensive clothing and moved into a rundown apartment with some of the other 9/11 hijackers (ibid).

The tragic pattern that emerges from these young men's lives is threats and inhibition to needs gratification in the form of unachievable self-interest that were established by external influences (unemployment, frayed social relations, and lack of meaningful sexual relationships). We can surmise that unemployment overlapped with the inability of these young men to marry; in Islamic culture, unmarried men are ostracized. Hanjour's family, in particular, is allegedly known to have pressured him about not being married or being in a meaningful relationship (Fainaru and Ibrahim, 2002).

The psychiatrist Jerrold Post has gathered a series of quotes from terrorists over the years. The common themes in these quotes are chilling, yet insightful. One member of Fatah states, "After recruitment, my social status was greatly enhanced. I got a lot of respect from my acquaintances and from the young people in my village" (2005, p.454). The common theme emerging from statements is that of intermediate social needs frustration.

Post also had the opportunity to consult with the Department of Justice as an expert on terrorist psychology involving the case of a Palestinian named Mohammed Rezaq (2005). He was accused of hijacking an Egypt Air passenger jet on which 50 people lost their lives. During the 1967 war, Rezaq was forced into an overcrowded Palestinian refugee camp. He engaged in training exercises in Jordan, but was treated as a second-class citizen. The evidence suggests that insecurity and social needs frustration played a part in forming the psychology of a mass murderer.

Post also introduces us to a Tanzanian embassy bomber. We are told that he was ordered to leave school by his brother to work at a grocery store. It is reported that he was "miserable—alone, friendless, isolated..." (2005, p. 456). The problem is that once a person is significantly frustrated while pursuing a particular needs level, it is difficult, by our modern standards, to bring that person back to healthy motivational development. It is unlikely that a person can be deprived of say, social needs, and then have their needs gratified by later immersion of such needs. Long-term needs frustration produces susceptibility to mental instability within people and is the root cause of their violent actions.

For example, we can reflect upon the case of the Tsarnaev brothers who allegedly bombed the Boston marathon. *The Boston Globe* reported that the Tsarnaev family was largely living off food stamps and welfare payments in the USA, and trying to survive well below the nation's poverty level (Allen, 2013). In addition to physical needs insecurity, the older brother, Tamerlan, is reported to have been severely socially needs frustrated in the USA. *The New York Times* quoted Tamerlan as stating, "I don't have a single American friend. I don't understand them" (Goode and Kovaleski, 2013). We also notice that the pursuit of self-esteem was heavily threatened for Tamerlan. His world view had concentrated around becoming a famous boxer, but those hopes were dashed when Tamerlan was arrested for a report of domestic violence. That incident prevented Tamerlan from obtaining US citizenship, and rendered him as a non-citizen unable to compete in a Golden Gloves of America boxing competition (Sontag et al., 2013).

The horrors of poverty, feeling like outcasts, and, most importantly, having damaged self-esteem pursuits turned two young adults into murderers. Dzhokhar Tsarnaev might have blended in better to US society than his older brother, and it appears he was less socially needs frustrated, but was easily persuaded to turn against his adopted nation. From the emerging evidence, it appears that Dzhokhar, who also had experienced severe financial insecurity growing up, possessed strong dispositional trust towards his brother, which was easily manipulated.

In addition to the qualitative analysis of individual terrorists, the quantitative data demonstrate that needs frustration causes people to engage in evil acts. Post cites the following as evidence:

So-called psychological autopsies, i.e. reconstructions of the lives of suicides, have been developed for some 93 suicide bombers of the

Palestinian suicide bombers in Israel (Merari, personal communica-
tion). While these demographic features are undergoing change, and
now the age range has broadened significantly and some women
have joined the ranks of suicide bombers, they were for the most part
carried out by young men between the ages of 17 and 22, unmarried,
uneducated, unemployed. (2005, p. 458)

Unfortunately, we can safely conclude that events such as 9/11, the
Iranian revolution in 1979, and a host of other instances of direct violence were completely preventable. The Iranian revolution occurred
because the USA and UK supported the Shah of Iran, who was widely
known to Western intelligence agencies to be a violent and unstable
dictator. By parity of reasoning, the support of the Saudi Royal family
and prevention of equitable distribution of that nation's oil income to
its own people appears to have frustrated generations and swelled the
ranks of terrorist organizations.

While visiting in Florida, I happened to meet a colleague who
was at a tennis match that some of the 9/11 hijackers had attended
before the terrorist attacks. He said the hijackers appeared detached
and uncommunicative. This reminded me of members of Charlie
Manson's murderous gang. For example, review the life of Tex Watson,
one of the mass murderers operating under the orders of Manson. He
had dropped out of university and had experienced a failed business
shortly before joining Manson's group. Were the 11 September 2001
hijackers indoctrinated into cult-like behavior as a direct result of
needs frustration?

We can only speculate, but it appears the hijackers willfully signed up
to engage in mass murder. Of course, whether they were indoctrinated
into a cult (which occurs when social and esteem needs, and egoistic
and egocentric altruistic motivation become threatened) or a catalyst
rubbed salt into otherwise open psychological wounds requires further
in-depth investigation. The important point we can consider at this
stage is that had the human needs of these individuals been satisfied,
the result would have been very different, and this lends credence to
Maslow's thoughts on pathology.

In reality, the young men who pledged support to the Nazis were not
much different from the 9/11 hijackers. After World War I, the allies
placed such harsh economic penalties on Germany that severe economic depression ensued. Members of the Nazi party were obsessed
with materialism, having been deprived themselves of basic physical
and security needs during their formidable years. Witness the early

Nazi industrial and service creations, such as the Volkswagen (i.e. the people's car), which was meant to gratify people's basic order needs.

US soldiers at Abu Ghraib, Guantanamo Bay, or rendition centers around the world also fit the profile of needs-frustrated young people. The US military purposefully sends recruiters into poor neighborhoods to mass-market military service to impoverished minority teenagers. The promise of education and career potential is offered as an escape for these young people.

The guards at Abu Ghraib were not transformed by some rapidly changing situation. They were already primed with a distorted view of the other owing to threatened needs gratification. Let's briefly review some of the backgrounds of what we know about some of the Abu Ghraib soldiers. US army reservist Charles Graner dropped out of university and is alleged to have engaged in domestic abuse (BBC News, 2005; Zimbardo, 2007, p. 360). Pfc. Lynndie England was divorced before the age of 21 and worked at a chicken processing plant before joining the military (Dao and von Zielbauer, 2004). Sabrina Harman was an assistant pizza shop manager before being called up to active duty in Iraq (CBSNews.com, 2009). This highly mechanistic-type job, which is based on quotas and a moderately low salary, probably further affected both Harman's sense of security and self-esteem.

Most of the alleged abusers argued that they were taking orders from higher officials who were never formally prosecuted (a topic I will delve into in Chapter 7). The brief summaries of the abusers, however, start to challenge the notion that throwing any individuals into a 'bad' situation would cause them to become evil. It takes long-term inhibition and threats to needs gratification for people to be negatively affected by environmental influences.

In hindsight, the USA should have directly sent George Bush's daughters (one of whom, incidentally, was protesting the Iraq invasion) to guard Abu Ghraib. Given the fact that both Bush daughters were well needs gratified, they would have been resistant enough to have rejected the unjust orders of the unnamed officials who ordered the torture at that facility. Unfortunately, we find that most individuals who wage illegal warfare are hesitant to send their own children into harm's way.

Inoculation Against Bad Situations

What do the rescuers who saved people from genocide tell us about the evil versus good dichotomy? Why are some people seemingly resistant to bad situations? We find that dispositional needs gratification explains more of the healthy mindset than situational factors.

Ervin Staub conducted extensive research on Christians living in Nazi-occupied countries during World War II who risked their lives to save Jewish people (Staub, 2004). He also had the opportunity to interview a rescuer from Rwanda. He found consistent evidence from childhood that the rescuers were well gratified in social needs and had parents who fostered self-actualizing notions of equality when dealing with out-groups. This ability to gratify needs along Maslow's hierarchy appeared to have also strengthened rescuers' internal locus of control and self-esteem, which have been found to be major dispositional factors in resisting illegitimate authority.

We can delineate from the evidence presented that the biggest threat to our psychological development to exocentric altruistic motivation is structural violence in the form of needs frustration. It produces a vicious cycle whereby large numbers of people can be turned from their drive to exocentric altruism into xenophobia.

What is the first and number one recommendation for a counter-terrorist policy? The medical community suggests that it is not added security. Rather, "Alienated youth must be able to envisage a future within the system that promises redress of long-standing economic and social inequality..." (J. M. Post, 2005, p. 463). This type of strategy applies not only to terrorism. In the USA, young people who are subjected to enslavement to student loan debt, high unemployment, and reductions in real wages must also hope for a future system that will rectify long-standing economic issues if we are to witness any measurable declines in domestic violence, aggression, and school violence.

Why Peace has Been Elusive for Peace Psychologists

Thus far in this chapter, we have observed that threat to basic- and intermediate-order needs gratification produces pathology, and that needs gratification makes people resistant and altruistic in negative situations. Where do we go from here?

Peace psychology is a discipline that aims to explore how to reduce episodic violence (direct violence, such as war) and structural violence (human needs frustration) (Christie, 2006). Recently, we find that the study of peace psychology is increasing in popularity. Dr. Herbert Blumberg at Goldsmiths College observed that there has been an increased interest in journal articles relating to peace psychology over the last two decades.

Let's go back to the origin of peace psychology and examine how it has developed and the direction that this discipline appears to be navigating in to see if we can chart a better course for its future. We can trace the emergence of peace psychology back to the Cold War (ibid). During this period, many psychologists started to break with the policies of Western governments. In hindsight, they were, arguably, right to do so.

By 1962, John F. Kennedy's government had placed missiles in Turkey and pointed them at the Soviet Union. In response, Nikita Khruschev ordered nuclear missiles to be placed 90 miles off the USA's coastline in Cuba. This prompted Kennedy's administration to seriously consider the concept of "mutually assured destruction." Orders were given to the US Navy to fire upon Soviet ships that did not heed their warnings.

In response to the tension between the USA and the Soviet Union, early peace psychologists believed that mutually assured destruction was avoidable. It was thought that the best way to move back from the brink of mutually assured destruction was to better meet the needs of people worldwide and thus put an end to superpower conflicts that resonated around scarce resources. However, after the collapse of the Soviet Union, many social scientists believed that capitalism, when left to its own devices, would be able to properly distribute the world's resources. Psychology professor Daniel Christie states, "In short, part of the answer to 'What is peace psychology the psychology of' depends on the geohistorical context in which the observer and actor are situated" (2006, p. 4).

We now find that modern man faces a far more dangerous context than during the period of superpower conflicts. At the University of Chicago there is a group of atomic scientists that has been forecasting a potential nuclear catastrophe for the last six decades. They use a figurative doomsday clock, with midnight representing the hour of our demise. At the height of the Cuban Missile crisis, the clock was set at 11:48 PM, and now it is set at 11:55 PM. The potential for regional conflicts between nations such as North and South Korea, Israel and Iran, and India and Pakistan have, in scientific opinion, put us on the fast track to the apocalypse. We stand closer to nuclear catastrophe even within the borders of the USA owing to the familiar theme of terrorism.

What will once again bring us back from the brink of self-destruction? We need to focus peace psychology in a direction to end threats to human needs, with the end goal to end inhibition of exocentric altruism. We know that threats produce pathology. For example, Hitler had been rejected from art school, experienced homelessness, and was gassed during World War I. Currently, we have the potential for his personality type to arise in any number of nations that are rapidly progressing towards nuclear weapons.

It logically follows that to counter the rise of another Hitler, peace psychologists need to devise ways to swell the ranks of exocentric altruists. The problem with peace psychology is that it does not appear to have an overarching mission. The mission of peace psychology in its current form is too broad and encompasses structural and episodic counters to violence. This is where defining the purpose of peace psychology to bring people to exocentric altruism is paramount.

An increasing number of exocentric altruists among the population will mean that several of them make it into spheres of influence, such as Martin Luther King, Mohandas Gandhi, and Nelson Mandela, and greatly improve further distribution of resources to larger numbers of individuals, thereby reducing threats and the potential number of pathological individuals.

Our demons throughout history have not been the by-products of rapidly progressing bad situations or some misguided sense of altruism. Humanity's demons have been grafted and molded by our mass greed and lack of equitable distribution of economic resources because our systems of governance and commerce, rooted in extrinsic rewards, run counter to our true intrinsic motivation to be good.

We find that episodic peace-building in the form of intergroup dialog, promotion of the status quo, and direct intervention in other foreign nations is treating the symptoms of direct violence, rather than solving the underlying cause. Christie (2006) notes that there are 107 million preschool children underweight and living in South Asia and sub-Saharan Africa. Our planet is home to more than three billion people who are living on less than $2.50 per day (Shah, 2013). Are we so ignorant in the West that we are unaware that our hoarding of vital economic resources will thwart psychological development and create the villains of tomorrow in those areas more than any situational factor?

A Future for Peace Psychology

Try to ponder the following thought before reading further. The great mistake of the social sciences throughout the past few centuries is the argument that the world's resources are scarce. Resources are scarce only as long as we in the West buy into the argument that our wants are unlimited. When we start to practice self-discipline our human wants become limited and resources unlimited. In the West especially, we have orchestrated a capitalist model from a flawed underlying principle.

As supposedly representative nations, we share the responsibility for the continuation of structural violence worldwide. Peace psychologists are advised to focus their mission around the hyperbola paradigm as justification to change the way we view our economic resources.

The current objectives of many peace psychologists to break down the status quo are insufficient without replacing it with a system that promotes cooperation and recognizes intrinsic motivation. Recently, Congresswomen Barbara Lee proposed creating a Secretary of Peace as a cabinet position for the White House, and was shot down by hawkish members of both parties. This would be an excellent idea.

However, a word of caution is necessary here. Such a cabinet position would need to employ the theories within peace psychology from a well-focused and defined perspective based on the human drive to become altruistic. And members of such an office would need to be well versed in the scientific method and statistical analysis to check whether polices are satisfying the department's mission. In Part 4, I will discuss more about governing, educational, and therapeutic systems that could be used by social scientists in recreating a new culture of cooperation that results in needs gratification and progression to exo-centric altruism.

7

The Special Case of Psychopathy

Are some people born innately evil? This paradoxical question is typically addressed by theology, but it casts a unique shadow over psychology and whether we are ultimately driven to be altruistic. The view taken here is that there exists a minority of psychopathic individuals, who, owing to brain impairment, could be classified as evil, and, throughout history, these individuals have operated to prevent the majority of people from achieving development to exocentric altruism.

The psychiatrist Ben Karpman is typically cited to distinguish between two different types of psychopaths. It is theorized that "... primary psychopaths [are] callous, manipulative, massively selfish, and routinely untruthful, and [Karpman] believed that secondary, or neurotic psychopaths engage in antisocial behavior under the influence of emotional disorder—typically manifested as extreme impulsivity—whereas pure primaries give no evidence of such disorder" (Karpman, 1948 cited in Levenson et al., 1995). Many non-institutionalized psychopaths likely possess both primary and secondary traits, although Karpman believed that only primary psychopaths were true psychopaths (Levenson et al., 1995). Psychopaths will also experience varying levels of shame when caught doing something wrong, and this produces the response to lash out at others.

Social psychologists would say that we are neither born good nor bad, but that people can be made to act psychopathic by encountering bad situations. My position is different from this point of view. In particular, primary psychopathy should be classified as a special case of pathology that can arise separately from threats and inhibition to needs pursuits and environmental factors. Brain scans suggest that primary psychopathy results from emotional empathy impairment. Psychopaths tend to manipulate needs frustrated people into evil actions and thus they inhibit members of the larger society from developing stronger cognitive empathy. The absence of the lower form of emotional empathy in a minority of psychopaths thus stunts the development of the higher form of cognitive empathy in others.

Maslow was arguably correct to theorize that there are several such special cases of pathology. For example, children can act against their best interest owing to lack of fully-formed personality development. Likewise, over-spoiling a child may also lead to the impairment of conscience, and, as a side note, it is important to mention that the goal of motivational psychologists is not to indulge people through over-gratification of human needs, but to create intentional systems that aid our intrinsic motivation to be altruistic.

Why include a chapter on the special case of psychopathy? Maslow had only cursorily mentioned this topic. We need to explore the phenomenon of psychopathy because, arguably, psychopaths cause structurally frustrated people to act against their intrinsic motivation to become altruistic.

This chapter will provide the results of a never-before-published pilot study conducted on law enforcement officials in a mid-Atlantic state.[1] The data from this study raise some red flags. They suggest that psychopaths may very well be attracted to positions of authority and are operating among us in larger numbers than we may realize. It also suggests that there are a few 'bad apples' out there who are ruthlessly damaging the psychological advancement of the rest of us on a larger scale.

When we are young, we learn to trust authority, such as parents, teachers, the police, and religious leaders. Trust is one of the strongest dispositional attributes, and too often it is abused by people in positions of authority. Many people wrongly believe that people in positions of authority will not let us go too far in harming others.

Let's hark back for a moment to the famous social psychology experiments of the 1960s and 1970s. In 1961, Stanley Milgram conducted an obedience study in which participants were told by a professor to administer shocks to a confederate (Milgram, 1994). It was reported that sixty-five percent of participants followed orders to administer a series of dangerous shocks all the way to the end of the experiment (ibid). More than 10 years later, Zimbardo conducted the Stanford Prison Experiment, where students were placed in makeshift prisons and played the roles of guards and prisoners (Zimbardo, 2007).

However, research on trust suggests that the participants in the Milgram experiment may have implicitly trusted the authority figure that the confederate would not be harmed (Blass, 1994). In the Milgram experiment, the experimenter explicitly told participants that "Although the shocks can be extremely painful, they cause no permanent tissue damage" (Milgram, 1994, p. 232 cited in Blass, 1994, p. 248). By parity of reasoning, it could be said that the students trusted that Zimbardo himself would eventually step in and end the experiment before irreversible harm would befall the prisoners.

A short time into the Stanford Prison Experiment, Zimbardo described how the guards attempted to take the beds of rowdy prisoners:

> [Prisoner] 819 screams wildly, 'No, no, no! This is an experiment! Leave me alone! Shit, let go of me, fucker! You're not going to take our fucking beds!'

> [Prisoner] 8612, 'A fucking simulation. It's a fucking simulated experiment. It's no prison. And fuck Dr. *Zimbargo* [sic]!'

> (Zimbardo, 2007, p. 61)

The prisoners were constantly reminding the guards that they were under the control of an experimenter, and, while the guards inflicted harm, it is conceivable that in their minds Zimbardo was always around the corner to pull the plug before things got too serious. And, eventually, that is exactly what happened. Zimbardo ended the experiment early.

There are many real-world examples of how dispositional trust is exploited by those in authority, but the plug is never pulled and the violence goes too far. Members of the Nazi hierarchy, such as Joseph Goebbels, had invented the story that Jewish people would not be slaughtered in death camps, but relocated to the cozy island known as Madagascar. The Nazi plan was a facade to trick Europeans into swallowing the bitter pill of mass genocide. Many German people fell for this trick and probably believed early on that no real harm was going to come to the Jewish people. On a visit to Auschwitz, I learned that the Nazis had placed the sign 'Arbeit Macht Frei' ('work makes free') above the entrance to death camps and played classical music as detainees arrived. Everything was purposefully organized in that regime to manipulate dispositional trust.

The manipulation of trust by psychopaths continues in our own time. Documents obtained by the *Washington Post* showed that Lt. General Ricardo Sanchez personally authorized the troops at Abu Ghraib to use military dogs, temperature extremes, reverse sleep patterns, and sensory deprivation against prisoners (Smith and White, 2004). This goes to the heart of the research about how dispositional trust can affect people who are needs frustrated.

Lower-level guards at Abu Ghraib were described in Chapter 6 as inhibited in motivational development. These same guards were apparently following orders on the contingency that their commanding general would not permit actual harm to come to the prisoners. This certainly does not excuse the lower-order guards or their actions, as they could have refused orders, but it goes a long way to understanding how people can act against their nature. There was an explosive combination at Abu Ghraib where guards with a propensity for xenophobia (fear of out-groups), due to needs frustration, were exploited by leaders with obvious signs of alleged psychopathic tendencies.

The situational factors of putting people in a laboratory setting with an authority figure dressed in a laboratory coat and giving orders have a lesser effect in determining human behavior compared with our internal dispositions. Trust is one of our greatest traits, permitting us to help and love other people, but it is also one of our greatest downfalls because, as we will soon see, while the majority of us are driven to become exocentric altruists, there is a small minority who are brain impaired, have infiltrated positions of authority, and seek to exploit our good nature, and have done so with relative ease.

Background

Upon finishing my doctoral work, I started a statistics firm and took up a part-time position teaching statistics at the University of Baltimore to undergraduate business students. At the time, a lot of these students showed an interest in the organizational psychology book *Snakes in Suits* (Babiak and Hare, 2007). It had hit the media by storm, and claimed that psychopaths were lurking within the business environment.

Although a quantitative researcher, the qualitative research in *Snakes in Suits* intrigued me. Was it possible that psychopaths would exist in larger numbers among business executives than prison populations? And then I got to thinking: What about the police? Most research on psychopaths has been conducted on criminals, but, in theory, police officers may tend to think like criminals to excel in their jobs. My curiosity went a step further. Rather than thinking like psychopaths, might there be elements of psychopathic tendencies among police officers themselves?

The presence of psychopaths in the police, military, and political professions is important because it suggests that there are predators waiting to pounce on structurally needs frustrated individuals. These individuals are chameleons in disguise who have compounded the issue of structure violence throughout history. Zimbardo would like to have us believe that anyone can turn evil given a situational manipulation, and he cites a lot of primary research in dealing with law enforcement experiments, in particular, to suggest that this is not a case of a few bad apples. The following research offers a counter viewpoint to Zimbardo. A pilot survey instrument designed to investigate levels of psychopathy among actual law enforcement officials is presented in the following sections.

Method

A mature student came to me with a police contact to potentially administer a survey. Rather than pursue this feasibility project as an adjunct faculty, my decision was to investigate the matter as a pro bono project for my statistics company. The ethics adhered to at my company were the same as those endorsed by the American Psychological Association. Essentially, my view was that a project should be undertaken as long as the potential benefits to society outweigh the harm, and, in this case, it was evident that exploring psychopathy among those who are supposed to serve and protect significantly outweighed any potential harm.

A survey instrument was administered to a non-random sample of law enforcement officials in the mid-Atlantic area. The sample contained 35 responses from active police officers, one parole officer, and one retired police officer. The initial study was envisioned as a pilot to test the questionnaire for a larger study, but the results provided some precursory insights, which are worth reporting.

The resulting sample was 51.4% male and 48.6% female; 51.4% white, 45.7% African–American, and 2.9% unresponsive; 2.9% low-income, 82.9% middle-income, and 14.3% high-income; 28.6% Republican, 48.6% Democrat, 17.1% independent, 2.9% apolitical, and 2.9% unresponsive; 40% single, 48.6% married, and 11.4% divorced; and 48.6% had children and 51.4% had no children. The age range was 23–55 years, with an average age of 38 years.

Personality Measures

The participants completed the twenty-six-item Levenson self-report psychopathy scale (Levenson et al., 1995). The scale has sixteen items that measure for primary psychopathy and ten items that measure for secondary psychopathy. Levenson et al. describe the scale as follows:

> The psychopathy assessment items were designed to produce, by means of a self-report procedure, two factors similar to those produced by the Hare Psychopathy checklist. The primary psychopathy

items were created to assess a selfish, uncaring, and manipulative posture towards others, and the secondary psychopathy items were designed to assess impulsivity and a self-defeating lifestyle. (Levenson et al., 1995, p. 152)

A four-point scale with reverse-scored items was used to control response sets. Unit weightings were summated to obtain scales for inferential analysis. A decision was made to also include the Gosling et al. (2003) Ten Item Personality Inventory (TIPI) to explore for possible relationships between potential psychopathy scores and personality dimensions. This inventory taps the 'big five' personality dimensions, such as extraversion, neuroticism, openness, conscientiousness, and agreeableness, and uses a seven-point Likert-type scale with paired items measuring openness, agreeableness, extraversion, conscientiousness, and emotional stability. Each pair contains a reversed-scored item. The TIPI pairs are averaged to obtain a composite score for the personality dimension under investigation.

In theory, a strong negative association between psychopathic items and the personality dimension 'agreeableness' would further confirm whether participants in this sample are empathy impaired. This is because the agreeableness item on the TIPI crosscuts empathetic emotion. Filler questions pertaining to white collar versus blue collar crime and gambling were also included, but go beyond the scope of this investigation and are not analyzed here.

Procedure

Items were presented in the same order to all participants. Although this was not a random sample, the selection of police officers in municipalities and cities nationwide mostly follow similar standards and psychological testing, and this sample was representative of the law enforcement officials in their given locale.

The participants were told that they were partaking in a survey about white collar crime. A disclaimer was given to participants at the end of the study. It indicated that the questionnaire they had just undertaken contained questions about psychopathy, narcissism, and gambling, and advised participants to visit their local medical center if they had any issues associated with these conditions, or for any reason whatsoever. The gatekeeper administering the survey was instructed not to pressurize participants, and to inform participants that participation was voluntary and that they could discontinue the survey at any time. Participants were asked whether their data could be retained for contact purposes in the future. None of the participants elected to allow their data to be retained.

Results

Descriptive statistics were employed to compare the average response rates to the twenty-six psychopathy items with reports of psychopathy in the general population and within prisons. In addition, correlation analysis between the psychopathy scale and TIPI was conducted to explore associations between these two scales.

Reliability and Validity of the Measures

The scales used here were time-tested, and have been estimated to be reliable and valid. Reliability in the form of standardized alphas was reported by Levenson et al. (1995). These estimates for internal consistency were reported at .82 for the primary psychopathy scale and .63 for the secondary psychopathy scale, and thus demonstrated moderate-to-strong internal consistency. A two-factor solution was also found to be consistent with the primary versus secondary psychopathy dimensions (ibid). The TIPI had a test–retest reliability estimated at .72 (Gosling et al., 2003). A comparison between the Big Five Inventory with the TIPI found convergent correlations (r = .77) that far exceeded discriminant correlations (r = .20) (ibid).

Descriptive and Inferential Analysis of the Measures

Hare (1998) suggested that one percent of the male population is psychopathic compared with fifteen percent as a baseline figure for the prison population. When viewing the results here, it is important to keep in mind that psychopathy is supposed to be a very rare phenomenon. Where do the law enforcement officials in this sample fall with regard to these frequencies? Table 7.1 shows a descriptive analysis of the psychopathy scale.

The table shows that 7.3% strongly agreed with primary psychopathy items. A further 11.8% moderately agreed with primary psychopathy items. These levels are far higher than for the general population. On average, participants agreeing with psychopathy items generally equalled 19.1%, which is approximately higher than what we see in prisons. The reversed items for response sets further confirm alleged psychopathy among this population. In regard to items that were more couched as pro-social, 18.3% and 10.3% disagreed strongly and

Table 7.1 Self-reported psychopathy items among a sample of law enforcement

	Strongly disagree	Moderately disagree	Moderately agree	Strongly agree
Primary psychopathy				
1. Success is based on survival of the fittest. I am not concerned about the losers.	48.6	37.1	8.6	5.7
2. My main purpose in life is getting as many goodies as I can.	80.0	11.4	5.7	2.9
3. Making a lot of money is my most important goal.	26.5	35.3	29.4	8.8
4. For me, what's right is whatever I can get away with.	80.0	8.6	0.0	11.4
5. I enjoy manipulating other people's feelings.	85.7	8.6	2.9	2.9
6. I often admire a really clever scam.	74.3	5.7	14.3	5.7
7. People who are stupid enough to get ripped off usually deserve it.	60.0	20.0	11.4	8.6
8. I tell other people what they want to hear so that they will do what I want them to do.	65.7	22.9	5.7	5.7
9. Looking out for myself is my top priority.	42.9	11.4	31.4	14.3
10. In today's world, I feel justified in doing anything I can get away with just to succeed.	71.4	20.0	2.9	5.7
11. I let others worry about higher values, my main concern is with the bottom line.	51.4	22.9	17.1	8.6
Indexed mean	62.4	18.5	11.8	7.3
Response set primary psychopathy items				
12. I would be upset if my success came at someone else's expense.	31.4	14.3	25.7	28.6
13. I feel bad if my words or actions cause someone else to feel emotional pain.	14.3	14.3	31.4	40.0

Continued

Table 7.1   Continued

	Strongly disagree	Moderately disagree	Moderately agree	Strongly agree
14. Cheating is not justified because it is unfair to others.	22.9	2.9	5.7	68.6
15. Even if I try to sell something, I would not lie about it.	14.3	11.4	17.1	57.1
16. I make a point of trying not to hurt others in pursuit of my goals.	8.6	8.6	17.1	65.7
Indexed mean	18.3	10.3	19.4	52.0
Secondary psychopathy				
1. I quickly lose interest in the tasks I start.	68.6	28.6	2.9	0.0
2. When I get frustrated, I often let off steam by blowing my top.	60.0	25.7	8.6	5.7
3. I am often bored.	48.6	25.7	20.0	5.7
4. Most of my problems are due to the fact that other people just do not understand me.	71.4	17.1	8.6	2.9
5. I find myself in the same kinds of trouble time after time.	71.4	14.3	14.3	0.0
6. I don't plan anything very far in advance.	28.6	40.0	20.0	11.4
7. I have been in a lot of shouting matches with other people.	42.9	25.7	14.3	17.1
8. Love is overrated.	52.9	20.6	17.6	8.8
Indexed mean	55.6	24.7	13.3	6.5
Response set secondary psychopathy				
9. Before I do anything, I carefully consider the possibilities.	2.9	5.7	54.3	37.1
10. I find that I am able to pursue one goal for a long time.	5.7	17.1	42.9	34.3
Indexed mean	4.3	11.4	48.6	35.7

moderately, respectively. You may be wondering while reading these descriptive statistics what ever happened to the motto "serve and protect."

The respondents also did not fare so well on the secondary psychopathy scale: 6.5% of respondents strongly agreed with secondary psychopathy items and 13.3% moderately agreed with secondary psychopathy items. Combined, this means 19.8% test positive for secondary psychopathy. Again, we observe participants well within the range expected of institutionalized populations, rather than law enforcement. A noticeable 4.3% and 11.4% disagreed strongly and moderately with reversed-scored pro-social items on the secondary psychopathy scale.

Measures of association in the form of t-tests and analyses of variance were performed between the demographic items and psychopathy scores. No significant results were observed. This was especially surprising for the gender item. Men should, theoretically, show higher psychopathy scores than women, but this was not the case here, and suggests that a minority of participants who enter law enforcement may be prone to higher levels of psychopathy, regardless of gender.

A correlation analysis between the psychopathy scales and TIPI resulted in some interesting correlations. The primary and secondary psychopathy scores possessed a moderately strong inverse relationship with agreeableness ($r = -.60$ and $r = -.50$, respectively). Agreeableness typically taps cooperative behavior and empathy, and people who score high on this scale believe that others are honest, trustworthy, and decent. An inverse relationship confirms that allegedly psychopathic participants are critical and quarrelsome, which is a feature of this personality type when cornered or experiencing shame.

There also existed a noticeable inverse relationship between primary and secondary psychopathy and emotional stability ($r = -.37$ and $r = -.39$, respectively). Those who are emotionally stable are typically calm and even-headed. The results here suggest that higher scores for psychopathy are characteristic of anxiety, jealousy, and envy. No significant correlations were observed with regard to openness, conscientiousness, and extraversion, but, of course, the sample size was relatively small. A larger sample size might demonstrate a relationship with extraversion because psychopathic individuals are thought to be cunning and manipulative. We often consider them wolves in sheep's clothing.

Discussion

From 3 February 2013 until 12 February 2013, the Los Angeles Police Department (LAPD) lived in fear of one of their own officers. Christopher Dorner, a former naval reservist, went on a shooting rampage to wage war against his fellow officers. Was Dorner a psychopath? Not necessarily. He returned $8,000 that he and a friend found that belonged to a Korean Church in in Oklahoma (Carroll, 2013a). Unless pressured by his friend, Dorner would have likely kept the cash had he been psychopathic. Can we say the same for his fellow officers?

Dorner rendered very strong allegations against fellow officers. He alleged that a training officer, Teresa Evans, had kicked a mentally ill homeless man identified as Christopher Gettler after he had been Tasered, handcuffed, and subdued on the floor (Carroll, 2013b).

Of course, this was not the first time the LAPD has made the news. How could we forget when, in 1991, Rodney King was videotaped being beaten by officers? Sergeant Stacy Koon, who led the alleged assault on King, stated that he had intended to "break bones" (Henry and Willwerth, 1993). He stated, "The intent I had was to cripple him, to make him unable to push off the ground. You can't push off the ground if your elbows are broken. You can't push off the ground if your knees are broken" (ibid). Koon's fellow officer, Lawrence Powell, spoke of how he left King in a police car for an hour while he traded stories with his colleagues (ibid).

Sadly, these events are not isolated to the LAPD. In 2011, armed police officers shot and killed Mark Duggan, who was not carrying a firearm (Dodd, 2011). That killing sparked the 2011 riots in London. In 2012, Drew Peterson, a former police officer in Chicago, was convicted after his fourth wife disappeared (The Associated Press, 2012).

In the state of Maryland, USA, Robert Saylor, a 26-year-old man suffering from Down syndrome died while being subdued by police (McCormack, 2013). Saylor had attended a movie with his aid; after the movie, the caregiver went to get the car (ibid). Saylor reportedly wanted to watch the film again. Three officers attempted to drag Saylor from the cinema and allegedly held him on the ground where he died from asphyxiation (ibid).

In the aftermath of Saylor's death, there has been a call for more police training, but is it not common sense to call a social worker or disabled services to diffuse the situation rather than tackle a severely mentally disabled person to the ground only because he wanted to watch a movie? On the surface, there appears to be a much larger problem within police departments, which would not be addressed by additional training.

We cannot conclude, without direct psychological testing, whether the officers involved in the above mentioned incidents are psychopathic. However, the data collected here do suggest that a noticeable contingent of the sample under investigation possessed significantly higher levels of psychopathy than the general population, and their scores are more aligned with what we would anticipate of a prison cohort. This raises a series of red flags. To reiterate, average ratings for primary psychopathy are 7.3% strongly agree and 11.8% moderately agree for a total of 19.1% in agreement with primary psychopathic items. The participants who tested positive for psychopathy in this study also presented neurotic and quarrelsome dimensions of their personalities. This suggests that there is something more dispositional going wrong than being transformed into villains by wearing a uniform, indoctrinated in boot camp, and obeying the orders of commandants.

Zimbardo subjected participants in the Stanford Prison Experiment to a series of personality measures, such as the F Scale, the Machiavellian Scale, the Comrey Personality Scales, and Mood Adjective Self-Reports. However, the participants were not directly tested for psychopathy and, to reiterate, they relied on the experimenter's exploitation of their dispositional trust. In addition, although participants were middle-class men, we were not told enough about the needs pursuits of each, or their feelings about economic and political insecurity, which may have affected their formidable life experiences. We now know that the Stanford Prison Experiment occurred during one of the worst inflationary periods to emerge as a result of the Vietnam War. It would only take one psychopath within a group of needs frustrated officers to persuade the group to engage in evil actions.

The point being made is that a power system cannot easily create primary psychopathic tendencies in people born with a conscience. Psychopaths do not transform into evil based on environmental factors. They are mostly evil to start with, and we need larger studies to explore whether this phenomenon occurs on a larger scale within police departments and military apparatuses worldwide. Specifically, we need to much better investigate whether psychopaths are instigating episodic violence by preying upon those subjected to structural violence.

The structurally-affected individuals are, arguably, not transformed in the moment of a bad situation, but their dispositional scaffolds have been figuratively weathered and made susceptible to the wrecking ball of psychopaths. At any time that we decide to better distribute economic resources and help people overcome threats and inhibition to needs gratification, we will render larger numbers of individuals resistant and capable of whistleblowing in the face of psychopathic manipulation.

We can root out psychopaths from power systems, and this is a good first step. But more effort must be made in making people resistant to the temptations of psychopaths, and that requires large-scale systematic reforms to advance larger numbers of people along the hyperbola paradigm.

Recommendations

In 2006, my position as the owner of a statistics firm collecting data for this feasibility study came down to whether the benefits to society outweighed the possible harm of exploring psychopathy among the police. Today, a funded study at the university level would require virtually insurmountable ethical approvals. It is such a critically important area that we must lessen the ethical burden to explore this phenomenon, and link emerging technologies in neuroscience in an effort to build a diagnostic toolkit that is biologically sound. Social and biological scientists require open access to the corridors of authority and power within the police and military apparatuses.

In addition to larger-scale studies, it would appear that psychological tests for selection of police officers and those serving in the military vary widely. We need a uniform system that measures for psychopathy across the board and is resistant to potential psychopaths learning how to cheat the test. We require biological evidence in the form of brain scans that demonstrate a lack of emotional empathy as a starting point. This may seem a bit unorthodox and potentially expensive, but investment in this area is substantiated given that human lives are, literally, at stake.

This is not to say that psychopaths are untreatable and it is certainly is not a crime to be a psychopath as long as the psychopath does not commit a crime. The point being made here is that humanity would be better off if such individuals, who are, arguably, untreatable under current medical paradigms, were not permitted into positions of vital authority and trusted to protect others.

Where do we go from Here?

We have ventured into some dark corners in exploring why, for much of human history, people have been acting against their drives to become exocentric altruists. There is light at the end of the tunnel.

For the last six decades, we have witnessed a relative economic miracle in the West prior to the 2008 recession, which positively shaped the formative experiences of young people and, arguably, rendered large numbers of individuals resistant to negative environmental influences. I will now turn my attention directly to the positive aspects of how overcoming threats and inhibition to needs has created widespread value shifts in favor of our development along the hyperbola paradigm before turning attention to governing, educational, and therapeutic systems, which have lagged far behind the populace's development.

Part 3

Sequential Confirmation of the Hyperbola Paradigm

8
Post-materialist Value Change

Political sociologist Ronald Inglehart took America by surprise in 1977 by declaring that an era of consensual politics had not formed. He posited that there was a silent revolution occurring between newly emerging higher-order needs gratifiers who were vying for resources with lower-order needs pursuers. In particular, his seminal work advised the political establishment of the USA how to keep one step ahead of the curve in forming public policy that would meet the changing needs pursuits of Western populations. Inglehart had no idea that his predictions, over time, would prove to be much more accurate than the mass media expected, except on one pivotal point. For 40 years, his attitudinal surveys have confirmed the first two tiers of the sequence of needs achievement along Maslow's original paradigm.

Unfortunately, Inglehart capped off his paradigm too early by rooting it in Maslow's needs hierarchy. He ended up with a premature picture of what future society would come to resemble. The mission in this chapter is to observe the accuracy of predictions for the rise of a post-materialist-type civilization in order to confirm the sequence of needs achievement along Maslow's needs hierarchy. Mass survey evidence will initially be offered to confirm collective advancement.

I will then turn my attention in Chapters 9 and 10 to original primary data which show the dangers of capping the paradigm too soon and the emergence of an undiscovered values type. We are about to venture onto a path that will suggest that policy makers, academics, and other key stakeholders with good intentions have fallen short. An argument will be made that Western civilization is not any closer to an era of consensual politics. Mass publics are all heading for profound confrontation between value types, and this has the potential to harm the healthiest of humanity unless stakeholders embrace the predictive power of the quantitative evidence offered in the next few chapters.

Introduction to Values Change

Two major concepts underpin Inglehart's paradigm. He essentially mapped development within mass publics based on the concepts of scarcity and socialization. Dalton sums up the process, stating, "The combination of both hypotheses—scarcity and socialization—produces a general model of value change. Individuals initially form their basic value priorities early in life and then emphasize those desired goals that are in short supply" (Dalton, 2006, p. 83) This concept states that overcoming scarcity through needs gratification shapes the perspective of individuals who pass off their needs concern levels to successive generations.

Inglehart argued that people "place the greatest value on those things that are in relatively short supply" (1981, p. 881). 'Materialist' concerns about economic and physical security are desired by the public in times of depression or warfare. Emphasis on 'post-materialist values,' such as freedom, self-expression, and quality of life, increases as demands for clean drinking water, food, and shelter are met (Abramson and Inglehart, 1995). However, these needs are not beyond self-interest, as the phrase 'post-material' would imply. Post-materialist concerns as originally envisioned by Inglehart are a form of enlightened materialism. This is because people are still pursuing self-interest—just on a higher level for meaning and purpose.

Values generally represent beliefs that are derived from human needs gratification (Inglehart, 1971, 1977). Inglehart states:

> Drawing on the work of Abraham Maslow, we reason that age cohorts who had experienced the wars and scarcities of the era preceding the West European economic miracles would accord a relatively high priority to economic security and to what Maslow terms safety needs. For younger cohorts, a set of [post-materialist] values relating to the need for belonging and to aesthetic and intellectual needs, would be more likely to take top priority. (1971, pp. 991–2)

The terms 'post-materialist' and 'materialist' were created to invoke a two-tier classification along Maslow's hierarchy of needs. Maslow's intermediate and higher-order needs, such as social, self-esteem, and self-actualization, define post-materialist concerns, and lower-order needs, such as economic and physical security, describe purely materialist goals.

Inglehart classifies twelve political values according to the tier with which they are most often associated. He states that "The twelve options themselves were designed to permit a fuller exploration of Maslow's need hierarchy" (1977, p. 41). Political values are further described:

> Six items were intended to emphasize the physiological or Materialist needs: 'Rising prices,' 'Economic growth' and Stable economy' being aimed at the sustenance needs; and 'Maintain order,' 'Fight crime' and 'Strong defense forces' being aimed at the safety needs. The remaining six items were designed to tap various Post- Materialist needs. We view the latter needs as potentially universal: every human being has a need for esteem, inherent intellectual curiosity, and aesthetic satisfaction: he or she will act on these needs unless circumstances force one to stifle them. (1977, p. 43)

Conflict arises along this paradigm because it is perceived that resources are scarce. Thus, materialists vie for financing for a strong economy and protection with post-materialists who want universal healthcare and childcare. When viewed in this way, scarcity appears to be causing a never-ending tug of war between the two camps. To reiterate, scarcity only exists because of the perception that our wants are unlimited. Approaching this conflict differently with limiting our wants through self-discipline would aid in human values development, but we cannot approach this conflict differently until our governing, educational, and therapeutic systems have a clearly defined purpose. I will turn to the topic of defining purposeful systems in Part 4.

We can correctly assume, as Inglehart does, that overcoming scarcity leads to positive experiences. We also know from Maslow's observations that people gain functional autonomy and immunity from overcoming threats to lower-order needs. During the 1990s, we witnessed something truly dramatic unfold. Between 1995 and 2000, real wages increased, income inequality declined, overall poverty decreased from 15% to under 12%, and workers enjoyed the liberties of a full employment economy (Galston, 2001). The decade prior to 2008 had historically low unemployment and inflation.

And the USA had not witnessed defeat in any major war since Vietnam. Although there were smaller conflicts in Panama, Bosnia, and First Gulf War, these were dealt with expeditiously, with little loss of life for the USA. Even political scandals had been rather lame since Watergate. The fact that President Clinton turned the White House into a frat house by having an affair with Monica Lewinsky was more like an entertaining soap opera than a real threat to the functioning of the government.

The formidable experiences of young people were very hopeful and optimistic throughout the late 1990s. Polls in 1999 suggested that Americans trusted each other to tell the truth seventy-one percent of the time (Levine and Cureton, 1998). Trusting others to tell the truth demonstrates advancement beyond materialist needs for security and protection.

Let's briefly look at the policy proposals of that time. President Clinton proposed universal healthcare and the Family Leave Act. Universal healthcare tore the nation apart because left-over materialist types controlling the congress believed it would destabilize the economy. Nevertheless, we witnessed the rise of more say at work, as W. Edwards Deming's Total Quality Management theories were replacing Frederick Taylor's traditional scientific management theory. Deming's concepts were based on promoting cooperation within the workplace rather than rugged individualism. Workers engaged companies at all levels through quality circles, flexible working hours, and flexible workstations (Dalton, 2006). My generation, in particular, witnessed the rise of movable coffee bars at work. To say the least, this was a good time to be living in the USA.

Time Series Analysis of Value Trends

Advancements in surveying techniques have permitted us to confirm over time the sequence of needs achievement according to Maslow's hierarchy. Michael Hagerty examined evolution along Maslow's needs hierarchy utilizing quality of life time-series analysis for eighty-eight countries spanning a period from 1960 to 1994, and confirmed "... significant agreement with some of Maslow's predictions, including his sequence of needs achievement" (1999, p. 249). In 1993, a separate study further confirmed these findings. On a scale of one to ten, young Americans aged 17–30 reported a high score of 7.66 on "overall satisfaction in life" (Friesl et al., 1993). It is also true that respondents in that survey reported a score of 7.88 on possessing a "subjective feeling of freedom" (ibid).

Russell Dalton, a professor of political science at the University of California, has provided us with more recent mass survey analysis of development along Inglehart's paradigm. He used data from 1990 to 2002 from the World Values Survey (WVS) to explore increases in the numbers of post-materialists relative to materialist types (Dalton, 2006). The WVS polls more than 60,000 people in the USA, and worldwide. We will also compare Dalton's data with Carmines and Laymen's analysis of National Election Studies (NES). The NES are conducted by the Center for Political Studies at the University of Michigan.

How have Americans ranked values such as a strong economy, national defense, crime, more say on the job, freedom of speech, environmentalism, and many others?

Carmines and Laymen summarized their findings as follows:

> In 1972, 35.2% of the respondents were materialists; by 1992, the proportion of materialists had declined by more than half to 16.3%. At the same time, the proportion of post-materialists has almost doubled from 9.5% to 18.4%. In 1972, the ratio of materialists to post-materialists was almost 4 to 1; in 1992 there were slightly more post-materialists than materialists in the electorate. (1997, p. 287)

Between 1972 and 1973, Inglehart concluded that about 31% were materialists, 12% post-materialists, and 39% mixed types. Between 1972 and 1999, we were certainly witnessing significant increases in post-materialism. Inglehart also suggested that the ratio of materialist to post-materialists types in the USA fell from 3.5 to 1 in 1972 to 1.5 to 1 in 1987 (Inglehart, 1990).

My own experiences as a member of America's youngest are in agreement with these findings. We can estimate three separate US generations based on census data as follows: baby boomers (born between 1946 and 1964), Generation X'ers (born between 1965 and 1976), and

Table 8.1   The US shift in post-materialist values over time (in percentages)[a]

Value type	1972	1976	1980	1984	1988	1990[b]	1992	1999[b]
Materialist	35.20	31.06	34.24	20.75	18.52	–	16.32	–
Mixed	55.32	59.17	56.09	63.44	64.30	–	65.25	–
Post-materialists	9.48	9.77	9.68	15.81	17.18	21.00	18.43	23.00

[a]Adapted from Carmines and Layman (1997) and Dalton (2006).
[b]The entries for 1990 and 1999 are from the World Values Survey and use percentages that place a higher priority on post-materialist goals, using Inglehart's twelve-item measure (see Dalton, 2006). Data for materialist and mixed items for 1990 and 1999 were not available. All other years use the averages for materialist, mixed, and post-materialist goals that were listed on the American National Election Studies surveys.

the baby boomlet (born between 1977 and 1994) (Edmondson, 1995). Aside from being a cute name, the label 'baby boomlet' is apt for my generation because our numbers rival the baby boomers. Television shows such as *Oprah* and *Dr. Phil*, which focus on self-fulfillment and personal growth, are popular largely among my cohort.

My fellow baby boomlets also engaged in strong civic engagement. This is important because civic engagement demonstrates self-acceptance and instrumentality. Baby boomlets became active voters when a young African–American Senator declared his interest for the presidency. It was largely the youth vote that agreed with Obama's post-materialist agenda for larger access to education and increased funding for college.

However, voting behavior among post-materialist baby boomlets is unpredictable, and they soon became disillusioned with the same corporately run federal government that continued the status quo of no real jobs growth, continued overseas conflicts, and Guantanamo Bay. Dalton argues:

> The participatory orientation of postmaterialists doesn't affect all participation modes equally. Voting turnout is often lower among postmaterialists because most established parties have not fully embraced postmaterial issues. In addition, postmaterialists are skeptical of formal hierarchical procedures and organizations, such as elections and most political parties.
>
> Instead, postmaterialist are more likely to participate in citizen initiatives, protests, and other forms of direct action. The 2005–08 WVS [World Values Survey] found that postmaterialists are more likely than materialists to participate in protest (Dalton, 2013, p. 100)

Baby boomlets protested much more than they voted. In 1999, the Seattle Independent Media Center helped to link anti-globalization protestors, including young environmentalists, laborers, civil rights activists, and other anti-corporate elements. The protests were so vociferous that members of my generation ground the World Trade Organization discussions to a halt.

The Seattle protests were only the tip of the iceberg. By 2004, 500,000 people took to the streets to protest the Iraq war and Republican National convention (McFadden, 2004). By 2012, we witnessed the crowning moment for the baby boomlet generation with the rise of Occupy Wall Street (OWS). The average age of the OWS protestors was 33 years (Goodale, 2011).

Unlike earlier protests, large numbers of baby boomlets were now unemployed and pissed off. Baby boomlets had inherited the motivational interests from their baby boomer parents and Generation X'er siblings. But high unemployment, inescapable student loan debt, and the mortgage crisis did not appear to cause baby boomlets to regress to fighting for materialist concerns. The peaceful and highly creative nature of the OWS protests provided strong evidence that many participants might have gained functional autonomy and immunity to threats to lower-order needs as a result of intergenerational change.

OWS protestors gave post-materialist demands to the media, including balanced distribution of economic resources, better jobs, and more free speech. They were, by and large, anti-war and opposed to the rise of a strong domestic police force. These protests rapidly spread worldwide and led to tense stand-offs with aggressive governments under the control of corporations with self-interest-driven cultures.

Reduced Xenophobia Confirms Values Change

Latterly, Inglehart's career has focused on exploring xenophobia or fear of out-groups among insecure societies. He theorized that individuals who had not overcome scarcity and were thus strong materialist types would develop stronger fears against individuals who were different from them and lash out with violence. This line of reasoning is summarized as follows:

> When resources are so scarce that it is a question of one group or the other surviving, discrimination against outsiders, strong in-group solidarity and insider-favoritism become increasingly prevalent. Xenophobia becomes widespread when threats to survival dominate people's lives (Inglehart et al., 2006, p. 496).

In the aftermath of the Second Gulf War, Inglehart had an opportunity to test his theory. The results of a national survey of Iraq's population showed the strongest xenophobia scores in comparison with eighty-five societies analyzed by the WVS (Inglehart et al., 2006). Domestic and foreign terrorism, a strongly devalued currency, and incredibly high unemployment were contributing to strife between Shiites, Sunni, and Kurdish segments of Iraq's population. Over the last decade, this has fuelled a dramatic and often violent internal struggle for power.

A strong contrast with xenophobia in the USA would further support that intergenerational value change had a tremendous positive effect on the population before the wars on terror, Iraq, and Afghanistan, and the economic collapse in 2008. Thanks to the Federal Bureau of Investigation publishing hate crime statistics from 1995 to the present online, the opportunity presented itself to perform a similar analysis comparing hate crime activity with economic indicators.

Figure 8.1 gives a fairly clear picture that xenophobia is on the decline in the USA. Between 1996 and 2011, the data show a dramatic twenty-nine percent decrease in hate crimes. And the numbers appear to keep falling year by year. Between 2010 and 2011, there was a six percent decline in hate crimes. Of course, retaliatory attacks following the 11 September 2001 terrorist attacks in New York and Washington, DC, were to be expected, with a sizeable minority of the population still interested in purely materialist concerns. But this only represented a temporary spike in the data.

It is evident that hate crimes are continuing to decline even in the aftermath of the 2008 economic collapse. A correlation analysis showed a moderate negative linear relationship between unemployment levels and incidents, offences, and victims to hate crimes, respectively ($r = -.58$). A paradox has emerged in that thirty-four perecent of the variation in decline in the numbers of hate crimes can be explained by rising unemployment levels.

To a member of the mass media, the rising unemployment correlation to declining hate crimes may seem unexplainable given the traditional

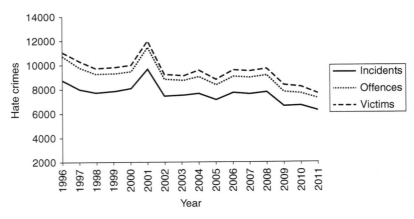

Figure 8.1 Time series analysis of hate crime statistics in relation to incidents, offences, and victims from 1996 to 2011. Data obtained from the Federal Bureau of Investigation Hate Crime Statistics (http://www.fbi.gov/about-us/cjis/ucr)

positive relationship between unemployment and xenophobia. Such a dichotomy is resolved when we realize that decades of economic growth prior to 2008 supports Maslow's theory of autonomy to threats to lower-order needs. Arguably, large segments of the population had gained immunity to needs frustration and the insecurity it produces.

The mass media would probably like to accredit the large decline in hate crimes to the election of the first African–American president. My intention is not to belittle in any way the contribution that Barack Obama has had on helping to reduce racism in the USA. However, the declines here are coincidental with his presidency, and would have occurred in any event given the decades of economic growth predating the 2008 economic collapse.

Figure 8.2 shows that among bias motivation, we observe the largest declines in hate crimes in relation to race. Between 1996 and 2011, there was a forty-six percent decrease in racial hate crimes, a twelve percent decrease in religious hate crimes, and a twenty-three percent decrease in national-origin hate crimes. The only area that has risen is sexual orientation. While the numbers of hate crimes for sexual orientation are considerably lower than racial hatred, there has been a 21% increase over 15 years.

We can only speculate, but a minority of materialist types may be retaliating by targeting gay, bisexual, and transgender people owing to the rapid inroads these groups have made in redefining state marriage laws and participating in the military. Materialist types would view

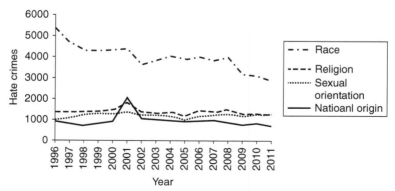

Figure 8.2 Time series analysis of hate crime statistics in relation to bias motivation from 1996 to 2011. Data obtained from the Federal Bureau of Investigation Hate Crime Statistics (http://www.fbi.gov/about-us/cjis/ucr)

these inroads as threats to a strong defense force and security within the home.

Correlation analysis showed a strong negative relationship between declines in racial hatred and rising unemployment levels (r = –.71). Nearly fifty percent of the variation in declines for race hate crimes can be explained by increasing unemployment levels. This dichotomy further adds to the evidence that large segments of the population gained functional autonomy and immunity to threats before the collapse of the USA's economy. No significance was found between unemployment levels and religious, sexual orientation, or national origin hate crimes.

Figure 8.3 breaks down hate crime events by race. Between 1996 and 2011, we witness a fifty-four percent decline in white hate crimes, a forty-three percent decline in black hate crimes, a sixty-one percent decline in Asian hate crimes, and a twenty-eight percent decrease in Hispanic hate crimes. The numbers of hate crimes against African–Americans are still much higher than hate crimes against other groups, and even one hate crime is one too many. Inferential statistics indicate the same pattern of rising unemployment and declining hate crimes in recent years. Correlation analysis demonstrated that rising unemployment levels shared a strong negative relationship with declining white (r = –.75), black (r = –.62), and Asian hate crimes (–.70). There were no significant relationships between rising unemployment and hate crimes against Hispanics.

All of these numbers provide a sense of optimism for the future of the USA and conform to predictions made by Inglehart. However, there is

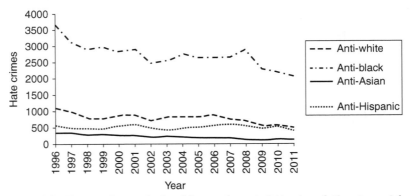

Figure 8.3   Time series analysis of hate crime statistics in relation to racial-type bias. Data obtained from the Federal Bureau of Investigation Hate Crime Statistics (http://www.fbi.gov/about-us/cjis/ucr)

degree of caution to be used here. We have thus far experienced a relatively short period of economic decline from 2008 to the present time compared with decades of strong economic growth, as measured by low inflation, unemployment, and strong gross domestic product in the economic miracle that spans World War II to 2008, and this period was only interrupted by relatively brief recessions and inflationary issues.

Should the high unemployment levels become the new norm or extreme national debt produce hyper-stagflation (high inflation and unemployment) over the next decade or more, we might start to witness breaches in functional autonomy and immunity to threats which will affect younger generations and reverse the gains the USA has made against xenophobia.

Corporate Media Pundits Blind to Values Change

The insurmountable evidence supports the notion that people are progressing from materialism to post-materialism at levels never before witnessed in history. This has increased civic engagement and reduced xenophobia. Dalton stated that "The current mix of values sometimes makes it difficult for political analysts and politicians to know what the public wants" (2006, p. 96). The corporate mass media "... tend to focus on dramatic or sensation national events without much reference to underlying processes" (Inglehart, 1977, p. 17).

For example, the media said in 1994 that the Republican Revolution was in full swing when a congressional election gave Republicans control of the United States House of Representatives. However, the Republicans miscalculated the public's desire to slash social programs in order to give citizens extra tax savings. By 1996, President Clinton won in a landslide against Senator Robert Dole. The Republican Revolution was dead in its tracks. And the 1996 election showed that many materialist successes are short-run events in the nation's drive towards post-materialism and beyond.

Critics might point to the rise of materialist-type presidents to suggest that an era of post-materialism has not arrived. The literature does not support this viewpoint. Materialist-type presidents ascend to power because citizens do not have decent alternative choices presented to them from their political parties. Inglehart argued:

> ... political behavior does not occur in a vacuum; it is shaped in crucial ways by the political context in which one lives. Even when the public does have relatively strong policy preferences and potentially

could engage in policy-voting (as may be increasingly true in the United States), they may be unable to do so because the major party candidates adopt Tweedledee-Tweedledum positions on the key issues. (1977, p. 180)

Today, it is almost impossible to see huge policy differences between Republicans and Democrats. Both parties are centrists and they have created in the voter's mind that neither party is aligned to post-materialism.

Inglehart made an interesting observation about the 1972 presidential election. He states:

In the public's perceptions, President Nixon's position on Vietnam changed very little from 1968 to 1972. But the attitude of the American public as a whole shifted appreciably from a position slightly on the hawk side of the continuum to one clearly on the dove side of the midpoint. This in itself would have favored McGovern. But his own position (as perceived by the public) was that of a dove extremist, much farther away from the median voter than that of the President. The result (here and on various key issues) was a strong net preference for Nixon. (1977, p. 258)

This phenomenon crops up over and over again with Reagan versus Carter, Reagan versus Mondale, Bush versus Dukakis, Bush versus Gore, and Bush versus Kerry. Voters in all these elections (with the exception of Gore, who won the popular vote) viewed the losing candidate as ineffectual and often a 'dove extremist.'

The media pundits have proven themselves unable to predict much of anything. The academic-turned-pundit, Robert Putnam's nostalgic work *Bowling Alone,* argued that society was failing to gratify intermediate-order social needs. He had argued that US society was in decline.

Of course, Putnam's view of bowling leagues and activities from the 1950s typically involved overweight white males who were members of the middle class. Putnam's recollection of bowling leagues could hardly be called inclusive or representative of any form of advanced social needs gratification. Lemann debunked Putnam's argument in *Kicking in Groups.* That article argued that social needs gratification was continually increasing among Americans, as evidenced by the rise in participation for inclusive sports, such as soccer (Lemann, 1996).

In Chapter 9, I highlight the new challenges that needs advancement poses to the West. And, in Chapter 10, I turn my attention to the use of advanced quantitative techniques to observe a new shift in values among a minority of people from post-materialism to exocentric altruism. The data offered in the next two chapters will suggest that the population's advancement has rapidly outpaced the ability of Western governing systems and policy makers to meet important challenges. The objective of these chapters is to lay the groundwork for arguing that new systems and the way policy is formed will need to be investigated.

9
New Challenges for the West

Despite the advancement towards post-materialism, we should not make the mistake of concluding that post-materialist types are the best specimens for optimal psychological health. The illusionary pursuit of maximized self-interest can come with a heavy price tag.

Along with the abundance of the 1990s came something that was lacking for many baby boomlets. For example, on Friday 8 April 1994, thousands of fans were greatly saddened to hear of the death of Kurt Cobain, the lead singer of the band Nirvana. It seemed like such a waste of extreme talent. In his suicide note, we see the tragedy of overindulgence in the pursuit of self-actualization. Cobain allegedly reported despair at not having "...felt the excitement of listening to as well as creating music along with really writing...for too many years now".[1]

Cobain mentioned empathy repeatedly throughout his suicide note. We can speculate that he was alluding to a frustration at self-actualization. He had disconnected from embracing a connection with all others. We will never know what exactly was going through Cobain's mind at the time of his death. Our sadness at his death, even several decades later, is immense. Can you imagine Cobain's potential impact had someone been able to counsel him that a higher calling in life was to serve all others?

This chapter will argue that post-materialists are in need of a special type of psychology because they can become stuck in a rut to restore their pinnacle as the effects of aging and mental decline remove their talents. Why do so some self-actualizers, such as Ernest Hemingway, commit suicide? Some of these individuals seek to live a certain way. They have acquired a method for success and want to continue to apply their will to power over a given situation, but when circumstances, for example declining ability with age, overload the will to power, we tend to witness a tragic end to people who could otherwise have progressed to the negation of will.

Try to imagine and put yourself in the shoes of Elvis Presley. Presley won three Grammy Lifetime Achievement Awards by the age of 36, but, with age, his ability started to decline, and locating meaning and purpose after fame became elusive. The inability to sustain achievement became pathogenic as the pop star pursued a prescription drug addiction, which resulted in death.

And thus we arrive at another interesting postulate. When lower- or intermediate-order needs are gratified, these needs become less motivating. However, self-actualizing concerns can operate differently from intermediate-order needs owing to the brain's dopamine system. People can easily become addicted to the maximization of self-interest by turning in on oneself, rather than using the external third station to become motivated to help others.

My deviation from Maslow is that self-esteem and self-actualization concerns can become frustrated in a different manner than lower-order needs. Frustration at lower-order needs is likely to cause pathology in the form of violence against others, whereas frustration directly in the pursuit of higher meaning and purpose, and self-gratification can lead to boredom, apathy, and self-destruction. People need to develop to a sense of permanence that comes from negating the self in order to gain immunity to threats to higher-order needs gratification.

Descriptive Analysis of Suicides in the USA

A descriptive and inferential quantitative analysis of a rash of suicides in the relatively brief 5 years of economic downturn demonstrates the fragility of post-materialists. These statistics start to paint the picture that intergenerational change has affected the dopamine systems of larger numbers of people at unsustainable levels. The disturbing trend is that many of the individuals committing suicide are not from poverty or the materialist cohort.

Members of white collar professions are more likely to commit suicide than those in blue collar jobs. Table 9.1 shows that professions with the highest suicide rates are those with graduate and postgraduate education levels and high incomes, for example physicians, veterinarians, and dentists—many of whom Maslow would have identified as self-actualized.

Figure 9.1 suggests that there was a trend towards higher suicide rates from 2002 to 2008—even before the recession. Suicides have increased by approximately nineteen percent. It would appear that the trend in suicides is attributable to declining abilities among baby boomers. In 2006, it was reported that white males over the age of 65 years commit suicide at triple the average rate. While mental illnesses, such as depression, schizophrenia, anxiety, substance abuse, and bipolar disorder, are

Table 9.1 Odds ratio (OR) of suicides for professional white males (Lubin, 2011)

Type of profession	OR
Natural scientists	1.28
Pharmacists	1.29
Lawyers	1.33
Real estate sellers	1.38
Urban planners	1.43
Chiropractors	1.50
Finance workers	1.51
Dentists	1.67
Veterinarians	1.54
Physicians	1.87

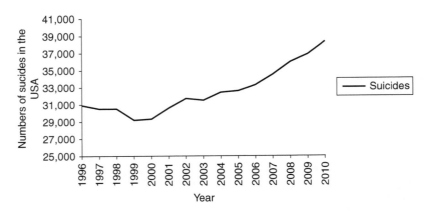

Figure 9.1 Increasing suicide rates in the USA over a 14-year period. Data from Centers for Disease Control and Prevention (CDC, 2009, 2010, 2013)

risk factors, the significant increases in less than a decade suggest that something else is exacerbating mental illness. Individuals at high risk of triggering depression and anxiety are achievers who suddenly find that they can no longer live life the way they so choose.

The intergenerational passing off of needs gratification also makes the youth of US society interested in post-materialism vulnerable. Materialists are too traditional and conservative in nature, and likely to shun therapy or be unable to afford it. A study by Dr. Matt Lock at Harvard University showed that fifty-five percent of US teenagers sought therapy before contemplating suicide or trying to kill themselves (Carey, 2013). Today, one in eight US teenagers harbors suicidal thoughts (ibid).

It is interesting that the one treatment that appears to be working with some success in treating suicidal teens is dialectical behavior therapy (DBT) (ibid). DBT therapy mixes cognitive therapy with Buddhist teaching on mindfulness and acceptance to help individuals get a grip on emotions and redefine meaning in life. It has been observed that college students treated with DBT showed significant reductions in suicide, depression, and the need for psychotropic medication (Pistorello, et al. 2012). Unfortunately, DBT is not largely used today because it is typically considered more expensive than other therapies.

Arguably, the success of the therapy lies in dealing with anxiety by encouraging the patient to develop meaning and purpose out of their circumstances. This is particularly effective for higher-order needs individuals whose early stage meaning and gratification has been impeded in some way, and who are trying to redefine new ways of living that satisfy the will to power. DBT mostly involves a patient moving towards self-acceptance. Of course, forgiving oneself and progressing beyond guilt is a fundamental first step before learning to negate the self. The main enhancement recommended for DBT would be to go further to concentrate self-actualizing patients on other-orientated mindfulness. DBT, in its current form, has not been tested over time, and thus we do not know the long-term implications of the therapy. The therapists need the skills to encourage altruistic motivation in order to produce immunity to future inhibition to self-actualization concerns or the patient may one day relapse when redefined meaning again becomes elusive.

The Case of Aaron Swartz

The life and death of Aaron Swartz demonstrates primarily how we are failing post-materialists. Swartz had fit the profile of a young self-actualizer.

By the age of 14, he had authored the RSS 1.0 web syndication specification (Schwartz, 2013). He went on to form the online company that merged with Reddit (ibid).

In many ways, Swartz's civic engagement fits the pattern observed earlier in this chapter. He became a research fellow at Harvard University's Edmond J. Safra Research Center for Ethics (ibid). Swartz also co-authored *Demand Progress*, a "hactivist" publication that organized people to take action online by pressuring politicians to maintain civil liberties (ibid). By the age of 21, he took on Pacer, a court repository system that was charging people 10 cents per page for federal judiciary documents (ibid). Swartz believed such documents should be free as we had already paid for them through taxation. Swartz wrote a program that downloaded 20 million documents from that website.

In 2010, Swartz filed a Freedom of Information Act request to learn of the treatment of military whistle-blower Bradley Manning, and is alleged to have assisted *WikiLeaks* (Anon, 2013; Leopold, 2013). Of course, Swartz was most infamous for downloading 4.8 million documents from the database JSTOR (Schwartz, 2013). The Middlesex County District Court initially agreed to drop the charges and said that Swartz should be "returned to civil society to continue his pioneering electronic work in a less legally questionable manner" (McCullagh, 2013). However, an aggressive Justice Department wanted to make an example out of Swartz and decided to pursue charges that would have likely resulted in 35 years in prison and $1 million in fines (Schwartz, 2013).

On 11 January 2013, Aaron Swartz, Internet prodigy and activist, committed suicide by hanging himself. He was 26 years old. In the first instance, the federal judicial system failed Swartz. The judicial system is based on antiquated laws that can cause significant mental harm to post-materialists. There appears to be no uniformity in the USA's system of justice other than retribution. Retribution is a catastrophic trigger to a self-actualizer because it overloads the individual will to power, which, in Swartz's case, led to self-destruction.

Rather than threatening Swartz with 35 years in prison and $1 million in fines, a better rehabilitation would have been to use Swartz's advanced knowledge of the Internet to help others. In hindsight, it is almost guaranteed that Swartz would be alive and mentally healthier and stronger today if the Justice Department had given him the task of volunteering to set up Internet networks and access to US libraries for the newly-formed nation in the south of Sudan.

Swartz's girlfriend, Taren Stinebrickner-Kauffman, said that Swartz was "... a man of joy, energy and inspiration ..." (Peterson, 2013). Swartz was one of many post-materialists searching for higher meaning and purpose; he was thwarted in his search over time by a threatening and obtrusive legal system that is more interested in punishment than rehabilitation.

Because policy makers are so ill-equipped to deal with post-materialists, we are, sadly, likely to see more cases like this one, as the US federal government continues to aggressively pursue members of *WikiLeaks*, *Anonymous*, and a host of other rogue hackers worldwide. The aggressiveness of the judicial system will neither assist the government nor the individuals participating in such organizations until mechanisms are created to encourage post-materialists to use their talents in progressing to exocentric altruism.

The entire justice system's view of punishment must change to rehabilitation with the purpose of getting people like Swartz to help others. We cannot continue to punish post-materialists with confinement and extensive fines and not expect such results to have devastating consequences for all parties involved.

Discussion of Challenges

Western governing, educational, and therapeutic systems have not advanced sufficiently to assist populations in achieving better states of mental health. The systems lack purpose and fail to utilize the scientific method to evaluate policy based on the consistent purpose to improve the population's drive towards altruistic motivation. This is partly because policy makers do not fully understand the human condition and our intrinsic motivation to be good.

The next chapter will demonstrate that Western governments are witnessing the rise of a new exocentric altruistic values type, and yet those in charge have absolutely no idea how to ensure that the populace continues its advancement towards better states of psychological health. The self-interested bases underlying our societal systems are contributing to an entrenchment among a minority of materialist types and precipitous over-indulgence among self-actualizers.

10
Political Values in a Threat Environment[1]

The 11 September 2001 attacks provided an environment conducive to exploring value change at a finer level than had been done with my predecessors, such as Inglehart. It might be easy to assume that the events of that day would have produced significant insecurity and caused the public to revert attention back towards materialist concerns.

However, the consequence of being a spectator to that awful event versus the experience of a direct bodily harm or first-hand economic needs frustration produces different psychological responses. My theory is that major life events that are indirect and produce transitory stress cause people to engage in higher critical reflection of our role in the world and its relation to us. Such events operate as catalysts not only to provoke critical reflection, but they can also cause psychologically healthy individuals to create positive events and positive reappraisal through negating the self. These events thus operate significantly differently than, say, exposing a newly minted individual at self-esteem or self-actualization to economic deprivation and withdrawal of such needs.

The ability to create our own worldview and use adapted reflection, and positive reappraisal and coping skills to negate self-interest is present in well-gratified self-actualizers who witness such events from a second-hand perspective. We have not yet identified what the precise threshold of self-actualization concerns that need to be crossed to obtain this result is, and it may very well vary from person to person.

Abramson and Inglehart argued that "predicted values in advanced industrialized societies would tend to shift away from 'Materialist' concerns about economic and physical security, toward greater emphasis on freedom, self-expression, and the quality of life, or 'Post-materialist

118

values'" (1995, p. 1). Should the hyperbola paradigm tread water, we should expect a parallel shift in a terrorist threat environment where a minority of the baby boomlet shift interest to exocentric altruistic political values.

In other words, the attacks on 11 September 2001 did not psychologically weaken most of the US population, but strengthened a sub-segment of the population who were well situated in needs gratification.

What follows are the results of a large national survey at the height of the war on terror. The results will offer an optimistic assessment that a sizeable minority of exocentric value types emerged from the post-materialist cohort and represent a previously undiscovered value type.

Method

Participants

The administration of the main survey instrument was quite large and involved numerous universities and colleges on the east and west coasts of the USA.[2] The students reported psychology, political science, sociology, history, and undecided majors. Analysis was eventually conducted on 400 usable surveys, and the researcher was 95.4% confident that the resulting sample represented the proportions of political values among the intended cohort with a ± .05 margin of error.[3]

The sample was 61.5% female and 38.5% male; 28% were 18 years old, 23.5% were 19 years old, 13.5% were 20 years old, 17.5% were 21 years old, 9.5% were 22 years old, 4.5% were 23 years old, 2.0% were 24 years old, 0.5% were 25 years old, 0.5% were 26 years old, and 0.5% were 27 years old; 69.1% were from middle-income backgrounds, 20.1% were from upper-income backgrounds, and 10.8% were from lower-income backgrounds; 68% were Caucasian, 4% were African–American, .03% were American–Indian, 7.3% were Asian, 8.8% were Spanish–Hispanic–Latino, 6.0% were Puerto Rican–American, and 5.5% were 'other'; 38.4% were Catholic, 23.1% were of no religion, 15.3% were Christian (probably mainly Protestant), 11.1% were of other religion, 6.8% were Jewish, 4.5% were Protestant, .5% were Mormon, and .3% were Orthodox; 51.6% were Democrat, 19.4% were Republican, 14.1% were Independent, 9.8% were apolitical, 5.0% were 'other'; 99.0% were single, 0.8% were married, and 0.3% were divorced; 99.3% reported having no children and 0.8% had children; 69.5% completed the form on the west coast and 30.5% completed the form on the east coast; 100% were US citizens.

Political Values Measure

The participants completed a nineteen-item Political Values (PV) instrument; Inglehart's original four goals were included as follows: (1) maintaining order in the nation (which is measured by national defense, crime and violence, drugs, and international terrorism); (2) giving the people more say in important government decisions (size of the federal government); (3) fighting rising prices (state of the economy and taxes); (4) protecting freedom of speech. Values (2) and (4) indicate a shift toward self-actualization because they enhance the concepts of democratic character structures. Values (1) and (3) represent materialist or lower-order needs to protect physical and security concerns.

Additional values from the Sherrod et al. (2004) study were also included to tap post-materialist values. These included childcare; healthcare and health insurance; protecting the environment; quality of schools; poverty; and racism and discrimination. These values typically involve community resource-sharing and tax spending in order for individuals to attain some marginal utility (i.e. better health, education, cleaner air, more opportunity in the workplace, and others). The objective is to use community resource-sharing in order to promote self-interest.

Because the concept of exocentric altruism is new, social scientists have yet to attempt to measure political values that would correspond to this motivation. This study took the bold step of including the following items on a political values scale to measure exocentric altruism: (a) providing free medications to people infected with HIV in Africa; (b) practising international non-violence; (c) declare Swiss-like military neutrality; (d) boycott companies exploiting poor countries; and (e) redistribute US wealth to poor countries. These items appear to represent the use of community resources in such a way that result in personal (i.e. tax dollar or military) sacrifice without potential benefits to individual US citizens.[4]

Procedure

The items were presented in the same order to all participants. Participants were able to complete the PV scale within about 5 minutes. The sample was not randomly selected; however, enrolment statistics at the colleges chosen for the sample indicate that social science subjects, such as political science, history, or psychology, are popular subjects, so the pool of subjects is already somewhat of a random sample of demographics at these institutions.[5]

The purpose of the survey was explained to the professors and lecturers (the 'gatekeepers') who administered the questionnaire. The gatekeepers were instructed to explain the purpose to students and not to pressurize them to complete the questionnaires. They were also requested to allow students to refrain from partaking in part or all of the administration of the survey. Participants were asked on a disclaimer form whether it would be permissible to retain data in order to possibly contact them at some point in the future. The measures were completed in groups of 15–130 participants.

Results

Split-half reliability and factor analysis were used to examine whether the PV scale was a reliable and valid measure. Descriptive statistics were employed to compare averages between the current data and Inglehart's 1972–73 survey results. Finally, multiple regression models and factor analysis were used to examine whether there exists a linear relationship that extends beyond Inglehart's paradigm.

Reliability and Validity of the PV Inventory

Split-half reliability was utilized to demonstrate the internal consistency of the PV inventory. Guttman's split-half reliability is .76 for the PV inventory. This estimate of reliability indicates that the revised PV scale has high internal consistency.

Factor validity was assessed by factor analysis of materialist, post-materialist, and exocentric type values using principle components of extraction and oblique rotation (oblique rotation is used to allow for possible correlation among factors).

As Figure 10.1 shows, the three-factor solution is consistent with three distinct political value factors on the PV instrument, which include materialist, post-materialist, and exocentric dimensions.

Therefore, the PV scale satisfies construct validity. It is important to note that correlations <.30 were omitted from the factor analysis results. The correlations in the pattern and structure matrices were highly similar, and, as a result, the decision was made to present the pattern matrix that represents the linear combination of variables. It is typically necessary to discuss differences between pattern and structure matrices if there were significant differences, but as there was little difference, it was deemed to be too repetitive to perform a comparison.

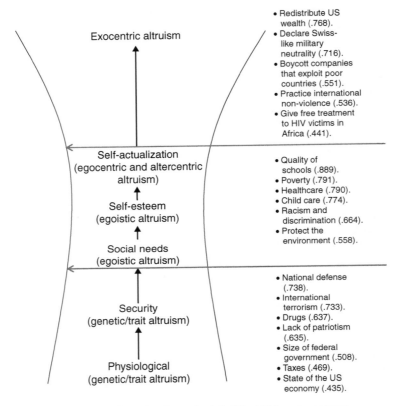

Figure 10.1 Factor analysis for the revised Political Values inventory

Descriptive Analysis of the Nineteen-item Political Inventory

Inglehart speculated that the threshold to a self-actualized political value change was about seventeen percent of the population (Inglehart, 1977). In comparison, increasing numbers of participants might be crossing a seventeen percent threshold to exocentric altruism in a terrorist threat environment. To explore this hypothesis, it is necessary to observe the frequencies of materialist, post-materialist, and exocentric altruistic types among a cohort aged 18–28 years. To reiterate, Inglehart's analysis of survey data from 1972 indicates that among the cohort aged 18–28 years, twenty-four percent were materialist and seventeen percent were post-materialist types (ibid). Table 10.1 shows that value preferences might have undergone profound change since the 1970s.

Table 10.1 Value types by indexed averages of political attitude importance ratings (percentages)

	Extremely important	Very important	Neutral	Not very important	Not important
Materialist political values					
National defense	28.6	23.1	25.1	15.3	7.8
Crime and violence	38.4	35.1	18.4	4.0	4.0
Drugs	18.1	22.9	31.3	16.5	11.2
International terrorism	31.4	23.9	25.6	12.6	6.5
Size of the federal government	11.4	16.2	40.3	18.7	13.4
Taxes	20.2	30.8	30.1	10.6	8.3
State of the US economy	33.6	30.8	23.7	7.6	3.8
Lack of patriotism or civic engagement	9.8	14.6	21.7	23.0	30.8
Indexed mean	**23.9**	**24.7**	**27.0**	**13.5**	**10.7**
Post-materialist political values					
Child care	49.9	26.2	14.9	5.5	3.5
Healthcare and health insurance	49.9	27.0	12.8	5.3	5.0
Poverty	50.0	25.6	15.6	5.3	3.5
Protecting the environment	41.4	29.3	17.7	7.1	4.5
Quality of schools	62.7	24.9	5.0	3.0	4.3
Racism and discrimination	49.1	28.2	13.6	4.5	4.5
Indexed mean	**50.5**	**26.9**	**13.3**	**5.1**	**4.2**
Exocentric political values					
Give free treatment to HIV victims in Africa	31.0	24.9	24.4	12.3	7.3
Boycott companies exploiting poor nations	21.9	24.6	32.9	11.8	8.8
Practice international non-violence	34.6	25.0	21.2	12.1	7.1
Redistribute US wealth to poor countries	17.6	16.4	22.7	24.4	18.9
Declare Swiss-like military neutrality	11.5	14.6	29.5	18.5	25.9
Indexed mean	**23.3**	**21.1**	**26.1**	**15.8**	**13.6**

Table 10.1 shows that approximately fifty-one percent of the sample rate 'post-materialist values' as extremely important. This is more than double the percentage of participants who selected post-materialist values in the 1972 survey. The percentages of materialist types have not declined since the 1972 survey, but post-materialist types have significantly increased in number. It is important to mention that in 1972 the majority of people likely fell into a mixed materialist/post-materialist value-type category. Whereas the 1972 data suggest that materialist types slightly outnumbered post-materialist types, the 'extremely important ratings' for each category indicate that materialist types are evenly split with exocentric value types: twenty-four percent are materialist types and twenty-three percent are exocentric value types.

The improvement of the theoretical underpinnings of the scale, increased number of scale items, and a likely reduction of 'mixed value types' over time might have led to self-reported ratings that reflect major changes in political preferences. These data show that post-material values are clearly more important to the majority of the sample than materialist items in 1972. It also suggests that materialist and exocentric value types represent bi-polar opposites or extremes on the continuum. If seventeen percent was considered a threshold in 1972 for the rise of a post-materialist type, then a twenty-three percent 'extremely important' average rating for exocentric values reveals that this threshold has been crossed for today's social science college students on the east and west coasts.

This distribution corresponds to a needs hierarchy that reflects what is expected of a highly post-materialist sample. The needs for growth and knowledge generation are assigned the greatest value, while needs for materialist and exocentric altruism pursuits are given the least value. Of course, historical events affect the frequencies. The materialist-type goals of national defense and preventing international terrorism are likely to be rated higher because the USA continues to fight a war against terrorism.

Establishment of an Updated PV Indicator

The satisfaction of construct validity generally permits indexing political values by summing importance ratings. For example, the ratings that tap post-materialists, such as child care, healthcare and health insurance, poverty, protecting the environment, quality of schools, and racism and discrimination, are summed in SPSS to form one post-material response variable. The sample process is repeated with items that tap the exocentric dimension. Below, indexing has been used to form material and exocentric response variables, respectively, for use in multiple regression models. In each model, individual materialist and post-materialist variables are used to predict the indexed post-materialist and exocentric response variables, respectively.

Multiple regression models highlighted linear advancement along the political value paradigm. Below is a regression model that predicts the post-materialist dimension from the materialist dimension.

Table 10.2 shows that thirty-eight percent of the variation, adjusted owing to chance, is explained by a direct linear relationship between the

Table 10.2 Post-materialism regression results

Model summary: predicting post-materialism from taxes, lack of patriotism or civic engagement, crime and violence, size of the federal government, international terrorism, state of the US economy, drugs, and national defense

R	.626
R square	.392
Adjusted R square	.379
Standard error of the estimate	4.07015

Analysis of variance: predicting post-materialism from taxes, lack of patriotism or civic engagement, crime and violence, size of the federal government, international terrorism, state of the US economy, drugs, and national defense

	Sum of squares	Degrees of freedom	Mean square	F	Significance
Regression	3994.372	8	499.296	30.140	.000
Residual	6195.743	374	16.566		

Test regression statistics: predicting post-materialism from taxes, lack of patriotism or civic engagement, crime and violence, size of the federal government, international terrorism, state of the US economy, drugs, and national defense

	Beta	T	Significance
Crime and violence	.494	10.735	.000
Drugs	−.005	−.111	.912
International terrorism	.042	.751	.453
Lack of patriotism or civic engagement	−.080	−1.754	.080
National defense	−.172	−3.137	.002
Size of the federal government	−.040	−.920	.358
State of the US economy	.280	5.801	.000
Taxes	.015	.329	.742

post-materialism ratings and materialism items. The F-statistic (30.14) and small *p*-value (.000) indicate that there is a significant relationship between post-materialism and materialist items. The test regression statistics indicate that there exists a directly linear relationship between crime and violence, national defense, and the state of the US economy and post-materialism (t = 10.74, –3.14, and 5.80, *p* < .05). Materialist items such as drugs, international terrorism, lack of patriotism, size of the federal government, and taxes are insignificant (*p* > .05).[6]

Table 10.3 Exocentric altruistic value-type regression results

Model summary: predicting exocentric value type from racism and discrimination, child care, protecting the environment, healthcare and health insurance, poverty, and quality of schools

R	.640
R square	.409
Adjusted R square	.400
Standard error of the estimate	3.51182

Analysis of variance: predicting exocentric value type from racism and discrimination, child care, protecting the environment, healthcare and health insurance, poverty, and quality of schools

	Sum of Squares	Degrees of freedom	Mean square	F	Significance
Regression	3226.364	6	537.727	43.601	.000
Residual	4661.833	378	12.333		

Test regression statistics: predicting exocentric value type from racism and discrimination, child care, protecting the environment, healthcare and health insurance, poverty, and quality of schools

	Beta	T	Significance
Child care	.107	2.046	.041
Healthcare and health insurance	–.001	–.022	.982
Poverty	.312	5.342	.000
Protecting the environment	.342	6.765	.000
Quality of schools	–.299	–4.964	.000
Racism and discrimination	.266	4.878	.000

The aforementioned regression models suggested a linear pattern leading from materialist to post-materialist value ratings. The more important question for analyzing a current political value change is to examine whether the linear pattern continues between post-materialism and exocentric altruistic value ratings, and thus supports the sequence of needs achievement along the hyperbola paradigm. Table 10.3 presents the results of a regression model predicting the exocentric altruistic type variable from post-materialist items.

The model summary indicates that forty percent of the variation, adjusted owing to chance, is explained by a direct linear relationship between post-material item ratings and ratings for the exocentric altruistic value-type variable. The F statistic (43.60) and small p-value (.000) indicates that exocentric altruistic value-type ratings can be predicted from post-materialist value ratings. The test regression statistics show that child care, poverty, protecting the environment, improving the quality of schools, and racism and discrimination share a direct linear relationship leading to exocentric altruistic value type ratings (t = 2.05, 5.34, 6.77, −4.96, and 4.88; $p < .05$). The healthcare and health insurance items are insignificant and fail to show a direct linear relationship leading to exocentric altruism value type ratings ($p > .05$).[7]

Rise of the Exocentric Altruistic Values Type

The leading researchers at the time of 11 September 2001 believed that the terrorist attacks had a negative effect on the college students. Blanchard et al. (2004) concluded that "Overall, these results show a noticeable psychological toll was taken by the September 11, 2001 attacks on college age students around the country within the first few months. There were high levels of ASD (acute stress disorder) symptoms and noticeable levels of PTSD [post-traumatic stress disorder] symptoms" (p. 203). But higher stress levels have not produced a noticeable shift toward security needs among participants of this study. Well-gratified post-materialists who were indirectly affected by the attacks show themselves to be impervious to threats to security needs because they have built what Maslow termed 'functional autonomy' and immunity to threats during early childhood development.

Take something directly away from a higher-order needs gratifier, such as income, or threaten them with direct violence, and a loss of meaning may provoke an existential crisis. However, indirectly expose a self-actualizer to a tragic event or someone else's loss and we seem to get critical reflection on high universal principles—the ability to empathize with the suffering of the other and the desire to negate self-interest. This starts to provide us with hints about how to assist higher-order needs gratifiers through therapy. We need to better tailor cognitive therapies to expose self-actualizers to using cognitive empathy in a safe environment. We need to assist self-actualizers in building upon their use of imagination long before their abilities start to decline or they get stuck in a rut of over-gratification.

Given the predictable value of the regression model above, it appears that an exocentric political values shift is underway among post-materialist types in this sample. The primary research and literature suggest that the terrorist threat environment enhances the ability of satiated post-materialist types to become exocentric.

I cannot understate the need to further investigate this phenomenon. We are not close to an era of consensual politics and require significant revisions to the way our governing systems operate. What we require is to get our institutional systems caught up to serve the psychological advancement of the population.

11
The Rejection of Barabbas

After the makeshift tents of the Occupy Wall Street (OWS) movement had folded, a not so silent exocentric altruistic values shift started. *The New York Times* reported that after Hurricane Sandy hit, "...Occupy Wall Street protestors rushed to apply their rabble rousing hustle to cleaning out houses, clearing debris, and raising more than $1.5 million for relief efforts. In some minds, Occupy members had become less a collection of disaffected class warriors than a group of efficient community volunteers" (Nir, 2013).

It was also reported that this has left a rift among OWS protestors (ibid). The post-materialist-type OWS protestors have started showing interest in exocentric altruism, as predicted in the Chapter 10, while the materialist types desire confrontation and conflict to gain economic security. Although a lot of economically frustrated individuals subscribe to the platform offered by the Republican Party, no one political party maintains exclusivity over materialist types. Materialists who are disenfranchised with traditional US politics will float towards movements that advocate economic security. And we find in OWS a strange mixture of values for economic security and post-materialist concerns. OWS cross cuts a section of all three political values types, and we find that exocentric altruistic activities cause materialist types to cringe within the movement. Thus far, a new paradigm for psychological health has been demonstrated and its predictability of values development tested through survey research. We will now turn to whether larger society is keeping pace with the psychological advancement of exocentric altruists.

We are all highly familiar with the lives of Socrates, Mohandas Gandhi, Martin Luther King, and Robert Kennedy. Let's say, hypothetically, that we could somehow bring one of these historical figures into our own

129

time. Would our brand of collective humanity be more inclined to listen to them this time around? Or, would members of the society or the state itself conspire to kill such individuals again? The answers to these questions have profound psychological implications as to the readiness and maturity of society to become purely altruistic.

It is conceded that the human track record even over the last 100 years has not been good. Nelson Mandela and Aung San Suu Kyi were imprisoned in their respective nations. The Dalai Lama was forced from his homeland. The Soviet Union allegedly conspired to assassinate John Paul II. Perhaps, we can again turn to an old source that might help us explore episodic violence against arguably exocentric types and whether our society is undergoing the type of change necessary to keep pace with the psychological advancement of individuals. We turn to the story of Barabbas:

> At festival time Pilate used to release a prisoner for them, any one they asked for. Now a man called Barabbas was then in prison with the rebels who had committed murder during the uprising. When the crowd went up and began to ask Pilate the customary favor, Pilate answered them, 'Do you want me to release for you the king of the Jews?' For he realized it was out of jealousy that the chief priests had handed Jesus over. The chief priests, however, had incited the crowd to demand that he should release Barabbas for them instead. Then Pilate spoke again, 'But in that case, what am I to do with the man you call king of the Jews?' They shouted back, 'Crucify him!' Pilate asked them, 'What harm has he done?' But they shouted all the louder, 'Crucify him!' So Pilate, anxious to placate the crowd, released Barabbas for them and, after having Jesus scourged, he handed him over to be crucified. (Mark 15: 6–15)[1]

The story of Barabbas provides us with several unique insights into a choice between materialist- versus exocentric-type individuals. The name Barabbas in Aramaic translates to 'son of the father.' He was considered a son of the Israeli fatherland. At the time, Israel was under foreign occupation by Rome. This meant that the Jewish people suffered financial, as well as security, hardships and, arguably, were threatened and insecure in their needs development. Barabbas, who is suggested to be a rebel and bandit, is thought to have been viewed as a hero by the Jewish people for physically confronting his nation's occupiers.

Jesus was viewed as a different type of radical. We can infer a few nontheologically-based observations about Jesus. He is speaking to women in the middle of the day at a well and is often seen visiting households owned by women. The only women to own property at that time were likely prostitutes. Jesus is also seen as breaking bread with tax collectors (Matthew), individuals with short tempers (Peter), and continually critical of the power elites. Jesus, even by our modern standards, is a radical exocentric altruistic revolutionary who was challenging the status quo and distribution of resources.

We can surmise that there must have been a lot of variables at play in the Barabbas story. We can assume that those voting for Jesus to live were likely his female disciples and young people who had cheered his entrance into Jerusalem the week prior. Those opposed and instigating the crowd were the religious and academic leaders known as the Sadducees and Pharisees, respectively. Although these groups were better off materially than the rest of the Jewish society, they were under the crushing blow of insecurity of their Roman occupiers, and feared anything that would challenge their authority as leaders. In essence, they were leaders stuck within the rut of their own meaning. It is assumed that those who turned against Jesus among the laity were dispositional materialist types who would likely only help others if the situation would end in some gain or benefit for the self.

What surprises me are some of the underlying commonalities between the Barabbas story and our modern time. While the war on terror was raging and Osama bin Laden was still on the run, an opportunity arose to conduct a brief, but insightful, study. bin Laden had killed more than 3,000 US citizens and his attacks on oil plants in Saudi Arabia and pursuit of weapons of mass destruction were very real threats to the financial stability of the West. Al-Qaeda created a similar insecurity for the West that the Roman occupiers would have created among the Jewish people.

President George Bush said that bin Laden was wanted "dead or alive." A $25 million reward was offered for his capture or death. Through the use of the media, every single authority figure in the country was ordering US citizens to rally in the effort to capture or kill bin Laden.

In 2007, the very real terrorist threat environment and heightened attacks in Iraq offered an ideal environment to survey Americans who found themselves under several strong situational constraints. The threat itself presented a situation where we had been given orders. And, at the same time, the data presented in the Chapter 10 suggest to me that the population was becoming highly resistant to situational factors.

For example, my theory was that if offered a choice between a Barabbas confederate who had knowledge of bin Laden's whereabouts versus a Jesus confederate who was a civil rights activist, the majority of

Americans would reject the commands of authority and favor the Jesus confederate. This has important implications not only with regard to our readiness to accept exocentric altruistic leaders, but also whether studies undertaken by famous researchers, such as Stanley Milgram, under laboratory conditions would hold true under a terrorist threat environment.

Milgram's experiments had theorized that Americans would be no different from Germans in the 1940s in obeying authority. At Yale University, he recruited forty male participants and ordered the naïve participants to administer electric shocks to a confederate at voltage levels that ranged from 15 to 450 volts. The unknowing participants had no idea that the machine was only a simulated shock generator. Milgram reported that 65% of the naïve participants followed orders all the way to the end to administer lethal shocks.

Zimbardo reported a follow-up study using a puppy instead of a human confederate. The puppy needed to perform an unsolvable task or receive a shock. In that study, the naïve participants did not know that the shock box was set to a lower voltage so as not to actually kill the puppy. That study reported that half the males (54%) and all of the females would shock the puppy to 450 volts. I have already discussed the issues of trust as compromising the outcomes of obedience studies, and readers are referred to Chapter 7 for a fuller discussion of the flaws of these experiments.

Several hypotheses are tested in this chapter to explore whether society is shifting towards acceptance of a potential coming age of altruism based the emergence of stronger dispositional scaffolds. The first hypothesis is that the majority of modern Americans would select a Jesus confederate rather than a Barabbas confederate, regardless of orders given by the government that had focused on the killing or capture of bin Laden. That is, larger numbers of Americans stand ready to reject the orders of their leaders and the media all the way up to the presidency itself.

The second hypothesis is that we should find no significant demographic differences with regard to gender, age, education, or geographic location. Historically, women in US society earn less than men and are, arguably, more needs frustrated. However, as the society has advanced in needs pursuits, it is theorized that the potential differences which may have once existed where women would be more susceptible to situational factors have started to become less of an influence.

The final hypothesis is that the party affiliation might play a role in the preference for a hypothetical confederate. To reiterate, the platform of the Republican Party is highly concentrated on the protection of materialist pursuits, and, in theory, these types would be more likely to release a confederate whose aims are to protect the country and its national defense. A party affiliation item was used to explore this phenomenon.

Method

Participants

A non-random convenience sample was selected to test this phenomenon at the height of the war on terror. The survey was created via surveymonkey.com and students from Loyola University in Baltimore, MD, USA, were initially invited to take it. The survey was expanded to blogs and open forums via the Internet, where the sample size swelled.

The consent statement read, "As a participant, you agree to participate in a study of individuals to gather information regarding reactions to September 11, 2001. The purpose of this study is to evaluate general reactions and motivations six years after the events of September 11, 2001. The project director hopes to use the information obtained from this study to better model political and societal development."

Administration of the survey was quite large, and many respondents were from the east coast of the USA. The demographics showed that 79.6% were from the east coast, 10.9% were from the west coast, 5.9% were from the Midwest, 2% were from the south, and 1.4% came from elsewhere in the country or did not report which section of the country they came from. Analysis was eventually conducted on 357 useable surveys.[2] My calculations showed 94.12% confidence that the resulting sample represented the proportions of political values among the intended cohort with a ± .05 margin of error.[3]

The age range for this sample was 18–67 years, with an average age of 26 years. The sample was 50.1% female and 49.9% male; 77.6% were single, 18.2% were married, 3.6% were divorced, and .6% were non-responsive; 18.55% had children, 81.2% had no children, and .3% were non-responsive; 88% were white, 2.8% were African–American, .3% were Native–American, 2.2% were Asian–American, 1.1% were Spanish/Hispanic/Latino, 1.1% were Mexican–American–Chicano, .3% were Puerto Rican–American, .6% were of other ethnicity, and 3.6% were multi-ethnic; 71.1% reported having a college education, 14.8% reported having a high school education; 12.9% reported having a graduate education, .8% reported some high school education, and .3% were non-responsive; 58.5% were Catholic, 13.4% were non-specific Christian,

11.2% were of no religion, 7.3% were Protestant, 2.85% were of other religion, 2.5% were Jewish, 6 1.7% were Mormon, 1.1% were Orthodox, .8% were Buddhist, and .6% were Muslim; 35% were Republicans, 28.3% were Democrats, 18.8% were Independent, 13.2% were apolitical/didn't know, .8% were of the Green Party, and .6% were non-responsive.

Procedure

Participants responded to the items in the same order. Cookies were enabled and IP addresses recorded to prevent participants taking the survey more than once. The survey was presented in sections to the respondents in the following order: (a) demographic items, (b) prisoner scenario, and (c) personality measures. Participants were told that they were free to withdraw consent and discontinue participation in the survey at any time.

After recording brief demographic items, the respondents encountered the following scenario:

Please read the following hypothetical short story and follow the directions listed after the story.

The United States Congress became angry because the President had been providing too many pardons to death row inmates. Congress voted to permit the President to provide only one pardon per year. The President has a problem because he wants to pardon two people this year. He has decided to let you decide which person should be pardoned.

Prisoner Background Information

First prisoner: Robert is a decorated war hero from the Afghanistan conflict. While on assignment in Afghanistan, he managed to capture a high-ranking al-Qaeda operative. Robert tortured the operative to death in attempting to get information about the whereabouts of Osama bin Laden. Robert was arrested for torturing and murdering an enemy combatant and sentenced to death. Robert maintains that the operative gave him the location of Osama bin Laden but that he will not release this information unless the President grants him a pardon. Robert filed his last appeal, but the Supreme Court held that Robert should face the death penalty.

Second prisoner: Peter is a civil rights leader who actively protested the Iraq and Afghanistan conflicts. He made very powerful enemies among America's corporate elite. Peter advocated peaceful civil disobedience through boycotting companies supporting the war effort.

Approximately, 1 million American college students started to follow Peter's recommendations, and companies supplying food, clothes, and other goods to the war effort saw their profits plummet. Shortly after the boycott began, Peter came home and found his house surrounded by federal agents. They claimed that Peter had been supporting the enemy in a time of warfare. Peter had been using donations from protestors to ship medical supplies to the Iraqi people, but the United States government contended that Peter was supplying insurgents. Peter was arrested and sentenced to death for treason. After his trial, two of five FBI [Federal Bureau of Investigation] agents who arrested Peter retracted their accusations and said that there had been a concerted effort by the government and big business to frame Peter. However, the Supreme Court (filled with pro-business judges) unanimously rejected Peter's last appeal.

You need to vote for pardoning (i.e. releasing) only one prisoner.

I vote to release:
(a) Prisoner one (Robert, the war hero), or
(b) Prisoner two (Peter, the civil rights activist).

This story was created with the original Barabbas story in mind. On one hand, Robert represents the Barabbas confederate. He is described as a hardened and decorated war veteran, and politically motivated to protect the fatherland. This theme must have had resonance at the time because US war casualties in Iraq and Afghanistan were hitting high points throughout 2006 and 2007 (when the survey was undertaken).

On the other hand, we have Peter who is an exocentric altruist and peaceful revolutionary. He is challenging the status quo of materialism and recruiting an increasing number of followers to his cause. It is apparent that Peter is not treasonous and that he is being framed by the government for challenging big business. He represents a modern version of the Jesus confederate.

Results

Who did the participants select to live? Two hundred and thirteen (59.7%) selected Peter (the Jesus confederate), 127 (35.6%) selected Robert (the Barabbas confederate), and seventeen (4.8%) abstained from responding to the question.

These frequencies support that the notion that dispositional scaffolds had made the majority of the populace resistant to the prevailing orders of its political establishment. Respondents overwhelmingly selected the Jesus confederate, even when the Barabbas confederate was said to have information on the whereabouts of bin Laden. Although a majority selected the Jesus confederate, a degree of caution is recommended when interpreting descriptive statistics.

We should probably not declare that our society is fully willing to accept exocentric altruists. A sizeable minority, most likely materialist types, selected the Barabbas confederate, and that could spell trouble for exocentric values types. The Barabbas supporters may be more radical and militant in their views, and willing to carry out violence against exocentric value types to protect their materialist needs pursuits. The assassins of Mohandas Gandhi and Yitzhak Rabin were ultraright extremists.

We also must remember that the participants took this survey in front of their computers, which is widely different than standing in a shouting crowd. The Barabbas supporters may be highly vocal and rowdy, and able to suppress the supporters of the Jesus confederate if assembled in a large crowd. And we know that threats to materialist types could make them susceptible to the ideology of a state. For example, the petty criminal Mehmet Ali Ağca joined the left-wing Popular Front for the Liberation of Palestine and became swept up in communist ideology. Ağca eventually attempted to assassinate Pope John Paul II.

A correlation analysis was conducted between the age of respondents and their candidate preferences. There was no statistically significant association found between these variables. Chi-square (χ^2) tests were run to explore whether significant relationships existed between the nominal demographic items and the pardon question. All of the demographic items were insignificant except for one variable, which I will discuss shortly. It would appear that the gap between racial and gender achievement is closing, and that women, in particular, are not as susceptible to the orders of authority, as observed by Zimbardo in *The Lucifer Effect* (2007).

There was a significant association between political party affiliation and which candidate was pardoned: χ^2 (5) = 39.43, $p < .001$. This represents the fact that, based on the odds ratio, Republicans were 5.23 times more likely than Democrats to select the Barabbas confederate rather than the Jesus confederate. It also appears that Republicans were 2.79 times more likely than any other party affiliation combined to select the Barabbas confederate rather than the Jesus confederate.

What can we delineate from association between party affiliation and the candidate selected? Today's Republican Party's platform supports a materialist agenda, such as a strong defense force, lowering of taxes, and a strong domestic police force. It also advocates support for US institutions, and compliance with authority among the grassroots of the party. The Republican Party crosscuts an interesting dynamic of people. The leadership of that party tends to be wealthy, whereas the mass support for the party comes from those who feel their needs gratification is under threat. It is not a stretch to assume that materialists, wherever they are found, represent a threat to the existence of exocentric altruists.

Discussion

During the height of the terrorist threat environment and increasing casualties in Iraq, we noticed researchers, such as Zimbardo, rushing to study needs-frustrated prison guards at Abu Ghraib claiming that the situation made them do it. In hindsight, Zimbardo should have turned the lens towards the homeland, where he would have found a lack of support for obedience studies.

The entire country had become a laboratory. Members of the executive and legislative branches of government dress in suits and yield the tremendous power to give orders to the populace from their offices in Washington, DC. By 2007, motivation to obey the orders to kill or capture bin Laden was, arguably, never stronger among the populace. These were orders, given the actions of al-Qaeda, that were perfectly acceptable to the US public. And, of course, participants, as US citizens, have a certain obligation to help protect the country.

The sample here was caught up in its moment in history. There is no question that the participants in this experiment certainly wanted to help in capturing bin Laden. These participants were in no way hostile towards the government. Many of the subjects came from the east coast, which was attacked on 11 September 2001; thus, their obligation to contribute to the capture of bin Laden was even stronger based on geographic association.

By 2007, the subject of torture had also arisen in regard to prisoners at Guantanamo Bay, and those in rendition camps and in Iraq. It was clear that the US government had already been overstepping its own acceptable limits in the attempt to kill or capture bin Laden, and this was transmitted to the public through the media.

Why would the majority of the public reject a person who had knowledge of bin Laden's whereabouts compared with a person providing assistance to an out-group? The participants' dispositional scaffolds are stronger as a result of needs gratification. Mass-survey research shows political values trending towards post-materialism and exocentric altruism. The sample was more capable of making its own decisions and resistant to power of the situation. My observations in conducting this type of research suggest that individuals who are less resistant to the power of the situation are associated with materialist needs pursuits.

In addition to shedding light on the situationalist versus dispositionalist debate, the study hints at something else that is equally as important. We know that there is now a three-way competition for the distribution of economic resources.

Aside from some violent outburst towards post-materialist liberals during the 1960s and 1970s, the conflicts between materialist and post-materialist types have been largely resolved through the democratic process as the numbers of post-materialists have increased with widespread needs gratification since World War II. This might not continue to hold true with the emergence of exocentric-type individuals. We may witness materialist types engaging in episodic violence to protect their illusionary needs gratification. In one sense, materialist types probably have no inkling that what they are doing is wrong. The pressure for the maximization of the self is overwhelming to those who have experienced needs frustration.

However, this demonstrates the need to recreate our governing, education, and psychodynamic systems to help materialist types progress towards post-materialism, and from that launching pad, exocentric altruism. We are thus progressing towards a coming age of altruism and held back only by the illusions of materialism, which are reinforced by an outmoded adversarial political system that promotes self-interest over cooperation.

Limitations

This non-random sample is not generalizable to the US population. The sample was 58.5% Catholic. From one perspective, Catholics are taught to be highly obedient to authority, and it was surprising to see this cohort challenge the status quo in such a direct fashion. Some US Catholics who attend church at Easter time might be familiar with the Barabbas story and, theoretically, may have relayed this scenario to that story in their own minds. However, a debriefing of some of the Catholic participants who listed their contact information did not reveal that they had made the connection to the Barabbas story when presented with this study's hypothetical scenario. And there were no significant differences located between Catholics and other religious affiliations in selecting who to release.

A larger limitation of the study is that it did not explore the situational factor of rushed conditions. The participants in this experiment were not timed with regard to answering the pardoning question. It is theoretically possible, although unlikely, that a rush condition might modify the results. Most respondents to surveys tend not to linger on individual question items for too long.

Recommendations for Future Research

Approximately thirty-six percent voted to release the Barabbas confederate. This rather disturbing figure shows there is a sizeable minority who would send an innocent man to death to protect collective self-interests.

However, there appears to be something more associated with the threat environment that is possibly affecting societal advancement towards pure altruism. Logic dictates that materialist types are pursuing self-esteem, along with security and social needs, gratification. It is highly possible that the pursuit of self-esteem and its relation to defining existential meaning at intermediate-order needs gratification may be playing a stronger role in inhibiting societal progress than previously known. And this role may be conflated by societal systems that promote self-interest rather than cooperation.

It has been argued "... that the importance of self-esteem lies not only in whether trait self-esteem is high or low but also in the pursuit of self-esteem—what people do to achieve boosts to self-esteem and avoid drops in self-esteem in their daily lives" (Crocker and Park, 2004, p. 393). Unfortunately, self-interested systems in the USA promote an unhealthy preoccupation with the pursuit of self-esteem through fame. Such unattainable drives result in reduced self-esteem and tendencies towards pathology and possible harm towards exocentric altruists.

For example, American boys and girls are told to become famous sports players or supermodels, respectively, and are inundated with the images of such people everywhere they turn. The Internet and television screens feed Americans shows such as *American Idol* and *The X Factor*, and reality television stokes the pursuit of internal self-esteem. Video game heroes further create a cult of vanity.

Today, it would seem that there is a measurable subsection of the population who believe they are entitled to become figurative gods.

However, the pursuit of self-esteem, especially when an individual is unsuccessful, can have serious consequences.

It appears that extreme capitalism in the advertising and entertainment industries during a terrorist environment are heavily reinforcing, by targeting the pursuit of self-esteem, the value standards of materialist types and indirectly damaging their dispositional scaffolds. We thus find that materialist types may feel more compelled to protect their worldview, and may go to extremes to silence those who are perceived as different or threatening to the successful pursuit of self-esteem.

Research has emerged to show the pitfalls associated when self-esteem pursuits are thwarted, but social scientists have not yet fully investigated whether unattainable self-interested goals are causing the entrenchment of materialist values. Future experimental research should follow up with dispositional measures of narcissism and personality measures, such as the Big Five personality inventory, to explore for potential harm to people's internal personality structures.

As we discover new ways to rebuild the power and economic systems of our society and open opportunity to larger subsections of the populace, we might discover how to foster security among materialist types while meeting the needs of the larger population. This is a topic to which I will turn in Chapter 12.

Part 4
The Coming Age of Altruism

12
Aligning Governing Systems and Altruistic Values

A little more than a decade ago, I attended the statistics lectures of a professor who had studied under W. Edwards Deming at New York University. Deming had a unique career. He once headed the United States Census Bureau before traveling to Japan in the aftermath of World War II. He argued against quotas and self-interested reward systems, and helped to automate most of Japan. His scientific management theory mostly fell on deaf ears in the USA, and several decades later we watched a once-booming US auto industry enter bankruptcy.

The cornerstone of Deming's approach was promoting cooperation over competition by getting leaders to recognize that people are intrinsically driven to be good. He lashed out at governing philosophies that promoted self-interest:

> What is the most underdeveloped nation? With the storehouse of skills and knowledge contained in its millions of unemployed, and with the even more appalling underuse, misuse, and abuse of skills and knowledge in the army of unemployed people in all ranks in all industries, the United States may be today the most underdeveloped nation in the world. (1986, p. 6)

We can extend Deming's theory based on my research. Never before in history are so many self-actualizers and exocentric altruists present among Western populations, and yet people languish at intermediate- and higher-order needs gratification with governing systems that seek to satisfy security concerns, promote extrinsic rewards, and advocate rugged individualism.

Deming was a prophet who was rejected by his homeland and made welcome abroad; unless the Western publics wake up to the

143

incompatibility of their governing systems with their psychological advancement, we will continue to witness the horrific toll that the philosophy of egocentrism has wreaked on modern society. In particular, the USA could become the most developed and altruistic nation in the world should its populace choose to change course.

High unemployment has become the new norm for the USA. The country's debt level is nearing an unsustainable $17 trillion. The point is that none of the quotas established by an adversarial power system that promotes self-interest and competition are met, and this once-great nation is rapidly becoming a banana republic with nuclear weapons. We can go a step beyond Deming's comments. The US governing system has become a glorified version of the once bankrupt and defunct Argentina. The ignorance that pervades the US government is by far not harvesting the talents of its higher-order needs gratifiers and is doing absolutely nothing to bring about true happiness among its population, which is attained by successfully overcoming illusionary needs gratification.

The USA and many Western nations like to pride themselves on being meritocracies. It is more the case that Western nations are multi-layered ruling systems. The modern USA has layers of artificial aristocracy, demeritocracy, and meritocracy. Artificial aristocracy is when individuals are advanced to positions of authority based on birth and wealth. In the last decade, the son of a president (George W. Bush) became president, and the wife of a president (Hilary Clinton) became secretary of state. The Kennedy's, and other politically-connected families, churn out representatives in the legislative branches of government.

The US is also a form of demeritocracy—a concept not in conflict with artificial aristocracy. The two notions go together. This is when people advance in society based on successful gambling, rather than ability. A strong case can be made that the economic crisis is a result of gamblers in the banking, accounting, and legal industries tricking and manipulating the public to gain big from their wagers in the derivatives market. We find that demeritocrats have often become the artificial aristocracy. Witness the lives of Andrew Carnegie, J.D. Rockefeller, and Joe Kennedy, to name a few, who became lucky from successful business gambles. Kennedy's rise to power came from illegally producing alcohol during the era of prohibition.

The well-established artificial aristocracy promotes some degree of secondary meritocracy as a form of buy-out of the middle classes. For example, scholarship funds have been set up to help students who score high on standardized tests attend university and graduate school.

Within the workplace, bonuses and individual promotions are the cornerstone of rewarding the average US middle-class worker who out-performs colleagues.

In 1958, Michael Young coined the term meritocracy to mean that individuals would be advanced based on their merit or ability. But Young had ridiculed the concept. In theory, this type of system has existed in the past. Ancient China relied heavily on bureaucratic test-ing to select pupils for future roles in the civil service. What did that nation accomplish? The upper echelon of educated elites dominated the system and made it so that they could select whoever would receive the best training in order to past the test.

Artificial meritocracy, demeritocracy, and meritocracy all run counter to psychological development to exocentric altruism. We do not require more bureaucratic measurement systems, designed by the wealthy and aloof, to fix our society.

What do we do when none of the currently prevailing systems of influence suffice to meet the human drive to become altruistic? This chapter will serve as a rough guide for future exocentric value-type leaders to revisit Deming, revise his profound knowledge, and apply it to the governing system in light of the hyperbola paradigm. It is antici-pated that exocentric value types may be looking for a new type of system that helps others by advancing cooperation, but may be short on choices given the types of governance that pervade the international community. I am going to venture into the very unique position of pro-viding a brief guide as to how policy could evolve in the future to better meet the needs of the entire population. I am going to evaluate how to create systems that operate for the continual psychological improve-ment of people.

In 1996, the head of the Canadian Deming Society, Wayne Levin, proposed optimizing the Canadian political system in a short piece he wrote for the *Journal of Quality and Participation*. He was so close to providing a workable paradigm, but fell short by defining purpose for Canada's governing system by maximizing full human potential. He capped off the purpose of the governing system too prematurely. I am going to argue for revising governing systems' purpose to achieve pro-liferation of exocentric altruism.

It will be posited that the recent Icelandic revolution was a step in the right direction, but—without consultation—fell short of achieving a better governing system according to human psychological develop-ment. The hyperbola paradigm offered throughout this book is the first psychology that brings Deming's philosophy to life and offers the best set of recommendations to get any given national system on the fast track to its most important goal—the psychological development of the human to negate self-interest.

We must remember that although governing systems may be "living systems," to borrow James Miller's terminology, these types of systems are mechanistic. They operate similar to the rules of evolution's original intentionality and do not have the adaptive ability to create their own purpose or negate it. Only humans, who make up organizational systems, can create purpose for such systems, but the system itself cannot transcend its purpose because it does not possess the cognitive ability to do so. In a nutshell, living organizational systems are non-human, albeit comprised of humans, and must operate according to the mechanistic rules that we establish for them. They are a tool to serve the human altruistic condition and are thus a work in progress that should be continually improved to meet our own continual psychological advancement.

The recommendation for a new system of governance is timely. Today, we are witnessing new forms of leadership emerging in nations like Iceland, which may be open to Deming's theory of profound knowledge and may attract adherents in other nations. And it will only be a matter of time before the US political leadership collapses under the weight of its own ignorance. The hope is that when this happens, the Americans might align themselves with exocentric-type leaders to forge a new and improved system.

The evidence indicates that humans are intrinsically motivated to be good, larger numbers are pushing the boundaries of psychological development, and, thus, the final piece of the puzzle is to replace the outmoded and outdated system of governance that is stagnating human development.

The System is Killing Itself

The US economy continues to tank, with unemployment hovering close to eight percent and gross domestic product (GDP) growth flat. Corporate profits were at a record high in the third quarter of 2013, but that growth came at the expense of wage-earners (Maydew, 2013). The US government reports that wages have fallen to a record low of 43.5 percent of GDP; the wealth of white versus black families has grown from $85,000 to $236,000 in 2009; the poor live, on average, 4.5 years less than the wealthy; the trade deficit with China has displaced 2.7 million workers; and the deficit continues to spiral out of control (ibid).

By now, you probably have a headache the size of Mount Rushmore in reading how Western governing systems cannot meet any of their pre-established targets. Would anyone dare to call this a successful form of government? Trying to fix the US or Europe's problems with patchwork over artificial quotas does not cut it.

The reason why I focus here on the US is because its individualistic and self-interest system of governance has served as a model for the rest of Western civilization. While it sets a series of macro-level quotas that go unfilled, the US system tells its citizens to be more productive to compete with individuals coming capitalist systems in Latin America and Asia. The entire quota system has dehumanized the US population and is symptomatic of a much larger dysfunction. Humans are not mechanized self-interested machines that need to be maintained. This has resulted in an entire subclass of individuals who have absolutely no idea of the conditions in which they exist. The materialist types live in a complete state of ignorance.

The establishment of a quota system by the artificial aristocracy adds to the pursuit of individual self-esteem and causes many people to create their own egocentric worldview, and, in this world, if one is already perfect, why would there be any need to strive to become better or to actualize, and to seek the negation of self-actualization? In this type of system, self-esteem is fulfilled by mediocrity. All one has to do to achieve a bonus or keep one's job safe is same thing one has always been doing, and, in the end, one has no form of continual improvement in the human condition.

The US government is so frustrated by its failings that its leaders are missing the bigger picture. The government is a 'living system' similar to that of a monkey—no pun intended. It operates within the confines of intentionality and does not possess the more advanced adaptive ability to create its own purpose yet alone negation of that purpose. Common sense tells us that if we dehydrate a monkey by withdrawing water, the first effect would be psychological deterioration. Its mind would slow in conducting learned tasks. After a while, organ failure and then death would befall the unlucky primate. Let's apply this example to the federal government of the USA.

In the run up to Christmas 2012, the top media story was the debt ceiling. Both political parties increased fear among the populace by telling them that sections of the government would shut down, or, worse, the elderly would not receive Social Security payments. The Speaker of the House, John Boehner, gave in to a compromise agreement with President Barack Obama. The agreement was to raise $600 billion over

10 years with cuts to spending and an increase in the payroll tax of US citizens (Stevenson and Harwood, 2013). In the end, the agreement will only cover little more than 1 year's interest payment on the current national debt. More troubling, $5.8 trillion will come due over the course of the next 5 years and the adversarial system is unable to find any consensus to tackle the problem (Baum, 2012).

The US federal government is leading the nation toward internal decimation. We know that every great empire has fallen from within. The cost-cutting and tax increases will inevitably increase unemployment and the misery of materialist types. A basic study of macroeconomics by any first-year university student shows the effects of retractionary fiscal policy.

The current leaders are like alcoholics—one little drink is OK, and then the entire bottle is gone. Raising government revenues stifles growth and crowds out the private sector, while reduced government spending increases unemployment. All that is being accomplished is that the power itself is shifting from an artificial aristocracy in the private sector to one in the public sector, and the upper echelon is relying more and more on the theme of a second-class meritocracy in an effort to keep the shrinking middle class in line. In other words, the status quo is changing hands between the private and public sectors, but the new public system does not embrace the unique talents, abilities, and altruistic desires of its population. The government is not fulfilling what should be its purpose to meet the higher-order motivational concerns of its populace.

The Case of Iceland

The US has no defined purpose. It is a flagship without direction. The American Constitution was adopted 226 years ago and lists liberty as its chief concern. Other than individual liberty, there is no mention of any purpose for the country. The founding fathers would have had no idea that our psychological development inspires us to become altruistic. Their scientific means of understanding human psychological development are still basic, even from the modern standpoint. The USA has ended up with a call to liberty, without direction, and this call has been inverted with the financial enslavement of the population to insurmountable national and personal debt.

How are other nations around the world reacting to the alleged financial enslavement of their populations? By 2008, the tiny nation of Iceland held a debt of roughly $100 million (Villa, 2010). The Icelanders took the streets banging pots and pans together, and throwing eggs at

Prime Minister Geir Haarde, who was forced to resign, along with his cabinet ministers (Jordon, 2009).

Icelanders nationalized their three largest banks and defaulted on insurmountable international debts. This infuriated the corporate puppet masters so much that the Prime Minister of the UK, Gordon Brown, seized Iceland's assets under the *Anti-Terrorism, Crime and Security Act of 2001* (Villa, 2010). Icelanders watched in horror as the British government essentially categorized their nation alongside terrorist organizations such as the Taliban and al-Qaeda (ibid).

The new Icelandic government has attempted to establish a meritocracy and has sought to re-write the nation's constitution online to make it more inclusive of its population. The preamble to Iceland's new constitution establishes several purposes:

> We, the people who inhabit Iceland, wish to create a just society where every person has equal opportunity. Our diverse origin enriches our society and together we are responsible for the heritage of generations, our country and its history, nature, language and culture. Iceland is a free and sovereign state with freedom, equality, democracy and human rights as its cornerstones. The government shall endeavour to strengthen the welfare of the country's inhabitants, encourage their culture and respect the diversity of the life of the people, the country and its biosphere. We wish to promote harmony, security and happiness amongst us and coming generations. We are determined to work towards peace with other nations and respect for the earth and all mankind. (Stjórnlagaráð, 2011)

Although this preamble is noble and defines a series of broad purposes, Iceland should have requested outside consultants and views from around the globe. One of the reasons I left the USA at a young age was so that it would be possible to view the country from the outside and recommend a more permanent solution to its present-day predicaments.

Typically, an intentional system cannot fix itself from within, just as a person with a gallstone cannot perform their own surgery. Iceland's mission is too broad, and while that nation is enjoying a period of growth, a new meritocrat class, or, worse, an artificial aristocratic class, will once again arise to reverse this tiny nation's huge accomplishment. The attempt at a better nation was aimed in the right direction and only needs to be tweaked by better understanding the human condition.

The USA is in a somewhat worse condition than Iceland. The USA prides itself on the scientific method, and yet this method is not used at all in governing the country. The federal government is all over the place. It is involved in an active war in Afghanistan; it is trying to reduce unemployment; it is trying to promote equality; it is trying to improve education; it is trying to create universal healthcare; and the list goes on and on. The country is trying to put out a thousand smoldering flames—any of one of which could erupt into massive blaze.

The US government is raising significant funds it simply cannot afford to finance projects that do not adhere to a single purpose and thus cannot be tested for effectiveness using a proper scientific method. Do we not yet understand that the Roman and Greek systems failed for a reason? Those systems also had no formal purpose. Why would we want to continue with a similar form of government which leads to the same failed outcome? Are we satisfied in the creation of a flawed system that can, at most, last a few hundred years? What Americans have done in continually rehashing the same purposeless system of governance fits the definition of insanity: doing some failed event over and over again expecting a different result.

The USA has become a nation of inconsistency because of its ill-defined purpose. Let us take just the tip of the iceberg. The USA experienced a horrendous drought last year, which sent the price of corn, and food products containing corn, soaring. Our political leaders argue that we must help the poor through elevating the costs of food. But the USA has also created a multibillion dollar ethanol fuel industry, which produced more than 13.9 billion gallons of gasoline in 2011 (Young, 2012). Marie Brill at ActionAid USA argues, "Considering the United States is the biggest exporter of corn, it is grossly irresponsible for our government to mandate that 40 per cent of U.S. corn crop to go to fuel instead of food or feed even in times of a natural disaster" (Brill, 2012). The end result is that instead of improving the environment, enhancing education, and getting the economy on track, the populace is often left frustrated and worse-off.

Consistency of Purpose for Intentional Systems

We now have a tested psychology, which pivots human psychological health around intrinsic development to exocentric altruism. It is not rocket science to understand that the next best step going forward is to better define directionality for an intentional governing system. Any governing system should facilitate human intrinsic motivation. It should strive to 'continually' develop to help as many people as possible become exocentric altruists. This cannot be done relying on the time-tested failures of an adversarial system, which prides itself on promoting the illusionary self-interests of its constituents.

This, of course, brings me to the main point. We overcome the self-interest and the psychological debilitation of frustrated materialist types and advance the nation toward the most optimal recognizable psychological outcome for individuals by getting the governing system to operate based on a system of cooperation. Essentially, we need to rewrite the first sentence of the preamble to the US Constitution. For this task, I took inspiration from the Abbé Pierre, a Franciscan Priest who saved thousands of people worldwide through his exocentric altruistic motivation.

The aim of the USA should be as follows: "We the people of the United States will ...'Give instant help to those nearest and in need. Show them how to help themselves. Afterward let them help others'" (Time, 1978). Inherent in this aim is, of course, the drive to have people self-actualize so that they build a store of something to negate. There is nothing communist or socialist about this mission. We are not saying we are going to give every person in need a new house, car, and large savings account. A nation that is $17 trillion in debt could not afford such a proposal. But we can alleviate the suffering of the extreme lowest rung and show all others how to help themselves and others, and we can create opportunities through cooperation. Using cooperation and sound scientific management theory we can reorder the public and private sector to fulfill this mission. Upon ratifying the aim of the governing system, any policy put forth by the public, members of the legislature, and lobbyists should spell out precisely how it aids this mission.

For example, using the scientific method, we could turn to Walter Shewhart's Plan, Do, Check, Act (PDCA) paradigm to develop better governmental services. PDCA would first require that legislation be defined according to whether it meets or exceeds the country's stated mission. The second step of PDCA would involve testing the effects of legislation through experimental research and simulations. The third step would evaluate the success of legislation through experimentation and, if the legislation serves its purpose, it should then be passed by the legislature. In the last step, public policy makers should retest the success or pitfalls of the outcomes of the legislation to discover whether it is effective. Should the legislation not produce the desired outcome then move to repeal. Deming argued that "Continuation of the four steps leads to a helix of continual improvement..." (1986, pp. 180–1).

There may arise a few obstacles that likely would hold the current government back from employing PDCA in new policy developments.

Deming states: "Any step in the Shewhart cycle may need guidance of statistical methodology for economic, speed, and protection from faulty conclusions from failure to test and measure the effects of interactions" (1986, p. 89). Specifically, the entire nation, and especially its leaders, require advanced knowledge of the inherent evilness of variation.

Approximately eighty-five percent of variation randomly occurs as a result of the system itself, and yet we treat outcomes as a common cause when it came from the system (Deming, 1994 cited in Braughton, 1999). It is not the fault of US citizens that their nation is faltering. The lack of psychological well-being and advancement rests squarely with the leaders who run the system. Unfortunately, most modern elected representatives are lawyers with virtually little or no statistical training. The quotas established by the political system's leaders are useless without the leaders developing a better understanding of how to improve the system.

Example of Self-Interested System Failure

In 1972, President Richard Nixon declared the war on drugs. What did this declaration accomplish? It increased extrinsic rewards for self-interested cartels to earn large amounts of cash by thwarting the USA's drug laws.

In 2007, the USA spent approximately $16.5 billion on law enforcement initiatives to fight the war on drugs (Miron and Waldock, 2010). In 2011, 1.5 million drug arrests were made in the USA (Ferner, 2012). The USA now imprisons more of its population than any other major post-industrialized nation worldwide. An American is arrested for marijuana usage every 42 seconds (ibid). We have also witnessed the rise of gang violence within inner cities. Thousands have been displaced in Latin America and Columbia. And drug consumption has declined little since Nixon declared his war.

The war on drugs is highly similar to the era of prohibition. The USA's antiquated laws encouraged the same extrinsic rewards that led to Al Capone's killing spree. It has been estimated that legalizing drugs would yield a tax revenue of $46.7 billion yearly (Miron and Waldock, 2010). We could easily use a portion of that revenue to create mental health facilities to properly treat and eradicate drug addiction among the poor, similar to how the USA has significantly decreased tobacco dependence over the years. The legalization of drugs could lead to such significant declines in criminality in the cities that it would reduce insecurity and threats to physical needs, and remove significant obstacles that threaten materialist types. We could easily use statistical control through pilot studies and testing to ensure that such a policy meets the overall goal. Several states, such as California, Colorado, and Washington, have tested marijuana legalization policies that have proved successful.

However, the federal government, lacking consistency or purpose, has sought to crack down harshly on marijuana growers in states with poorly-worded laws. Attorney General Eric Holder and a host of so-called experts called before the Justice Department and White House have come up with all sorts of purposeless tweaks to the failed war on drugs. These people allegedly aim to advance their own self-image and, thus, the outcome of numerous panels involving the scientific and law enforcement communities cannot possibly make a difference. This is because the experts do not fundamentally understand the complexity of the system or the notion of variation. They set unachievable quotas that end up harming US citizens. A reduction through prohibition of, say, ten percent significantly increases the size of the prison cohort and associated costs. A change in policy to scientifically test and measure an end to the war on drugs, and dramatically change the system is likely to reduce drug addiction, gang violence, and the size of the prison cohort at the same time. By eliminating the fear of arrest, the political system would encourage drug addicts to become cooperative partners in seeking mental health assistance.

Wayne Levin (1996) states, "The system of government is integrally linked to all social outcomes, therefore, government is in the best position to affect the kind of positive social change that comes from system optimization." To reiterate, the key is fundamentally revising the philosophy of the governing system.

Recommendation for the Future

The USA and most Western nations are today in need of their own version of a peaceful 'pots and pans revolution.' But a very important point needs to be stressed. The aim or objective of the revolution needs to be defined exactly according to our knowledge of human psychological development and how to further our intrinsic development to be altruistic, or else the revolution will fail as quickly as Occupy Wall Street (OWS) tents were removed from public view.

We cannot expect the current mix of material and post-material leaders in the USA or most Western nations to adapt to scientific reasoning because it is so foreign to the way the governing system has been conducted for far too long. And with a very small minority participating in elections, it is unlikely that the populace will vote to change the current lack of purpose and inconsistency unless it becomes the law that every citizen must vote or be fined.

It is conceded that the likelihood of a pots and pans revolution or mandatory voting law in the USA is relatively remote. Unfortunately, the materialist types are insecure and living in a state of fear produced by a system overly focused on self-interest. The results of the Barabbas study show that a sizeable minority is willing to execute an innocent person to protect security. Our political system is comprised of fear and it is spreading fear among a sizeable minority.

Of Deming's fourteen points, the most important is to drive out fear. Americans are afraid to speak out against their political system. Any criticism of the financial or economic system may list an individual as a "financial terrorist." OWS protestors were labeled criminals for putting forth new ideas. Americans are asking themselves, 'Will my unemployment check last another week?'; ' Will I be able to pay my student loan bill this month?'; 'Why is our government erecting fusion centers to house people?'

Our future depends on dismantling the current system of fear. This means eradicating the departments of homeland security, the large-scale domestic security apparatuses, and returning to a nation where a free flow of ideas and free speech permits optimal debate and a wide array of testable proposals to serve the nation's goal of helping people achieve exocentric altruism.

We may see critics who will allege that Deming's system of profound knowledge led Japan into economic crisis in the 1990s. Nothing is further from the truth. The writer Eamonn Fingleton (2013) provides substantial evidence to demonstrate that Japanese citizens enjoyed improvements in living standards throughout the 1990s.

Today, Western politicians are more like managers than leaders. They are carefully scripted tacticians who focus on outcomes. What we require are visionaries with the knowledge of the scientific method to carry out a well-defined mission. The good news is that the survey research suggests exocentric altruistic visionaries now exist. The key now will be for a number of them to rise up and align the aims of our mechanistic governing system with the human desire to become altruistic.

13
Promoting Altruistic Constructivist Education

The US education system is similar to its political system and is taking a turn for the worse. How do we expect people to attain better states of psychological health at exocentric altruism while an antiquated educational system holds them back?

Today, rankings have extended beyond student performance. Universities are heavily ranked by magazines such as *U.S. News & World Report*, which employ standardized test scores, such as the SAT (Scholastic Assessment Test), LSAT (Law School Admission Test), GMAT (Graduate Management Admissions Test), and GRE (Graduate Record Examination) for positioning purposes. In order to sustain accreditation, universities also have to go through laborious procedures to ensure that students receive exact contact time, have access to a certain number of journals in the library, and have a certain number of PhDs on staff. The quotas at university institutions are endless. Universities have developed advanced institutional research departments that keep and maintain diversity statistics so that affirmative action quotas can be achieved. In a nutshell, we have erected self-interest-based educational institutions that are failing to educate the public yet alone assist us in advancing to exocentric altruism.

The professors working at universities nationwide tend to grade on a curve because they know that student satisfaction is so important to their future career advancement. Professor Harvey Mansfield at Harvard University provides two marks to students: a mark the student should have achieved and a higher mark that is provided to the registrar (Mansfield, 2001). Is this serving the ability of citizens to psychologically advance or produce quality work on the world stage? The USA's students have become warped by the artificial nature of a self-interested educational system that reinforces materialism and illusionary needs gratification.

This aim of this chapter is to recommend an exocentric altruistic constructivist approach to education based on the discovery of our intrinsic motivation. We will first turn to the case of for-profit education to demonstrate an extreme case of how an education system based on self-interest threatens and inhibits development to exocentric altruism. I will then turn my attention to traditional colleges and discuss the policies they should undertake to improve education based on cooperation.

The Cases of Three For-profit Educational Corporations

Let's turn to a new development in the USA: the rise of for-profit education over the last decade. Proprietary schools offer online education, or hybrid online and on-ground courses, and tend to offer training for trades such as culinary arts, nursing, or graphic design. Proprietary schools tend to be owned by corporations such as Educational Management Corporation (EDMC), Career Education Corporation (CEC), and Corinthian Colleges, to name a few. These corporations are incredibly cash-rich, concerned with increasing the profits of shareholders, and celebrate self-interest among employees and their customers.

What does this system of self-interested education produce? The leaders of proprietary and traditional education try to pad the numbers to increase the profits of shareholders or increase their own compensation packages and sense of job security.

For example, it has been alleged that the former chief executive officer (CEO) of CEC, Gary E. McCullough, resigned because CEC was "...artificially inflating job placement rates at several of its health and arts schools in order to remain in good standing with college accreditors" (Kirkham, 2011).

The public sector also pads the numbers. For example, in Atlanta, GA, thirty-five educators at a public school, including the principals, were recently arrested and charged "...with essentially running a conspiracy in which standardized test scores were secretly raised as a way to get bonuses and ensure job security" (Severson and Brown, 2013).

There are other elements in operation at for-profit institutions, which are equally as unethical as fixing standardized test scores. Admissions officials at for-profit institutions are given very strict quotas by campus directors, who rarely possess education at the doctorate level. With few, or no, entry requirements, the admissions officials target first-generation students, and, when accepted, immediately load them up with debt through federal student loans. We find that the students who are being targeted are materialist types who are often stunted in their needs gratification. Through the use of proprietaries, the USA has alleg-edly created a second-tier educational system that reinforces insecurity and self-interest.

Little peer-reviewed research is produced by full-time academics working at for-profit institutions, and no job security is offered to lec-turers. The lecturers live in a state of fear, especially in "at-will" states, where they can be terminated at any time; thus, they tow the line and do the bare minimum to stay employed. There is little or no academic freedom, and textbooks for courses are generally set by the centralized curriculum designers at these institutions. The online instructors are little more than mere robots rehashing textbook knowledge to consum-ers who are overpaying and who could read the textbooks directly. This is actually an amazing digression in human educational history.

The lecture itself was invented at Oxford University at a time when reading materials were scarce. The lecturer, or sage, provided informa-tion from the literature to the students, and was also supposed to impart critical analysis of the literature to eager minds in order to spark Socratic enquiry. That type of new idea generation is all but crushed under for-profit institutions. Assessments for online courses very often take the form of multiple choice tests or quizzes, and the objective is to pass as many students as possible to maximize the profit. A recent survey of online courses suggested that seventy-two percent of online professors did not believe their students had learned anything (Ferenstein, 2013).

What happens to proprietary students when they graduate? Let's take the case of Jeffrey West. He was working at a pet store for $8 per hour when an allegedly predatory admissions official from Corinthian College paid a visit to him at his house (Goodman, 2010). Mr. West recalled the visit: "'They said they had a very high placement rate, somewhere around 90 per cent...That was one of the key factors that caused me to go there. They said I would be earning $50,000 to $70,000 a year'" (ibid). Mr. West graduated and his loan payments equal $600 per month; today, he earns $12 per hour weatherizing foreclosed houses (ibid).

One of CEC's schools, Le Cordon Bleu, states, "Our students are given the tools needed to become the future leaders in the industry...Many graduates have attained positions of responsibility, visibility, and entre-preneurship soon after completing their studies" (ibid). In contrast, *The New York Times* reported, "From July 2007 to June 2008, students who graduated from the culinary arts associate degree program landed jobs that paid an average of $21,000 a year, or about $10 an hour. Oregon's minimum wage is $8.40 an hour" (ibid). It is clear that the USA's self-interested education system enslaves young people to debt and reduces the nation's competitiveness compared with countries such as India and China.

The self-interested motivation of rewarding individual CEOs of these institutions is also part of the problem. The head of EDMC, 47-year-old Mr. Edward West, earns $1.25 million per annum (Yahoo! Finance, 2013a). The head of Corinthian Colleges, 64-year-old Mr. Jack Massimino, earns $2.28 million (Yahoo! Finance, 2013b). Let's contrast these salaries with those of more traditional educational institutions. Sixty-five-year-old Dr. Drew Faust, President of Harvard University, earned $874,559 (salary and expenses) in 2010 (Weinberg, 2011). The head of my alma mater, Rutgers University, 65-year-old Dr. Robert Barchi, could earn up to $747,000 (salary, expenses, and bonus) (Alex, 2012). There are huge differences in the academic achievements of Drs Faust and Barchi versus West and Massimino, but the overarching point is that pay schemes, in general, are faulty.

West and Massimino do not possess doctorates, and a search on *Google Scholar* fails to turn up any significant publications for either of these so-called educational industry leaders. In comparison, Dr. Faust has co-authored six books and is one of the foremost experts in the history of the southern USA. Dr. Barchi is a leading neuroscientist, with a long list of publications and teaching experience. It would be futile here to compare the job placement success of Harvard and Rutgers versus EDMC and Corinthian Colleges. The evidence clearly indicates that institutions purely reliant on self-interest unjustifiably reward their leaders with salaries higher than that of traditional universities and produce poorer quality education. The pursuit of profit, for the shareholders and the leaders of for-profit companies has prevented any form of consistency and purpose at these institutions.

Deming got it right when he argued that the US system of leadership has failed, and this is especially applicable to educational leadership across the board. Today, the most successful people in the private sector are those who do not challenge the status quo. By towing the line, these non-threatening yes-men arise to lead corporations such as CEC, EDMC, and Corinthian Colleges without any impetus to invoke statistical control or quality improvement. These corporations are devoid of leadership and storming the public treasury through federal student loans. They are contributing to unemployment. Debt-burdened students have become the reality of a self-interested for-profit education system that extrinsically rewards the individual over teamwork.

An important point to make is that this chapter is not meant to be an attack on the privatization of education, but rather the philosophy of self-interest practice by US companies. Japanese companies have effectively built upon Deming's concepts of cooperation to a great deal of success, which could, today, be emulated by US companies, and produce educational standards and continual improvement that would significantly rival the rest of the world.

The traditional universities are only nominally faring a bit better than for-profit educational establishments. Where individual bonuses are used at traditional universities, such as Rutgers, we see the promotion of individual self-interest without any real innovation. The key for the president of Rutgers University is allegedly to set a standard of fundraising and stick to it to achieve his bonus. There is no real motivation beyond that point.

Recently, nations such as UK, which permitted significant hikes in student tuition fees, and are transforming their education system into self-interest-based for-profit institutions, are pursuing the same path, which leads to a devastating brain drain and national incompetence. When for-profit education fails—and, inevitably, these systems will all fail—the pendulum will swing back to socialist education with predefined outcomes and quotas based on meritocracy. And, again, that type of system will also fail by creating a new super-class of intelligentsia, as was so eloquently described in George Orwell's *Animal Farm*.

The cycle of insanity in education will not be broken until the educational system generates consistency and purpose that recognizes our higher intrinsic motivation. The self-interested system based on extrinsic motivation and individualistic rewards must be uprooted and replaced with a system of cooperation.

Education Lacks Directionality

Traditional universities, and—far worse—for-profit institutions, tend to lack purpose, or, where they have defined purpose, it is vague and promotes self-interest. The thought is that if students pay a fee, they must somehow receive only a self-interested benefit without any consideration by the educational institutions with regard to the importance of cooperation. All we are accomplishing is the propagation of insecurity and social frustration among already dispositionally weakened materialist types. Table 13.1 provides samples of mission statements from for-profit colleges.

There exists no innovation or vision in these vague mission statements. Short-run self-interest through career focus is advanced over promoting cooperation. CEC is very explicit in stating that it seeks to

Table 13.1   Educational Management Corporation (EDMC), Career Education Corporation (CEC), and Corinthian College mission statements

EDMC[a]	CEC[b]	Corinthian Colleges[c]
EDMC operates with a singular mission in mind: education that builds careers and transforms lives of those who teach, learn and work here	We are a dynamic educational services company committed to quality, career-focused learning and led by passionate professionals who inspire individual worth and lifelong achievement	Our mission is to help students prepare for careers in demand or to advance their chosen field

[a]EDMC (2013).
[b]CEC (2013).
[c]Corinthian Colleges (2013).

advance "individual worth." What is the outcome that EDMC seeks to produce by the transformation of lives? The institutions themselves are thus doomed to failure. We have witnessed significant declines in CEC's stock performance over the last few years.

In comparison, traditional universities are also falling short. Today, universities are emerging from the B.F. Skinner model, which promotes memorization and ratings, and moving towards constructivism (i.e. permitting students to define their own worldview) as a new imperative for higher education. Ratings still form a part of the constructivist agenda, but, worse than quotas, we find a drive to have students develop an individualistic and self-interested worldview.

For example, part of the constructivist drive includes a race to define the attributes of a graduate. Instead, however, universities are unwittingly creating self-service buffets to maximize self-interest. Too often the attributes provided to us by higher education administrators are too numerous and capped too early at personal fulfillment to incur any significant improvements in the human psychological condition post-graduation. We are left with a mismatch between higher education and the needs advancement of Western populations.

Constructivist Approach

A misapplication of self-interested constructivism is behind an agenda within higher education to have students create a self-interested worldview.

Lev Vygotsky inspired the theory of constructivism. It constitutes a theory of knowledge predicated on having students learn through experience. Malcolm Knowles (1998) posits that real-life situations and learning through experience are better than the traditional subject approach, which embraces didactic teaching. This is especially true for adult learners. Biggs builds upon the definition of constructivism by stating that it "...is thus a way of interacting with the world" and that bringing about changes in conceptions of one's worldview produces higher critical thinking skills, rather than "...the acquisition of information" (1999, p. 60).

It is important to note that constructivism is supposed to equip students to build upon dispositional scaffolds through critical thinking, reflection, and imagination to foster advanced motivational development and intellectual character (Chaney, 2013). It is in this context that "dispositional thinking interacts with situational conditions, like education, to enhance intellectual character" (ibid). I agree with Chaney that the primary objective of the constructivist educator is to help students strengthen dispositional scaffolds in order to learn how to react to real life situations in the first place.

Thus, the aim of constructivist education requires revision based on our intrinsic drives to negate self-interest. No matter how much the for-profit institutions have tried to strip the traditional lecturer of his or her role, we recognize that the instructor is still a sage who should facilitate inspirational learning through cooperation within a physical classroom. What good is it to only equip the student to locate artificial and self-interested meaning by interacting based on an illusionary worldview?

As a result, any given student's attempt to locate meaning would be all over the map given the current attribute schemes of many higher education institutions. Through experience, we need to teach students how to use focus in the development of meaning. The objective is not to standardize meaning for everyone, but to enhance the ability to focus so that students do not lose the point and end up apathetic and without meaning.

Our agenda as educators is to use innovation to get young adults using adaptive ability in the search for meaning. Thus, we are here to help students recognize a worldview which is mindful of others. The experience of one's worldview is important, and experiential learning and simulations in the curriculum are encouraged. But educators must remain attentive that the worldview for many students is illusionary; thus, young people require guidance. Educators are responsible for aligning the curriculum to afford students the opportunity to develop an altruistic worldview that illuminates their internal motivation to do good.

The trick is for educators to produce deep learning through cooperation and serving others. In the first instance, educators should create a safe environment to let students play around with their vision of the world; teachers then need to slowly explore with the students how everyone else's interest is similar their own. The educator next turns to extending the focus of deep learners by encouraging them to use their imaginations to empathize with others.

Knowles conceded that altruism is important in higher education:

> We come into the world in a state of total self-centeredness, and one of our central tasks for the rest of our lives is to become increasingly able to care about others. Conditions that induce a spirit of rivalry toward others rather than helpfulness toward others—such as the competition for grades promoted by traditional schooling—interfere with maturation in this dimension. Incidentally, there are some psychiatrists (e.g. Franz Alexander) who hold that altruism is the single best criterion of mental health. (1980, p. 31)

This statement represents a dichotomy for Knowles. He had also indicated agreement with Maslow's needs hierarchy (Knowles, 1970, p. 85). Knowles, like so many social scientists before and after him, misinterprets altruism as encompassing a transpersonal and metaphysical development at self-actualization.

However, the evidence from experimental research shows something different—pure altruism forms a negation to self-actualization. Given the emerging evidence, we need to revise constructivist theory and focus it.

Cheating is Commonplace

The current educational systems, even those drawing inspiration from self-interested constructivism, are encouraging students to cheat rather than use their ability to psychologically develop. Many students are now turning to cognitive enhancers to stay competitive, meet all the attributes desirable of a graduate, make the grade, and delve deeper into the learning experience relative to their colleagues. Instead of progressing towards reality, students are now turning towards substances that reinforce their illusionary view of the world, and the decline into over-indulgence is precipitous and disastrous for many young people.

Students at my morning lectures regularly enter the lecture theatre with a 'Venti' (i.e. large) Starbucks coffee in hand. Other students have a large can of red bull at the waiting, and students in the USA now have access to Smart Gum, a product laced with caffeine, which is supposed to give a brief cognitive boost. And most disconcerting appears to be to be the use of 'off-label' drugs called nootropics.

The New Yorker reports that "College campuses have become laboratories for experimentation with neuroenhancement ..." (Talbot, 2009). Adderall, Ritalin, and Modafinal have become the favorite drugs among university students. Adderall and Ritalin are stimulants made from amphetamine salts (ibid). Modafinal is a narcolepsy drug, which has been reported to boost cognitive performance of those with minor cognitive deficits.

The use of stimulants to enhance performance within a self-interested system is reminiscent of history. The Nazis regularly distributed amphetamines to Schutzstaffel (SS) officers who would mix the substances with coffee. It was how the Germans advanced so rapidly throughout Western Europe in a relatively short period of time; but look what happened at the end of the war. The Nazis encountered burnout as the US and allied troops landed at Normandy. The same will happen with the future of our young people if dependence on off-market prescriptions of stimulants is not curtailed through a revision of our educational system's mission.

In *The New Yorker* article (ibid), we are told about the case of Alex, who simply copied his brother's symptoms to obtain Adderall. We also see college students regularly doctor shopping, trading these drugs, or ordering them from shady sites on the Internet. The pressure to meet quotas, and succeed and obtain all the defined attributes of a graduate is so intense that students are overlooking the potential side effects of these medications.

Modafinal permits people to stay awake for up to 48 hours without developing the symptoms of sleep deprivation. However, the human body is not made to withstand such sleep deprivation and the body's organs will eventually react.

The abuse of Adderall has been associated with suicides. Take the case of Kyle Craig. He had a 3.5 GPA (grade point average), but wanted to compete with friends achieving higher grades and who were vying for careers on Wall Street (James, 2010). Kyle managed to get a prescription from a doctor by faking symptoms of attention deficit hyperactivity disorder (ADHD) (ibid). Kyle's abuse of the substance eventually led to significant personality changes, and, at the age of 21, he committed suicide by jumping in front of a passenger train (ibid).

Unfortunately, Kyle's case was preventable. The quantitative data presented throughout this book have demonstrated that along with increasing post-materialist development is a parallel rise in suicides. The current systems actively encourage only illusionary gratification, and when talented and higher-order needs gratifiers cannot obtain glory, meet artificial quotas, and attain extrinsic rewards, tragedy strikes in the ultimate form of self-destruction.

Who is responsible here? The young adults like Kyle possess faulty dispositional scaffolding. However, it is the educational administrators who develop and encourage the faulty system of self-interest who share some of the responsibility along with the doctors who are duped into providing false prescriptions.

Educating for Exocentric Altruistic Constructivism

The first, and most important, objective of altruistic constructivists is to understand the system in which they operate and to select for their system an optimal mission. The first step in understanding the system is to promote statistical literacy. We are reminded of the wisdom of H.G. Wells:

> The great body of physical science, a great deal of the essential fact of financial science, and endless social and political problems are only accessible and only thinkable to those who have had a sound training in mathematical analysis, and the time may not be very remote when it will be understood that for complete initiation as an efficient citizen of one of the new great complex world-wide states that are now developing, it is as necessary to be able to compute, to think in averages and maxima and minima, as it is now to be able to read and write. (2004 [1903])

Educators will not be producing the altruistic leaders of the future unless they fully comprehend the necessity to create a system where the average citizen is required to understand the concept of variation. Because lawyers make up the majority of elected positions, they should not be permitted to pass law school unless they have successfully passed advanced statistical analysis classes. This is one of the few ways that elected leaders will realize that the faulty outcomes of polices are not the fault of citizens, but the system they control.

The lack of numerical literacy among Americans is as a result of George W. Bush's 'No Child Left Behind' policy. That policy created an artificial quota system based on standardized test scores. To reiterate, the establishment of quotas and individualized competition in early education encouraged self-interest and resulted in greater illiteracy across the board.

The best way to improve statistical literacy is to turn to Deming's theory of profound knowledge. Over the last two decades, there has been an explosion of literature in relation to applying Deming to higher education institutions, but most of his theories continue to be overlooked by administrators in practice. We are not going to overly rehash Deming's concepts here, but, briefly, his concepts include the elimination of rankings, individual bonus schemes, slogans, barriers to success, and fear within the workplace. It is also important to provide statistical training and knowledge of variation to all academic staff members.

Once educators understand the system in which they operate and are able to help stakeholders comprehend the system, the next step is to define the mission of that system. The mission should be to utilize cooperation among students and staff that guides students towards an exocentric altruistic worldview. Broadly following in the footsteps of constructivism, educators should actively engage students in the learning process. Active engagement assists students in obtaining higher critical thinking and reflection skills that are necessary to make the most out of advanced adaptive abilities to help others.

How the student learns within a constructivist paradigm is contingent upon the ability to focus the mind. It is not the position of an educator to define a worldview for the students, but to help facilitate the student to discover their intrinsic drives. Once the student starts to explore their world in a safe and supporting environment, he or she is in a better position to start experimenting with helping others.

Our responsibility as altruistic constructivists is to help students simultaneously include the other in the worldview they generate. We can use simulations and experiential learning to help focus students on success and achievement along the illusionary needs hierarchy and create a safe environment for them to explore their illusionary self-interest. But our responsibility is to also facilitate students in understanding the illusion of self-interest by encouraging them to empathize with human suffering. This is mainly accomplished by incorporating significantly more volunteerism in the curriculum which is tailored to the student's learning experience.

Educators should also revise collaborative learning. Too often, students are requested to reflect on what they have gained from working in a team. Would it not be better to get the students to observe what they give to the team and how to improve on their contributions to teamwork? The trick is to get the student to start reflecting early on others, as well as the self, so that when they eventually build a store of maximized self-interest, they know that the option is there to negate the self.

Today, we see educational administrators attempting to define the attributes of a graduate. Educators should be forewarned not to treat graduate attributes like a self-service food buffet or gas station. The educator should seek to define charity, love for one's neighbor, cooperation, and teamwork as the most important qualities a graduate should work at over the course of their lifetime.

Our task as educators is to continually innovate to have the students experientially build upon altruistic drives while ameliorating the negative tendencies and pathologies derived from operating out of self-interest.

14
Helping the Afflicted Transcend Self-interest

We have observed throughout this book that human dispositional scaffolds have been weakened by the West's embrace of egocentrism. The way to rebuild individual dispositional scaffolds is to shift consciousness among people from serving the self to serving others. The Abbé Pierre provided us with a foundation to help shift people's consciousness. He had a colorful career and had a tremendous influence on France following World War II. In the words of one lawyer, " '[the Abbé Pierre] almost singlehandedly mobilized the entire government and people of France to do something for the poor' " (Time, 1978). Unsurprisingly, the the Abbé Pierre was born to a wealthy family and had most of his needs gratified at a young age. He later decided to give away his inheritance.

One would think that his roles as priest, politician, and newspaper publisher would keep a person highly occupied. In addition to these roles, he is most famous for creating Emmaus to house the poor. One of the first people that the Abbé Pierre helped was a failed suicide (Emmaus Village Carlton, 2013). The recipient had allegedly killed his own father 20 years earlier; after serving a sentence of 20 years' hard labor, he was freed and subsequently tried to kill himself (ibid). The Abbé Pierre never judged the intended recipient for his crime. He said to the former prisoner:

> As a Member of Parliament, I am not poor because I am paid a parliamentary allowance. But I have nothing but debts. All my money is spent before I even receive it, to repair the house and to lodge those in need. Look this is where I live, dividing my life between Parliament, my constituency in Lorraine and the reception and maintenance of my Hostel. I am tired and can't respond to all these

calls for help. But you, because you want to die, there is nothing holding you back. So please, wouldn't you like to help me to help others? (ibid)

It is important to observe that the Abbé Pierre invites the former convict to help him help others. The Abbé Pierre took an approach that we in the West too often neglect. We are too ready nowadays to give hand-outs that we cannot afford or to turn people in need away from assistance altogether. Our self-interested-based reward systems are broken and produce the extremes of left versus right politics.

The Abbé Pierre recognized the intrinsic motivation of people and the benefits derived from a system based on cooperation. Rather than erecting an outcomes-based system, the Abbé Pierre deferred to the people he was helping to find creative ways to help others. He innovated to encourage others to cooperate and his commune spread to five nations that housed thousands of people.

For example, in 1951, the Abbé Pierre had lost his assembly seat and income (Time, 1978). Where did he turn to keep the commune running? A ragpicker housed in his commune (ibid). The ragpicker taught colleagues at Emmaus how to rummage through trash and locate items that could be repaired and resold.

By now, you are highly familiar with the Abbé Pierre's credo, " 'Give instant help to those nearest and in need. Show them how to help themselves. Afterward let them help others' " (ibid). I have briefly explored applying this theme to better align governing systems with the rapid advance of human psychological development. We can also build upon and adapt this mission in social work, psychodynamic therapy, and clinical counseling.

Today, the self-interest promoted by the governing system has left a lot of individuals disillusioned and over-gratified. We do not have effective therapeutic systems to help people pursuing self-esteem and self-actualization advance to exocentric altruism. The time has arrived to bring the Abbé Pierre's mission into modern psychology for the benefit of people suffering from apathy and boredom at the higher states of human psychological development. The objective of this chapter is to render a few simple suggestions to help people who have become afflicted with transient pathology due to (a) over-gratification of self-interest or (b) individuals who have become stunted in psychological growth due to frustrated needs pursuits.

The Current Mental Health Crisis

It has been reported that between 1985 and 2008, the sales of anti-depressants and antipsychotics multiplied by fiftyfold to $24.2 billion (Horgan, 2001). We have simultaneously witnessed a 19% increase in suicides. It is also alleged that 6.4 million US children (i.e. 11% of the population) have been diagnosed with attention deficit hyperactivity disorder (ADHD) (Schwarz and Cohen, 2013). Approximately one third of those children are on psychotropic medicine (ibid). Dr. Ned Hallowell, a psychiatrist, told parents that some stimulants (i.e. amphetamine salts) were "safer than aspirin" (ibid).

Many parents whose children are alleged to have ADHD tend to seek out psychodynamic therapy within 1.5 years of starting psychotropic medicine because of recidivism (Widener, 1998). A report in the *Journal of Health Economics* claimed that twenty percent of children on psychotropic medicine have been misdiagnosed (Elder, 2010). The purpose of our intentional therapeutic systems should be to bring about improvement in the health of patients. The field of psychiatry is not supposed to medicinally lobotomize the population. Currently, there is a plan underway by the *American Psychiatric Association* to change the definition for ADHD to allow more people to receive a diagnosis and medication (Schwarz and Cohen, 2013).

In addition to overmedicating the population to serve the self-interest of large pharmaceutical companies, people seeking help are typically overwhelmed by a selection of potential psychodynamic therapies, such as psychoanalytic, Adlerian, existential, person-centered, gestalt, behavioral, cognitive behavioral, reality, feminist, postmodern, and family systems to name a few.

The underlying theme for most therapies is how to get people to maximize self-interest. For decades, we have witnessed a litany of research assessing the success of each form of therapy in relation to outcomes (i.e. reduction in symptoms, recidivism, and associated costs). If any of these therapies, or the pharmacological route, are successful, then why do we continue to witness rises in pathology on a crisis level? The mental health field looks at symptom reduction and outcomes, and ignores the fundamental cause of many forms of mental illness. My decade of research leads me to suggest a new approach for therapists called System–External–Removal–Variation–Innovate–Continual–Exemplify (SERVICE) therapy to help individuals progress to increasingly better states of psychological health.

Service Therapy

System

Therapists must gain an insight into the overall human system. The human system has progressed beyond the intentionality of evolution's initial purpose for us. This means understanding that we are intrinsically motivated to negate illusionary needs and progress to exocentric altruism. Understanding systems is derived both from Deming's profound knowledge and by William Glasser's reality therapy.

Our point of departure from Glasser is that the drive for power is illusionary. Therapists cannot bring people to higher states of human psychological development by centralizing their focus on the satisfaction of power, belongingness, or any combination of self-interested needs alone. The epitome of self-interested needs gratification will result in apathy, boredom, and over-self-gratification. The therapist should help a client build a store of self-interest, with an eye towards helping the client explore exocentric altruistic motivation. Thus, the mission of therapy should follow the Abbé Pierre's wisdom.

Today, those pursuing a career in the therapeutic disciples are often taught how to eventually run their own practice as a business. This does not often result in helping those who are nearest and in need. We should be teaching therapists how to develop effective sliding fee scales so that those most in need can afford help.

For example, the costs of dialectical behavioral therapy (DBT) can run into thousands of dollars. Are most DBT therapists helping the nearest in need or only those who can afford assistance?

My observations are that too many therapist trainers attempt to act empathetic during simulations in classes. The empathy practised by such therapists becomes inauthentic. Empathy is not learned in the classroom. It is learned through experience, and not the type of experience that comes from an ever increasing pay scheme for therapists.

The second point of the therapeutic system is to show the client how to help themselves. We must help the self before we can help others. There is no need here to rely on just one form of type of therapy to meet the second part of a therapist's mission. We should draw upon the currently existing toolkit of therapies to bring about advancement through illusionary needs.

We know that pathology occurs from inhibition or over-gratification of self-interested needs gratification. Therapists can certainly seize upon the opportunity to explore a client's attitudes in relation to needs gratification and help work with the client to make better choices. That is an excellent first step. We also have at our disposal a series of mindfulness therapies, such as DBT. The goal of DBT is to help the client find meaning and acceptance to develop a life worth living (Linehan, 1993 cited in Chiesa and Malinowski, 2011).

However, there needs to be a second stage to DBT therapy. Once a client starts to establish a meaningful life, the therapist is advised to encourage other-orientated mindfulness. The current meditative practice used by DBT comes from Zen Buddhism, but the therapy often overlooks the need to focus on others. The other-orientated mediation component of SERVICE distinguishes it from DBT and will likely render this therapy more successful over a client's lifespan. It opens the client to a limitless motivational concern beyond the self.

Therapists must ask the question, 'What truly would become of, say, a borderline personality disorder client if they obtain a more meaningful life for, say, a period of time, but, with declining ability and age, again encounter frustration?'. There are so many ways that therapists can encourage other-orientated mindfulness among clients. In addition to meditation, actively encouraging clients to volunteer at soup kitchens, clothing drives, hospitals, and senior centers are good first steps to move from possessing a pro-social attitude to directly experiencing pro-social behavior. Even if the initial pro-social behavior is endocentric, any form of altruism is likely to help build the capacity to better reflect and imagine the plight of others.

External

The Western therapist needs to recognize that cultivating external motivation is destructive. How often do people tell their children to become sports players or doctors, lawyers, or some other profession that earns a lot of money, prestige, or power?

We know that extrinsic motivation does not serve the self or others. Remember the Darley and Batson experiment where sixteen Seminarian students offered rigid help and refused to listen to the needs of the confederate. Our society's drive to encourage individual incentives as a means to an end (i.e. high salary, good appraisals at work, fame and glory) are fundamentally destroying our internal drives to become good.

The objectives of therapists should be to minimize, wherever possible, a client's dependence of faulty extrinsic motivation, which arises from needs frustration. A client will be wasting valuable energy and time if they are primarily extrinsically motivated. The tell-tale signs of extrinsic motivation will typically come from a client who will complain of feeling tired all the time or unable to achieve satisfaction, perhaps even when they have a decent job or income. Or, a therapist may see a divorced, middle-aged individual in crisis, pursuing meaningless sexual encounters and partying.

To an extent, our consumer-driven culture and the commodification of the human has resulted in an extrinsic reward system that has left most people unsatisfied with their lives. Deming observed this phenomenon decades ago. He stated:

> People whether in management or on the factory floor have become, to management, a commodity. I met with 40 skilled tradesmen in a company that is doing well. Their main complaint was that they do not know till Thursday of any week or whether they will work the next week. 'We are a commodity,' one of them said. That is the word that I had been seeking—commodity. The management may hire them at the price posted, or may not, depending on the need. If not needed next week, they go back on the market. (1986, p. 77)

A therapist needs to evaluate the client's intensity for extrinsic motivation and help the client view alternatives, such as changing the nature of their work, stepping forward to help change the culture of individualistic rewards, or finding renewal in a meaningful relationship that is based on cooperation, rather than power.

Removal

Removal of barriers is a concept borrowed from Deming, but the meaning here is different. Instead of removing barriers to pride in workmanship, the objective is removal of barriers in therapy that block our intrinsic development.

Many insurance companies now put a limit on the number of sessions for a therapist to treat clients. This tends to be why cognitive behavioral therapies are supported over other forms of therapy. Each client's internal scaffolds are different. Some are well constructed, while others are weak and in need of improvement. How can therapists engage in the continual improvement of a client's mental health if they are concentrated only on meeting some artificial quota to maximize individual income? The system is set up against achieving psychological advancement.

Variation

Most therapeutic systems are established without an understanding of variation. Most systems of therapy use a disease paradigm without any focus or purpose, and these systems are all over the place. Aside from genetic forms of mental illness and special cases, such as primary psychopathy, the vast majority of psychological pathology is caused by self-interested needs frustration or over-gratification. With so many therapies attempting to address various different mental health issues that can be traced back to needs frustration or over-gratification, the variation in successful treatment varies considerably. Large variation in successful treatment is owing to the flawed system of therapy, rather than the individual's mental illness. The promotion of cooperation and altruistic action among therapists and clients as the ultimate purpose of therapy would lead to declines in the variability of therapeutic success and therapeutic approaches could be tailored with a view to reducing variation.

Innovate

A client may be facing any given sequence of future illusionary needs gratification before arriving at exocentric altruism. We need to translate the future needs of the client into measurable characteristics. People's needs will change all the time based on decreasing levels of satisfaction as they approach self-actualization and, eventually, its negation at exocentric altruism. People also go through different life events at every stage of the process.

Therapy needs to be incrementally tailored to help the client recognize each state of needs achievement and how choices affect different levels of achievement. To reiterate, innovative adjustments to endocentric altruism pursuits are encouraged to heighten the client's drive to pure altruism. Would we want to take a young medical doctor with huge amounts of student loan debt and a new spouse and throw him or her into Doctors Without Borders overseas? The therapist has to engage in some preplanning based on the client's history. Perhaps, having that young doctor participate in a local charity so that he or she could list volunteerism on their resume would be more effective at their current stage of development. As the doctor progresses, earns an income, and becomes financially stable, the next move over 15–20 years would then be to encourage such a client to volunteer to help others overseas.

Continual

The words 'catharsis' and 'cure' should go out the window. These terms are used mostly only to satisfy the requirements of self-interest-driven insurance companies. The human's mental health continually improves throughout life. It is a never-ending work in progress.

A therapist can help a client view a choice or cognition that shows disconnection to some human need for belonging, esteem, or actualization. However, therapy does not end there. We have mentioned Shewhart's Plan, Do, Check, Act (PDCA) cycle in this book. PDCA can also be applied to therapy.

A therapist should tailor therapy for each particular client based on their level of needs gratification. For example, a person pursuing early stage self-actualization might be introduced to altruism by asking them to volunteer to read to senior citizens for pleasure. As long as the participation in endocentric (self-interested) altruism is not overtaxing, it will eventually contribute to better development of cognitive empathy and eventual exocentric altruistic motivation.

Next, a therapist should test the success of therapy based on simulations with the client—send the client out into the real world. And, finally, test the result of service therapy by evaluating the client's altruistic progression and rendering adjustments to the therapy. These steps should lead to continual refinement and improvement as the client approaches and expands beyond the negation of the self.

Exemplify

A good therapist will exemplify exocentric altruism. They should shun the trappings of wealth and take every opportunity to serve others. A therapist should not try to impress clients with an expensive home, Mercedes in the driveway, or plush couch. Some therapists in Hollywood earn hundreds of dollars per hour. Are they really employing higher forms of empathy to help others?

We desperately require more exocentric altruistic leaders among modern therapists. We have an abundance of evidence which demonstrates that we know the directionality of human psychological development. The aim of a therapist is to use his or her knowledge of intrinsic motivation to build upon the client's internal depositional scaffolds and let the client, in their own time, come to experience the drive to help others.

Training, of course, cannot be understated. Following Deming's critique of faulty systems, we have so many therapists today who are experts in their selected discipline, and yet their institutions or affiliations require constant continual professional development in the same areas to fulfill bureaucratic protocols. Training for the sake of training accomplishes nothing when the therapist has maximized his/her learning curve in a particular discipline. A therapist should be actively engaged in training in new areas, such as technology, nutrition, and exercise, to name a few, in order to bring about a holistic mind—body transformation for their clients.

The Other Overlooked in Therapy

Western society does not encourage altruism or pro-social behavior in therapy, generally, unless it is a task the client wishes to undertake. Western therapeutic systems are mental health industries that place too much emphasis on the self-interests of therapists and clients, and such systems may cause more harm than good. SERVICE therapy seeks to replace self-interest that is at the heart of therapeutic systems with cooperation, and by encouraging therapists to engage in self-discipline and altruism to become empathetic inspirations to their clients.

Getting a materialist client to focus their mind or sharpen cognition towards enlightened motivational concerns such self-actualization is progress. Helping a client simultaneously build other-orientated focus through meditation unveils the illusionary nature of their self-interest and how to overcome it.

How do we know that SERVICE therapy would work in practice? We can defer to the time-tested success at Emmaus all over the world. Emmaus has demonstrated that having people help others results in a positive outcome for both the helper and recipient. When helping another, even for a brief period, we are freed from the self-interested thoughts and faulty cognitions that contribute to depression and anxiety.

All the concentration on pathological altruism is a smokescreen—it looks at the pro-social actions as the cause of pathology, when, in almost every single example, frustrated and thwarted self-interest or over-gratification are the causes of the underlying pathology. Western populations are seeking out a new form of healing which has taken over from theological faith-healing. Are the majority of therapists listening to what clients want? Or, are therapists going through the motions to meet some insurance company's quota? A profound transformation in the way therapists help others is found within the simple concepts of SERVICE therapy. SERVICE therapy would enable therapists to address the concerns of, in particular, intermediate- and higher-order needs gratifiers who have become disillusioned, bored, and apathetic by the unhealthy extrinsic rewards produced by self-interested systems.

The USA got lucky during the last century. It prevailed during World War II, which flung the nation's industry into overdrive and helped to meet the needs of its citizens from 1945 to 2008, with only small economic crises in-between. But US industry lost its way and competitiveness to Japan by moving from the national unification experienced during World War II to promoting a system of self-interest.

Now, that same faulty system threatens to unhinge the good psychological advancements Americans have achieved during the period of economic growth. Therapists can contribute to help populations with a therapy that has people focusing on others should long-term economic depression become the new norm.

Winning the Exocentric Revolution

The coming age of altruism is a peaceful revolution that is already underway. Twenty-three percent of college students on the east and west coasts of the USA rated political values associated with exocentric altruism as extremely important. What we do not want is for materialist types to wage episodic violence against exocentric value types. This is not so much of a 'silent revolution' that once existed between materialist and post-materialist types. It is likely to become a vocal revolution, with exocentric value types voicing their concerns. We watched exocentric altruistic individuals crop up at Occupy Wall Street (OWS) protests, and they interacted with mostly post-materialist types who desired to improve the nation's living standards.

However, the OWS movement was without purpose or focus. There are things we can do to help the exocentric value types, and this is where my role as an academic crosses over into an advocacy role.

Phillip Zimbardo states, "For reasons we do not yet fully understand, thousands of ordinary people in every country around the world, when they are placed in special circumstances, make the decision to act heroically" (2007, p. 488). My disagreement with Zimbardo is that we do know why they act heroically. At the root of heroism we find self-sacrifice: take any fictional or real hero and, at their core, they will sacrifice the self for others. Zimbardo has been too quick to overlook the importance of altruism. The emerging evidence in evolution, neuroscience, and psychology demonstrates that we are internally and dispositionally driven to become exocentric altruists and resistant to evil influences.

However, the last thing that we want is for potential OWS protestors or some other disenfranchised group to overthrow the prevailing system only to replace it with more of the same. That would be a cycle of systematic insanity and, given that the OWS protestors have little or no defined vision in the media, my fear is that is exactly what would end up happening.

Humanity needs to become cleverer to usher the coming age of altruism. This means we require new purposeful systems to replace artificial aristocracy and demeritocracy. The exocentric altruistic value-type leaders need to step up and centralize a theme for purposeful systems, which incorporates cooperation, eliminates fear, spreads statistical literacy, and innovates so that we can continually transcend our full potential through helping others.

Notes

Preface

1. According to Khalil (2003/2006) "...'sympathy' denotes common or sameness of feeling (from the Greek *sypatheia: syn,* together + *pathos,* feeling). In contrast, the word 'empathy' indicates the actor's ability to enter someone else's experiences...(from the Greek *empatheia: en-,* in + *pathos,* feeling)" (p. 2). Because empathy is a better word to express Smith's concept, empathy will be used in place of sympathy throughout this book. Specifically, cognitive empathy is referred to in this book because it goes further in denoting the ability to estimate the mental states of others. For a fuller description of station switching see (Smith, 1976[1759]).

3 Expanding the Scope of Biological Evolution

1. Readers are invited to investigate the literature that describes evolution as a continuum. According to Forrest (2000), "Humans were intentional beings before they became conscious ones, so we can refine our earlier understanding of meaning by viewing it as a continuum, with simple intentionality on the lower, or evolutionarily earlier, end, semantic or symbolic (representative) meaning on the ascent toward the higher, or evolutionarily more recent, end, and existential meaning on the highest, or most recent, end" (p. 864). Forrest (2000) also hints that our use of language, imagination, and ability to symbolize meaning have played a role as positive adaptations in human evolutionary development at the higher end of the continuum. I depart from Forrest's theories by viewing the negation of self-interest in the service of others as an even higher recognizable step along the evolutionary continuum. Thus, in my view, the state of human evolutionary development transcends the personal existential meaning that we have devised for ourselves at the higher end of the evolutionary continuum. In my view, the notion of self-preservation that formed at the lower end of the evolutionary continuum has remarkably given way to self-sacrifice at the highest end of the continuum as humans became conscious beings capable of selecting for themselves, through positive adaptations, to live for others.

2. A recent publication has addressed the concept of neo-Darwinian overreliance on the mechanistic foundation for evolution. Low (2008) argues that neo-Darwinian theory has trapped science in a "prison of mechanism" (p. 9). Low views evolution itself as highly creative rather than mechanistic. I go a step further in arguing that not only is evolution creative, but humans, in particular, have evolved so uniquely that we can select for ourselves through imagination to negate self-interested personal meaning by serving others. Humans can thus transcend self-ascribed purpose.

4 'The unlikely Samaritans'

1. The information and primary research for this chapter are derived from 'The unlikely Samaritans' experiment. Some of this information comes from observations made by me during the experiment. An introduction has been added to my article in this chapter and the article has been modified, revised, and reprinted here from Babula, M. 'The unlikely Samaritans,' *Journal of Applied Social Psychology*, 2013, 43(4), 899–908. © 2013 Wiley Blackwell. Reprinted by permission.
2. Bible, Revised Standard Version (RSV).

7 The Special Case of Psychopathy

1. The state and location are not named owing to the sensitivity of this data and to help ensure anonymity of the participants.

9 New Challenges for the West

1. Kurt Cobain's suicide note, as read by Courtney Love. Available at: http://www.youtube.com/watch?v=MnctjPOaPNY (accessed 2 February 2013).

10 Political Values in a Threat Environment

1. Article revised and reprinted from Babula, M. (2007) 'Political values in a threat environment', *PS: Political Science & Politics* 40, 2, 319–24. © 2007 Cambridge University Press. Reprinted by permission.
2. The surveys were administered to social science classes at Whittier College, University of San Diego, University of San Francisco, St. Mary's College, Rutgers University, and Georgetown University. In total, 600 questionnaires were administered, 123 were returned by people who did not meet the sampling criteria (because they were not in the USA on 11 September 2001, were over the age limit, and/or were not US citizens), and the response rate for the remaining 477 people was eighty-four percent owing to seventy-seven people either refusing to answer and/or improperly filling out the questionnaire. The data showed that fifty people on the west coast and twenty-seven people on the east coast refused to answer and/or improperly filled out the questionnaire. A decision was made by the researcher to input data from 400 properly filled out and completed questionnaires into SPSS (of course, these questionnaires also met the sampling criteria).
3. The confidence interval for the sample size is demonstrated: $400 = [(Z)^2(.5)(.5)]/.05^2$. Solving for the Z value, the equation becomes $Z^2 = [400(.05^2)]/(.5)(.5) = 2$. With a Z value of 2, the cumulative area from the left of the Z table is .9772. In order to determine the confidence level, the objective is to calculate the critical value (α), which is the number on the borderline, separating sample statistics that are likely to occur from those that are unlikely to occur. The amount not contained under the cumulative area from the left of the curve equals $1 - .9772 = .0228$. The total area not contained within the

normal distribution curve is $\alpha = [(.0228)(2)] = .0456$. The resulting confidence level is demonstrated as $1 - .0456 = .9544$.

4. It is important to mention that perception will be a highly important factor here. These values might measure exocentric altruism if the potential respondent perceives that they produce a greater cost than benefit. Habermas argued that "Individuals owe their identities as persons exclusively to their identification with, or internalization of, features of collective identity; personal identity is a mirror image of collective identity" (Habermas, 1987). It follows that collective political altruism, which involves sacrifices without regard to the self or some national gain, is a 'mirror image' of individual exocentric altruism. Nevertheless, in the absence of previous research on the matter, the best way to test this phenomenon is to administer the PV scale and perform factor analysis. The factor validity and regression models justify these choices. The fact that this study follows an ex post facto design and is an exploratory analysis permits some exploration when it comes to measuring a potential exocentric altruistic continuum.

5. It is recognized that non-random sampling introduces a bias, but it was the researcher's intention to obtain a biased sample in order to evaluate movement along the higher ends of the hierarchy and political values paradigms. The researcher wanted to tap a sample of potentially post-materialist types. It has been argued that higher education is one of the best measures to locate potential second-tier needs gratifiers in a given population, hence the researcher targeted institutions and subjects that were likely to enroll intellectual, progressive, and creative college students (see Hagerty, 1999).

6. The betas show that a pattern exists where values that correlate weakly with a factor in Table 10.1 share a positive relationship with the next highest factor, and preferences that share strong correlations with a factor show an inverse correlation with the next highest factor. For instance, for every unit increase in rating crime and violence, there is a .494 increased rating for post-materialism. Factor validity confirms that crime and violence correlates least with the post-materialist factor. It also appears that an increase in per unit rating for the state of the US economy produces a twenty-eight percent increased rating in post-materialism. In contrast, for every increase in unit rating for national defense, there is a seventeen percent decrease in ratings for post-materialism. It appears that certain variables, such as national defense, tap materialist motivations so strongly that people render an 'opportunity cost' decision to temporarily forgo post-materialist concerns. As people gratify human needs and altruistic counterparts, items such as crime and violence and the state of the US economy become less correlated with the materialist factor, and people 'step-off' these value preferences in a switch to post-material concerns.

7. Again, the more a political preference correlates with a post-materialist factor in Table 10.1, the greater the possibility of an inverse relationship due to opportunity costs, and when values correlate least with post-materialism there exists a positive linear relationship with exocentric altruism. In other words, the weakening of the influence of needs gratification at a particular values-type level appears to lead to the switch in interests toward the next highest-order political value. For example, the beta indicates that for every unit increased rating for quality of schools, there was a thirty percent

decreased rating for the exocentric altruism dimension. The quality of schools' objectives correlates the strongest with post-materialist values (see factor analysis results in Table 10.1). In contrast, the variable that is least correlated with the post-material factor shares a positive relationship with exocentric altruism. For every increased per unit rating for the item labeled 'protecting the environment,' there is a thirty-four percent increased rating for exocentric altruism value objectives. The strong beta offers further support that as tendencies to rate post-materialism important weaken, a strong positive linear relationship forms with exocentric altruism ratings. The betas also reveal that for every unit increase in poverty, racism and discrimination, and child care ratings there exists a corresponding increased unit rating in exocentric altruism of thirty-one percent, twenty-seven percent, and ten percent, respectively.

11   The Rejection of Barabbas

1. New Jerusalem Bible (http://www.catholic.org/bible/).
2. Initially, 402 individuals responded to the online survey. However, twenty-one respondents reported that they were under the age of 18 years, or failed to report their age, and a further twenty-four respondents reported that they were not US citizens. As a result, a decision was made to conduct the analysis on the remaining 357 surveys, where participants reported that they were of the age of majority to participate and citizens of the USA.
3. The confidence interval for the sample size is demonstrated: $357 = [(Z)^2(.5)(.5)]/.05^2$. Solving for the Z value, the equation becomes $Z^2 = [357(.05^2)]/(.5)(.5) = 1.889$. With a Z value of 1.889, the cumulative area from the left of 1.89 (rounded up) is .9706. In order to determine the confidence level, the objective is to calculate the critical value (α), which is the number on the borderline separating sample statistics that are likely to occur from those that are unlikely to occur. The amount not contained under the cumulative area from the left of the curve equals $1 - .9706 = .0294$. The total area not contained within the normal distribution is $\alpha = [(.0294)(2)] = .0588$. The resulting confidence is $1 - .0588 = .9412$.

References

Abramson, P. and Inglehart, R (1995) *Value Change in Global Perspective* (Ann Arbor, MI: The University of Michigan Press).

Alex, P. (2012) 'Rutgers President's $747,000 Pay Package a Boost Over Predecessor's', available at: http://www.northjersey.com/news/education/college/Rutgers_chiefs_747000_pay_package_a_boost_over_predecessors.html (accessed 1 April 2013).

Allen, E. (2013) 'Family of Suspected Bombers Received Welfare, Food Stamps', available at: http://www.bostonglobe.com/2013/04/26/bombbenefits/VNPB285wfdHTQ0biFWJnLM/story.html (accessed 16 April 2013).

Allport, G.W. (1950) *The Individual and His Religion: A Psychological Interpretation* (New York: Macmillan).

Allport, G.W. and Ross, J. M. (1967) 'Personal Religious Orientation and Prejudice', *Journal of Personality and Social Psychology*, 5(4), 447–57.

Anon (2004) 'The 9/11 Commission Report: Final Report of the National Commission on Terrorist Attacks Upon the United States', Official Government Ed. (Washington, DC: U.S. Government Printing Office).

Anon (2007a) 'Will to Meaning', available at: http://www.youtube.com/watch?v=MmKta5tymPY (accessed 15 May 2013) [*YouTube* video].

Anon (2007b) 'Professor Liviu Librescu (1930–2007)', *Mechanics of Advanced Materials & Structures*, 14(4), 225.

Anon (2008) 'Courage Under Fire', available at: http://www.chabad.org/multimedia/media_cdo/aid/664614/jewish/Courage-Under-Fire.htm (accessed 2 February 2013).

Anon (2012) 'FBI Documents Reveal Secret Nationwide Occupy Monitoring', available at: http://www.justiceonline.org/commentary/fbi-files-ows.html (accessed 22 January 2013).

Anon (2013) 'Wikileaks Reveals Association With Aaron Swartz', available at: http://rt.com/usa/news/wikileaks-aaron-swartz-organization-448/ (accessed 23 January 2013).

Babiak, P. and Hare, R. D. (2007) *Snakes in Suits: When Psychopaths go to Work* (New York: HarperCollins).

Babula, M. (2007)'Political Values in a Threat Environment', *PS: Political Science & Politics*, 40(2), 319–24.

Babula, M. (2013) 'The Unlikely Samaritans', *Journal of Applied Social Psychology*, 43(4), 899–908.

Bartal, I.B.-A., Decety, J., and Mason, P. (2011) 'Empathy and Pro-social Behavior in Rats', *Science*, 334(6061), 1427–30.

Batson, C.D. (1976) 'Religion as Prosocial: Agent or Double Agent?', *Journal for the Scientific Study of Religion*, 15, 29–45.

Batson, C.D. (1991) *The Altruism Question* (Hillsdale, NJ: Lawrence Erlbaum Associates).

Batson, C.D. (1998) 'Altruism and Prosocial Behavior', in Gilbert, D.T., Fiske, S.T. and Lindzey, G. (eds) *Handbook of Social Psychology*, 4th ed., Vol. 2, pp. 282–316 (Boston, MA: McGraw-Hill).

Batson, C.D., and Schoenrade, P.A. (1991) 'Measuring Religion as Quest: 2) Reliability Concerns', *Journal for the Scientific Study of Religion*, 30, 430–47.

Batson, C.D., Schoenrade, P., and Ventis, W. L. (1993) *Religion and the Individual: A Social-Psychological Perspective* (New York: Oxford University Press).

Batson, C.D., Klein, T. R., Highberger, L., and Shaw, L. L. (1995) 'Immorality from Empathy-induced Altruism: When Compassion and Justice Conflict', *Journal of Personality and Social Psychology*, 68(6), 1042–54.

Baum, C. (2012) "Four Numbers Add Up to an American Debt Disaster", available at: http://www.bloomberg.com/news/2012-03-28/four-numbers-add-up-to-an-american-debt-disaster.html (accessed 18 March 2013).

BBC News (2005) 'Profile: Charles Graner', available at: http://news.bbc.co.uk/1/hi/world/americas/4176885.stm (accessed 15 February 2013).

Beardsley, M. (1960) *The European Philosophers from Descartes to Nietzsche* (New York: Random House).

Benjamin, J. (1990) 'An Outline of Intersubjectivity: The Development of Recognition', *Psychoanalytic Psychology*, 7(S), 33–46.

Biggs, J. (1999) 'What the Student Does: Teaching for Enhanced Learning', *Higher Education Research & Development*, 18(1), 57–75.

Blair, R.J.R. (2005) 'Responding to the Emotions of Others: Dissociating Forms of Empathy Through the Study of Typical and Psychiatric Populations', *Consciousness and Cognition*, 14(4), 698–718.

Blanchard, E.B., Kuhn, E., Rowell, D.L., Hickling, E.J., Wittrock, D., Rogers, R.L., et al. (2004) 'Studies of the VIcarious Traumatization of College Students by the September 11th Attacks: Effects of Proximity, Exposure and Connectedness', *Behaviour Research and Therapy*, 42(2), 191–205.

Blass, T. (1994) 'Understanding Behavior in the Milgram Obedience Experiment', in Lesko, W.A. (ed.) *Readings in Social Psychology*, pp. 240–63 (Boston, MA: Allyn and Bacon).

Braughton, W.D. (1999) 'Edwards Deming's Profound Knowledge and Individual Psychology', *Journal of Individual Psychology*, 55, 449–57.

Brickman, P., Coates, D., and Janoff-Brickman, R. (1978) 'Lottery Winners and Accident Victims: Is Happiness Relative?', *Journal of Personality and Social Psychology*, 36(8), 917–27.

Briggs, H. (2007) 'Chimps Beat Humans in Memory Test', available at: http://news.bbc.co.uk/2/hi/7124156.stm (accessed 30 August 2012).

Brill, M. (2012) 'Biofuel Production', available at: http://articles.chicagotribune.com/2012-08-06/news/chi-biofuel-production-20120806_1_biofuel-production-corn-crop-tortilla-prices (accessed 19 March 2013).

Brooks, D. (2013) 'Tribal Lessons', available at: http://www.nytimes.com/2013/01/13/books/review/the-world-until-yesterday-by-jared-diamond.html?pagewanted=all&_r=0 (accessed 11 January 2013).

Brunet, E., Sarfati, Y., Hardy-Baylé, M.-C., and Decety, J. (2000) 'A PET Investigation of the Attribution of Intentions with a Nonverbal Task', *Neuroimage*, 11(2), 157–66.

Burris, C.T. (1999) 'Religious Orientation Scale (Allport & Ross, 1967)', in Hill, P. and Hood, R. (eds) *Measures of Religiosity*, pp. 144–54 (Birmingham, AL: Religious Education Press).

Campbell, R.J. (1989) *Campbell's Psychiatric Dictionary*, 6th ed (Oxford University Press).

Carey, B. (2013) 'Study Questions Effectiveness of Therapy for Suicidal Teenagers', available at: http://www.nytimes.com/2013/01/09/health/gaps-seen-in-therapy-for-suicidal-teenagers.html?hp&_r=1& (accessed 20 February 2013).

Carmines, E.G. and Layman, G.C. (1997) 'Value Priorities, Partisanship and Electoral Choice: The Neglected Case of the United States', *Political Behavior*, 19(4), 283–316.

Carroll, R. (2013a) 'Christopher Dorner's Last Stand: How the Manhunt Unfolded into a Fiery End', available at: http://www.guardian.co.uk/world/2013/feb/14/christopher-dorner-last-stand-manhunt (accessed 15 February 2013).

Carroll, R. (2013b) 'Fresh Questions over Christopher Dorner's Dismissal as Hunt Continues', available at: http://www.guardian.co.uk/world/2013/feb/11/christopher-dorner-lapd-grievance-judge (accessed 15 February 2013).

Casey, B.J., Tottenham, N., Liston, C., and Durston, S. (2005) 'Imaging the Developing Brain: What Have we Learned About Cognitive Development?', *Trends in Cognitive Sciences*, 9(3), 104–10.

CBSNEWS.com (2009) 'She's No Stranger To Grisly Images', available at: http://www.cbsnews.com/2100-500257_162-616584.html (accessed 15 February 2013).

CEC (Career Education Corporation) (2013) About CEC, available at: http://www.careered.com/About-CEC (accessed 10 April 2013).

Centers for Disease Control (2009) 'WISCARS Injury Mortality Reports (1981–1998)', available at: http://webappa.cdc.gov/sasweb/ncipc/mortrate9.html (accessed 9 April 2013).

Centers for Disease Control (2010) 'WISCARS Injury Mortality Reports (1999–2007)', available at: http://webappa.cdc.gov/sasweb/ncipc/mortrate10_sy.html (accessed 9 April 2013).

Centers for Disease Control (2013) 'WISCARS Injury Mortality Reports, Centers for Disease Control (2008–2010)', available at: http://webappa.cdc.gov/sasweb/ncipc/mortrate10_us.html (accessed 9 April 2013).

Chaney, G.P. (2013) 'My Teaching Philosophy: Constructivist Pedagogy Empowering Intellectual Character, University of Michigan School of Education', available at: http://sitemaker.umich.edu/ginapchaney/teaching_goals___philosophy (accessed 1 September 2013).

Chiesa, A. and Malinowski, P. (2011) 'Mindfulness-based Approaches: Are They All the Same?', *Journal of Clinical Psychology*, 67(4), 404–24.

Christie, D.J. (2006) 'What is Peace Psychology the Psychology of?', *Journal of Social Issues*, 62(1), 1–17.

Church, R.M, 'Emotional Reactions of Rats to the Pain of Others', *Journal of Comparative and Physiological Psychology*, 52(2), 132.

Corinthian Colleges (2013) About Corinthian Colleges, available at: http://www.cci.edu/about (accessed 10 April 2013).

Crocker, J. and Park, L. (2004) 'The Costly Pursuit of Self-Esteem', *Psychological Bulletin*, 130(3), 392–414.

Csikszentmihalyi, M. (1999) 'If We Are so Rich, Why Aren't We Happy?', *American Psychologist*, 54, 821–7.

Dalton, R. (2006) *Citizen Politics*, 4th ed (Washington, DC: CQPress).

Dalton, R. (2013) *Citizen Politics. Public Opinion and Political Parties in Advanced Industrial Democracies*, 6th ed (Washington, DC: CQPress).

Dao, J. and von Zielbauer, P. (2004) 'The Struggle for Iraq: The Prison Guards; Abuse Charges Bring Anguish in Unit's Home', available at: http://www.

nytimes.com/2004/05/06/world/struggle-for-iraq-prison-guards-abuse-charges-bring-anguish-unit-s-home.html?pagewanted=all&src=pm   (accessed   15 February 2013).

Darley, J.M. and Batson, C.D. (1994) 'From Jerusalem to Jericho': A Study of Situational and Dispositional Variables in Helping Behavior', in Lesko, W.A. (ed.) *Readings in Social Psychology*, pp. 272–81 (Boston, MA: Allyn and Bacon).

Decety, J. and Svetlova, M. (2012) 'Putting Together Phylogenetic and Ontogenetic Perspectives on Empathy', *Developmental Cognitive Neuroscience*, 2(1), 1–24.

Deming, W.E. (1986) *Out of Crisis* (Cambridge, MA: Massachusetts Institute of Technology Center for Advanced Engineering).

Deming, W.E. (1994) *The New Economics for Industry, Government, and Education* (Cambridge, MA: Massachusetts Institute of Technology Center for Advanced Engineering Study).

de Waal, F. (2009) *The Age of Empathy Nature's Lessons for a Kinder Society* (London: Souvenir Press).

Di Pellegrino, G., Fadiga, L., Fogassi, L., Gallese, V., and Rizzolatti, G. (1992) 'Understanding Motor Events: A Neurophysiological Study', *Experimental Brain Research*, 91(1), 176–80.

Dodd, V. (2011) 'New Questions Raised over Duggan Shooting' available at: http://www.guardian.co.uk/uk/2011/nov/18/mark-duggan-ipcc-investigation-riots (accessed 15 February 2013).

Doll, J. (2012) 'A Treasury of Terribly Sad Stories of Lotto Winners', available at: http://www.theatlanticwire.com/national/2012/03/terribly-sad-true-stories-lotto-winners/50555/ (accessed 12 August 2012).

Dunn, E.W., Aknin, L.B., and Norton, M.I. (2008) 'Spending Money on Others Promotes Happiness', *Science*, 319(5870), 1687–8.

Early, J. and Davenport, J.B. (2010) 'Desired Qualities of Leaders Within Today's Accounting Firm', *The CPA Journal*, 80(3), 59–62.

EDMC (Education Management Corporation) (2013) 'Education That Builds Careers', available at: http://www.edmc.edu/pdf/corporate-partnership-brochure.pdf (accessed 10 April 2013).

Edmondson, B. (1995) 'The Next Baby Boom', *American Demographics*, 17(9), 2.

Elder, T.E. (2010) 'The Importance of Relative Standards in ADHD Diagnoses: Evidence Based on Exact Birth Dates', *Journal of Health Economics*, 29(5), 641–56.

Emmaus Village Carlton (2013) 'The Emmaus Movement', available at: http://www.emmausvillagecarlton.org.uk/about.html (accessed 10 April 2013).

Fainaru, S. and Ibrahim, A. (2002) 'Mysterious Trip to Flight 77 Cockpit', available at: http://www.washingtonpost.com/wp-dyn/content/article/2007/08/13/AR2007081300752_5.html (accessed 7 March 2013).

Ferenstein, G. (2013) '72% of Professors Who Teach Online Courses Don't Think Their Students Deserve Credit', available at: http://techcrunch.com/2013/03/22/72-of-professors-who-teach-online-courses-dont-think-their-students-deserve-credit/ (accessed 2 April 2013).

Ferner, M. (2012) 'One Marijuana Arrest Occurs Every 42 Seconds In U.S.: FBI Report', available at: http://www.huffingtonpost.com/2012/10/29/one-marijuana-arrest-occu_n_2041236.html (accessed 18 March 2013).

Fingleton, E. (2011) 'The Myth of Japan's "Lost Decades"', available at: http://www.theatlantic.com/international/archive/2011/02/the-myth-of-japans-lost-decades/71741/ (accessed 18 March 2013).

Fletcher, P.C., Happe, F., Frith, U., Baker, S.C., Dolan, R.J., Frackowiak, R.S.J., and Frith, C.D. 'Other Minds in the Brain: a Functional Imaging Study of "Theory of Mind" in Story Comprehension', *Cognition*, 57(2), 109–28.

Forrest, B. (2000) 'The Possibility of Meaning in Human Evolution', *Zygon*, 35(4), 861–80.

FoxNews.com (2012) 'Lottery's Biggest Losers: Big Wins don't Equal Better Lives', available at: http://www.foxnews.com/us/2012/03/29/lotterys-biggest-losers-big-wins-dont-equal-better-lives/ (accessed 23 July 2013).

Franken, R.E. (1998) *Human Motivation*, 4th ed (Pacific Grove, CA: Brooks/Cole).

Freud, A. (1946) *The Ego and the Mechanisms of Defense* (New York: International Universities Press).

Freud, S. (1933) *New Introductory Lectures on Psycho-analysis*, standard ed., Vol. XXII (London: Hogarth Press).

Freud, S. (1961) *Civilization and its Discontents* (New York: W.W. Norton).

Friesl, C., Richter, M., and Zulehner, P.M. (1993) *Values and Lifestyles of Young People in Europe* (Vienna: Federal Ministry for the Environment, Youth and Family.

Frith, U. (2001) 'Mind Blindness and the Brain in Autism', *Neuron*, 32(6), 969–80.

Gabriel, S. and Young, A.F. (2011) 'Becoming a Vampire Without Being Bitten The Narrative Collective-Assimilation Hypothesis', *Psychological Science*, 22(8), 990–4.

Gallagher, H.L., Happe, F., Brunswick, N., Fletcher, P.C., Frith, U., and Frith, C.D. (2000) 'Reading the Mind in Cartoons and Stories: an fMRI Study of "theory of mind" in Verbal and Nonverbal Tasks', *Neuropsychologia*, 38(1), 11–21.

Galston, W. (2001) 'Who's a Liberal?', *Public Interest*, 144, 100–8.

Goel, V., Grafman, J., Sadato, N., and Hallett, M. (1995) 'Modeling Other Minds', *Neuroreport*, 6(13), 1741–6.

Goodale, G. (2011) 'Who is Occupy Wall Street? After Six Weeks, a Profile Finally Emerges', available at: http://www.csmonitor.com/USA/Politics/2011/1101/Who-is-Occupy-Wall-Street-After-six-weeks-a-profile-finally-emerges/%28page%29/2 (accessed 9 February 2013).

Goode, E. and Kovaleski, S. 'Boy at Home in U.S., Swayed by One Who Wasn't', available at: http://www.nytimes.com/2013/04/20/us/details-of-tsarnaev-brothers-boston-suspects-emerge.html?pagewanted=all (accessed 19 April 2013).

Goodman, P. (2010) 'In Hard Times, Lured Intro Trade School and Debt', available at: http://www.nytimes.com/2010/03/14/business/14schools.html?pagewanted=all (accessed 30 March 2013).

Gosling, S.D., Rentfrow, P.J., and Swann Jr, W.B. (2003) 'A Very Brief Measure of the Big-Five Personality Domains', *Journal of Research in Personality*, 37(6), 504–28.

Greenleaf, R. (1977) *Servant Leadership: a Journey into the Nature of Legitimate Power and Greatness* (Mahwah, NJ: Paulist Press).

Habermas, J. (1987) *The Theory of Communicative Action* (Cambridge: Polity Press).

Hagerty, M.R. (1999) 'Testing Maslow's Hierarchy of Needs: National Quality-of-Life Across Time', *Social Indicators Research*, 46(3), 249–71.

Hare, R.D. (1998) 'Psychopaths and Their Nature: Implications for the Mental Health and Criminal Justice Systems', in Millon, T., Simonsen, E., Birket-

Smith, M., and Davis, R.D. (eds) *Psychopathy: Antisocial, Criminal, and Violent Behavior*, pp. 188–212 (New York: Guilford Press).

Hatfield, E. (2009) 'Emotional Contagion and Empathy', in Decety, J. and Svetlova, M. (eds) *The Social Neuroscience of Empathy*, pp. 19–30. (Cambridge, MA: MIT Press).

Hatfield, E., Cacioppo, J.T., and Rapson, R.L. (1994) *Emotional Contagion* (New York: Cambridge University Press).

Henry, W.A. and Willwerth, J. (1993) 'Putting Justice in the Doc', *Time*, 141(16), 32–3.

Homant, R.J. and Kennedy, D.B. (2012) 'Does no Good Deed go Unpunished? The Victimology of Altruism', in Oakley, B., Knafo, A., Madhavan, G., Wilson, D.S. (eds) *Pathological Altruism*, pp. 193–206 (New York: Oxford University Press).

Horgan, J. (2001) 'Are Psychiatric Medicines Making Us Sicker?', available at: http://chronicle.com/article/Are-Psychiatric-Medications/128976/ (accessed 26 March 2013).

Hosmer, D. and Lemeshow, S. (1989) *Applied Logistic Regression* (New York: Wiley).

Hunter, K.I. and Linn, M.W. (1980) 'Psychosocial Differences Between Elderly Volunteers and Non-volunteers', *The International Journal of Aging and Human Development*, 12(3), 205–13.

James, S. (2010) 'Adderall Abuse Alters the Brain, Claims a Young Life', available at: http://abcnews.go.com/Health/MindMoodNews/adderall-psychosis-suicide-college-students-abuse-study-drug/story?id=12066619#.UVr_QKKce8A (accessed 1 April 2013).

Inglehart, R. (1971) 'The Silent Revolution in Europe: Intergenerational Change in Post-industrial Societies', *American Political Science Review*, 65(4), 991–1017.

Inglehart, R. (1977) *The Silent Revolution Changing Values and Political Styles Among Western Publics* (Princeton, NJ: Princeton University Press).

Inglehart, R. (1981) 'Post-materialism in an environment of insecurity', *The American Political Science Review*, 75, 880–900.

Inglehart, R. (1990) *Culture Shift* (Princeton, NJ: Princeton University Press).

Inglehart, R., Moaddel, M., and Tessler, M. (2006) 'Xenophobia and In-group Solidarity in Iraq: a Natural Experiment on the Impact of Insecurity', *Perspectives on Politics*, 4(3), 495–505.

Jackson, L. (2001) 'A Mission to Die For', available at: http://www.abc.net.au/4corners/atta/transcript.htm (accessed 7 March 2013).

James, W. (1936 [1902]) *The Varieties of Religious Experience: A Study of Human Nature* (New York: The Modern Library).

Jordon, M. (2009) 'Global Financial Crisis Fells Iceland's Government', available at: http://www.washingtonpost.com/wpdyn/content/article/2009/01/26/AR2009012600531.html (accessed 18 March 2013).

Jost, J.T. and Jost, L.J. (2009) 'Virtue Ethics and the Social Psychology of Character: Philosophical Lessons from the Person Situation Debate', *Journal of Research in Personality*, 43(2), 253–4.

Kanungo, R.N. and Conger, J.A. (1993) 'Promoting Altruism as a Corporate Goal', *The Academy of Management Executive*, 7(3), 37–48.

Karpman, B. (1948) 'The Myth of the Psychopathic Personality', *The American Journal of Psychiatry*, 104, 523–34.

Karylowski, J. (1984) "Focus of Attention and Altruism: Endocentric and Exocentric Sources of Altruistic Behavior', in Staub, E., Bar-Tal, D., Karylowski,

J., and Reykowski, J. (eds) *Development and Maintenance of Prosocial Behavior: International Perspectives on Positive Morality*, pp. 139–55 (New York: Plenum).

Kavka, G.S. (1983) 'Hobbes's War of all Against all', *Ethics*, 93(2), 291–310.

Kehoe, P. (2012) 'Protestors' Stories: Dorli Rainey and Occupy Seattle', available at: http://www.guardian.co.uk/world/2012/jan/13/protesters-dorli-rainey-occupy-seattle (accessed 17 February 2013).

Khalil, E.L. (2001) 'Adam Smith and Three Theories of Altruism', *Recherches Économiques de Louvain*, 67(4), 421–35.

Khalil, E.L. (2003/2006) 'A Pure Theory of Altruism' (working paper).

Khalil, E.L. (2004) 'What is Altruism?', *Journal of Economic Psychology*, 25(1), 97–123.

Kirkham, C. (2011) 'Gary McCullough, For-Profit College Chief, Resigns Following Internal Investigation', available at: http://www.huffingtonpost.com/2011/11/02/for-profit-college-gary-mccullough-resigns_n_1072519.html (accessed 30 March 2013).

Klerman, G.L. and Weissman, M.M. (1989) 'Increasing Rates of Depression', *JAMA*, 261(15), 2229–35.

Knowles, M. (1970) *The Modern Practice of Adult Education* (Englewood Cliffs, NJ: Prentice Hall Regents).

Knowles, M. (1980) *The Modern Practice of Adult Education. From Pedagogy to Andragogy*, 2nd ed. (Englewood Cliffs, NJ: Prentice Hall/Cambridge).

Knowles, M. (1998) *The Adult Learner: The Definitive Classic in Adult Education and Human Resource Development* (Houston, TX: Gulf Publishing).

Kohut, H. and Seitz, P. (1963) 'Concepts and Theories of Psychoanalysis', in Ornstein, P. (ed.) *The Search for the Self*, Vol. I (New York: International Universities Press).

Konner, M. (2010) *The Evolution of Childhood: Relationships, Emotion, Mind* (Cambridge, MA: Belknap Press).

Lazarus, R.S. and Launier, R. (1978) 'Stress-related Transactions Between Person and Environment', in Pervin, L.A. and Lewis, M. (eds) *Perspectives in Interactional Psychology*, pp. 287–327 (New York: Plenum).

Lazarus, R.S. and Folkman, S. (1984) *Stress, Appraisal, and Coping* (New York: Springer).

Lemann, N. (1996) 'Kicking in Groups', *Atlantic Monthly*, 277(4), 22–6.

Leopold, J. (2013) 'Aaron Swartz's FOIA Requests Shed Light on His Struggle', available at: http://pubrecord.org/nation/10676/aaron-swartzs-requests-light-struggle/ (accessed 23 January 2013).

Levenson, M.R., Kiehl, K.A., and Fitzpatrick, C.M. (1995) 'Assessing Psychopathic Attributes in a Noninstitutionalized Population', *Journal of Personality and Social Psychology*, 68, 151–8.

Levin, W.J. (1996) 'Could a Dose of Deming Transform Government?', *Journal for Quality and Participation*, 19(1), 56–61.

Levine, A. and Cureton, J.S. (1998) 'Student Politics: The New Localism', *Review of Higher Education*, 21(2), pp. 137–50.

Li, M. and Rodin, G. (2012) 'Altruism and Suffering in the Context of Cancer: Implications of a Relational Paradigm', in Oakley, B., Knafo, A., Madhavan, G., and Wilson, D.S. (eds) *Pathological Altruism*, pp. 138–155 (New York: Oxford University Press).

Linehan, M. (1993) *Cognitive Behavioural Treatment of Borderline Personality Disorder* (New York: Guilford Press).

Low, A. (2008) 'Creativity and Intention in Evolution', *ReVision*, 30(1), 88–96.

Lubin, G. (2011) 'The 19 Jobs Where You're Most Likely to Kill Yourself', available at: http://www.businessinsider.com/most-suicidal-occupations-2011-10?op=1 (accessed 9 February 2013).

Luna, B. and Sweeney, J.A. (2004) 'The Emergence of Collaborative Brain Function: FMRI Studies of the Development of Response Inhibition', *Annals of the New York Academy of Sciences*, 1021(1), pp. 296–309.

McBride, J. (1997) *Steven Spielberg* (New York: Faber and Faber).

McCormack, S. (2013) 'Robert Saylor's Death Ruled a Homicide: Man With Down Syndrome Died in Police Custody', available at http://www.huffington-post.com/2013/02/18/robert-saylors-death-homicide-mentally-ill_n_2711629.html (accessed 20 February 2013).

McCullagh, D. (2013) 'Swartz Didn't Face Prison Until Feds Took Over the Case, Report Says', available at: http://news.cnet.com/8301-13578_3-57565927-38/swartz-didnt-face-prison-until-feds-took-over-case-report-says/ (accessed 2 February 2013).

McFadden, R.D. (2004) 'Vast Anti-Bush Rally Greets Republicans in New York', available at: http://www.nytimes.com/2004/08/30/politics/campaign/30protest.html (accessed 20 February 2013).

Mansfield, H. (2001) 'Grade Inflation: It's Time to Face the Facts', available at: http://chronicle.com/article/Grade-Inflation-It-s-Time-to/9332 (accessed 30 March 2013).

Maslow, A. (1954) *Motivation and Personality* (New York: Harper & Row Publishers).

Maslow, A. (1970) *Motivation and Personality*, 2nd ed. (New York: Harper & Row Publishers).

Mate, G. (2003) *When the Body Says No: The Cost of Hidden Stress* (Toronto: Knopf Canada).

Maydew, G. (2013) 'Troublesome Economic Signs', available at http://thegazette.com/2013/03/18/troublesome-economic-signs/ (accessed 18 March 2013).

Maynard, S. (1995) *Applied Logistic Regression Analysis* (Thousand Oaks, CA: SAGE).

Mikulincer, M,, Gillath, O., Halevy, V., Avihou, N., Avidan, S., and Eshkoli, N. (2001) 'Attachment Theory and Rections to Others' Needs: Evidence that Activation of the Sense of Attachment Security Promotes Empathic Responses', *Journal of Personality and Social Psychology*, 81(6), 1205.

Milgram, S. (1994) 'Behavioral Study of Obedience', in Lesko, W.A. (ed.) *Readings in Social Psychology*, pp. 229–39 (Boston, MA: Allyn and Bacon).

Mills, J. (2006) 'Reflections on the Death Drive', *Psychoanalytic Psychology*, 23(2), 374.

Milton, J. (2012 [1677]) 'Paradise Lost (XII.575–587)', in Luxon, T.H. (ed.) *The Milton Reading Room*, available at: http://www.dartmouth.edu/~milton/reading_room/pl/book_12/index.shtml (accessed 21 August 2012)..

Miron, J.A. and Waldock, K. (2010) 'The Budgetary Impact of Ending Drug Prohibition', available at: http://www.cato.org/sites/cato.org/files/pubs/pdf/DrugProhibitionWP.pdf (accessed 18 March 2013).

Moen, P., Dempster-McClain, D., and Williams Jr, R.M. (1992) 'Successful Aging: A Life-course Perspective on Women's Multiple Roles and Health', *American Journal of Sociology*, 97, 1612–38.

Mommsen, T.E. (1942) 'Petrarch's Conception of the Dark Ages', *Speculum*, 17(2), 226–42.

Musick, M.A., Regula Herzog, A., and House, J.S. (1999) 'Volunteering and Mortality Among Older Adults: Findings From a National Sample', *The Journals of Gerontology Series B: Psychological Sciences and Social Sciences*, 54(3), S173–S180.

Myers, D.G. (2000) 'The Funds, Friends, and Faith of Happy People', *American Psychologist*, 55(1), 56–67.

Myers, R.H. (1990) *Classical and Modern Regression with Applications*, 2nd ed. (Belmont, CA: Duxbury Press).

Nir, S.M. (2013) 'Storm Effort Causes a Rift in a Shifting Occupy Movement', available at: http://www.nytimes.com/2013/05/01/nyregion/occupy-move-ments-changing-focus-causes-rift.html?hp&_r=1& (accessed 30 April 2013).

Nisslé, S. and Bschor, T. (2002) 'Winning the Jackpot and Depression: Money Cannot Buy Happiness', *International Journal of Psychiatry in Clinical Practice*, 6(3), 183–6.

Oakley, B., Knafo, A., and Madhavan, G. (2012) 'Pathological Altruism—An Introduction', in Oakley, B., Knafo, A., Madhavan, G., and Wilson, D.S. (eds) *Pathological Altruism*, pp. 3–9 (New York: Oxford University Press).

O'Connor, L.E., Berry, J.W., Stiver, D.J., and Rangan, R.K. (2012) 'Depression, Guilt, and Tibetan Buddhism', *Psychology*, 3(29), 805–9.

Oman, D., Thoresen, C.E., and McMahon, K. (1999) 'Volunteerism and Mortality Among the Community-dwelling Elderly', *Journal of Health Psychology*, 4(3), 301–16.

Parr, L.A. (2001) 'Cognitive and Physiological Markers of Emotional Awareness in Chimpanzees (*Pan troglodytes*)', *Animal Cognition*, 4(3–4), 223–9.

Peterson, J. (2013) 'Girlfriend: Aaron Swartz's Suicide not Caused by Depression', available at: http://dailycaller.com/2013/02/05/girlfriend-aaron-swartzs-sui-cide-not-caused-by-depression/ (accessed 6 February 2013).

Pistorello, J., Fruzzetti, A.E., MacLane, C., Gallop, R., and Iverson K.M. (2012) 'Dialectical Behavior Therapy (DBT) Applied to College Students: A Randomized Clinical Trial', *Journal of Consulting and Clinical Psychology*, 80(6), 982–94.

Post, J.M. (2005) 'The New Face of Terrorism: Socio-cultural Foundations of Contemporary Terrorism', *Behavioral Sciences & the Law*, 23(4), 451–65.

Post, S.G. (2005) 'Altruism, Happiness, and Health: It's Good to be Good', *International Journal of Behavioral Medicine*, 12(2), 66–77.

Schopenhauer, A. (1965) *On the Basis of Morality*, trans. E.F.J. Payne (Indianapolis, IN: Bobbs-Merrill).

Schwartz, J. (2003) 'Generous to a Fault or Faulty Generosity?' available at: http://articles.latimes.com/2003/nov/30/news/adna-giver30 (accessed 30 August 2012).

Schwartz, J. (2013) 'Internet Activist, a Creator of RSS, is Dead at 26, Apparently a Suicide', available at: http://www.nytimes.com/2013/01/13/technology/aaron-swartz-internet-activist-dies-at-26.html?_r=0 (accessed 15 January 2013).

Schwarz, A. and Cohen, S. (2013) 'A.D.H.D. Seen in 11% of U.S. Children as Diagnoses Rise', available at: http://www.nytimes.com/2013/04/01/health/more-diagnoses-of-hyperactivity-causing-concern.html?pagewanted=all&_r=0 (accessed 3 April 2013).

Seligman, M.E.P. (1989) 'Explanatory Style: Predicting Depression, Achievement, and Health', in Yapko, M.D. (ed.) *Brief Therapy Approaches to Treating Anxiety and Depression*, pp. 5–32 (New York: Brunner/Mazel).

Sennott, C.M. (2002a) 'Before Oath to Jihad, Drifting and Boredom', available at: http://www.webcitation.org/5bTYljW3A (accessed 7 March 2013).

Sennott, C.M. (2002b) 'Why bin Laden Pilot Relied on Saudi Hijackers', available at: http://www.boston.com/news/packages/underattack/news/driving_a_wedge/part1.shtml (accessed 7 March 2013).

Severson, K. and Brown, R. (2013) 'Divisions Form in Atlanta as Bail Is Set in Cheating Case', available at: http://www.nytimes.com/2013/04/03/us/atlanta-cheating-scandal-jailing-educators.html?hp&_r=0 (accessed 3 April 2013)..

Shah, A. (2013) 'Poverty Facts and Statistics', available at: http://www.globalissues.org/article/26/poverty-facts-and-stats (accessed 1 February 2013).

Sherrod, L.R., Quiñones, O., and Davila, C. (2004) 'Youth's Political Views and Their Experience of September 11, 2001', *Journal of Applied Developmental Psychology*, 25(2), 149–70.

Singer, P. (2006) 'What Should a Billionaire Give – and What Should You?', available at: http://www.nytimes.com/2006/12/17/magazine/17charity.t.html?pagewanted=1&ref=magazine (accessed 17 February 2013).

Smith, A. (1976 [1759]) *The Theory of Moral Sentiments* (Oxford: Clarendon Press).

Smith, R.J. and White, J. (2004) 'General Granted Latitude at Prison', available at: http://www.washingtonpost.com/wp-dyn/articles/A35612-2004Jun11.html (accessed 9 March 2013).

Sober, E. and Wilson, D.S. (1999) *Unto Others: The Evolution and Psychology of Unselfish Behavior* (Cambridge, MA: Harvard University Press).

Sontag, D., Herszenhorn, D., and Kovaleski, S. (2013) 'A Battered Dream, Then a Violent Path', available at: http://www.nytimes.com/2013/04/28/us/shot-at-boxing-title-denied-tamerlan-tsarnaev-reeled.html?pagewanted=all (accessed 27 April 2013).

Sroufe, L.A. (2000) 'Early Relationships and the Development of Children', *Infant Mental Health Journal*, 21(1–2), 67–74.

Staub, E. (1974) 'Helping a Distressed Person: Social, Personality, and Stimulus Determinants', *Advances in Experimental Social Psychology*, 7, 293–341.

Staub, E. (2004) 'Basic Human Needs, Altruism, and Aggression', in Miller, A. (ed.) *The Social Psychology of Good and Evil*, pp. 51–84 (London: The Guilford Press).

Stelter, B. (2011) 'California University Puts Officers Who Used Pepper Spray on Leave', available at: http://www.nytimes.com/2011/11/21/us/police-officers-involved-in-pepper-spraying-placed-on-leave.html (accessed 15 February 2013).

Stevenson, R. and Harwood, J. (2013) 'In Search of a Debt Deal, Obama Walks a Narrow Path', available at: http://www.cnbc.com/id/100540850 (accessed 18 March 2013).

Stjórnlagaráð (2011) 'Proposal for a new Constitution for the Republic of Iceland', available at: http://stjornlagarad.is/other_files/stjornlagarad/Frumvarp-enska.pdf (accessed 19 March 2013).

Talbot, M. (2009) 'Brain Gain', available at: http://www.newyorker.com/reporting/2009/04/27/090427fa_fact_talbot (accessed 1 April 2013).

The Associated Press (2012) 'Illinois: Peterson Convicted', available at: http://www.nytimes.com/2012/09/07/us/illinois-peterson-convicted.html (accessed 20 February 2013).

Time (1978) 'The Quiet Miracle of Emmaus at Abbé Pierre's Communes, Old Junk Leads to New Lives', *Time*, 111(15), 68.

U.S. Army Center of Military History (2011) 'Medal of Honor Recipients World War II', available at: http://www.history.army.mil/html/moh/wwII-a-f.html (accessed 20 August 2012).

Vaish, A., Carpenter, M., and Tomasello, M. (2009) 'Sympathy Through Affective Perspective Taking and its Relation to Prosocial Behavior in Toddlers', *Developmental Psychology*, 45(2), 534–43.

Villa, E. (2010) 'The Cold Shoulder', *Harvard International Review*, 31(4), 9–10.

Vogeley, K., Bussfeld, P., Newen, A., Herrmann, S., Happe, F., Falkai, P., et al. (2001) 'Mind Reading: Neural Mechanisms of Theory of Mind and Self-Perspective', *Neuroimage*, 14(1), 170–81.

Walker, M. and Dorsey, J. (2001) 'A Student's Dreams or a Terrorist's Plot', available at: http://s3.amazonaws.com/911timeline/2001/wallstreetjournal091801.html (accessed 7 March 2013).

Weinberg, Z. (2011) 'Drew Faust Took Home $874,559 in Salary, Benefits Last Year', available at: http://www.thecrimson.com/article/2011/5/14/faust-harvard-university-salary-management/ (accessed 1 April 2013).

Weissman, M.M., Wickramaratne, P., Greenwald, S., Hsu, H., Ouellette, R., Robins, L.N., Escobar, J.I., et al. (1992)'The Changing Rate of Major Depression Cross-National Comparisons', *JAMA*, 268(21), 3098–105.

Wells, H.G. (2004 [1903]) 'Mankind in the Making', available at: http://www2.hn.psu.edu/faculty/jmanis/hgwells/Mankind-Making.pdf (accessed 21 March 2013).

Widener, A.J. (1998) 'Beyond Ritalin: The Importance of Therapeutic Work With Parents and Children Diagnosed ADD/ADHD', *Journal of Child Psychotherapy*, 24(2), 267–81.

Wilson, D.S. (2012) 'Pathology, Evolution, and Altruism', in Oakley, B., Knafo, A., Madhavan, G., and Wilson, D.S. (eds) *Pathological Altruism*, pp. 406–11 (New York: Oxford University Press).

Wispé, L. (1991) *The Psychology of Sympathy* (New York: Plenum Press).

Yahoo! Finance (2013a) 'EDMC Profile', available at: http://uk.finance.yahoo.com/q/pr?s=EDMC (accessed 1 April 2013).

Yahoo! Finance (2013b) 'COCO Profile', available at: http://uk.finance.yahoo.com/q/pr?s=COCO (accessed 1 April 2013).

Young, A. (2012) 'Why is Ethanol so Controversial?', available at: http://www.ibtimes.com/why-ethanol-so-controversial-742459 (accessed 19 March 2013).

Young, M. (1958) *The Rise of the Meritocracy, 1870–2033: A Lesson on Education and Inequality* (London: Thames and Hudson).

Zimbardo, P. (2007) *The Lucifer Effect* (London: Random House).

Index

Printed and bound by CPI Group (UK) Ltd, Croydon, CR0 4YY